Generating Transworld Pedagogy

Generating Transworld Pedagogy

Reimagining La Clase Mágica

Edited by Belinda Bustos Flores, Olga A. Vásquez, and Ellen Riojas Clark

LEXINGTON BOOKS
Lanham • Boulder • New York • Toronto • Plymouth, UK

KH

Published by Lexington Books
A wholly owned subsidiary of Rowman & Littlefield
4501 Forbes Boulevard, Suite 200, Lanham, Maryland 20706
www.rowman.com

10 Thornbury Road, Plymouth PL6 7PP, United Kingdom

British Library Cataloguing in Publication Information Available

Library of Congress Cataloging-in-Publication Data

Generating transworld pedagogy : reimagining la clase mágica / [27 authors] ; Edited by Belinda Bustos Flores, Olga A. Vásquez, and Ellen Riojas Clark
p. cm.
Includes bibliographical references and index.
ISBN 978-0-7391-8683-1 (cloth) -- ISBN 978-0-7391-8684-8 (electronic)
1. Critical pedagogy. 2. Multicultural education. 3. Digital media. I. Flores, Belinda Bustos, editor of compilation. II. Vásquez, Olga A., editor of compilation. III. Clark, Ellen Riojas., editor of compilation
LC196.G45 2014
370.115--dc23

2013046142

Printed in the United States of America

9/8/15

Contents

Foreword

La Clase Mágica: *An Enduring Prototype for the New Latin@ Diaspora*

Kris D. Gutiérrez

Several years ago at the annual meeting of the American Educational Research Association, I had the privilege of commenting on an emergent set of papers that now constitute this volume. *Generating Transworld Pedagogy: Reimagining La Clase Mágica* expands those set of conceptual ideas that were part of the conversation. Many of the comments I made then remain relevant and I wish to further elaborate on these here, as I believe that these core ideas animate the larger collection of ideas advanced in this book.

The larger collection of essays provides a portrait, if not a blue print, for imagining what forms of learning, social relations, and tools are relevant and fundamental to educating youth in a rapidly shifting society, where diasporic communities with new and hybrid practices are normative. Today's youth largely constitute the new Latin@ diaspora and are engaged in and leverage multilingual, multicultural, and multimodal practices. The "transworld pedagogy" this book advances is a curricular and ecological response to the new superdiversity that is defining this country's changing demographics. *Generating Transworld Pedagogy: Reimagining La Clase Mágica* directly addresses the geographical and sociocultural influences of the Latin@ diaspora, as well the potential of new media technologies to teach high status knowledge in STEM-related practices. Of significance, this compendium of work places teacher preparation at the center of what it means to teach and learn in a globally networked society.

Generating Transworld Pedagogy: Reimagining La Clase Mágica transforms ordinary places, spaces, and practices into a magical world characterized by intergenerational learning, mutual relations of exchange, and new media practices organized around a bilingual/bicultural sensibility. *La Clase Mágica* (LCM) is at once a hybrid space organized around a transworld pedagogy that leverages everyday and scientific knowledge, in the Vygotskian (1978) sense, as well as historicizes the everyday by locating and celebrating its Indigenous antecedents. In the tradition of humanist and equity-oriented understandings of learning, learning is understood as the organization of possible futures (Gutiérrez, 2008; O'Connor and Allen, 2010). From a related perspective, its transworld vision and pedagogical innovations take up the metaphor of "learning as movement" (Gutiérrez, 2008) in which what takes hold as youth and families move within and across a range of ecologies is an essential part what counts as learning and the repertoires of practice developed in that movement.

First, in line with a cultural historical tradition—from Vygotsky (1978), Cole and Engeström (1993) to third generation activity theorists such as Engeström (2011)—I focus on the history and contribution of *La Clase Mágica* (Vásquez, 2003) that for more than several decades has served as prototype for a new model of education for Latino youth and families, as well as university students, whom Flores, Vásquez, and Clark (this volume) term *aspirantes*. Vásquez (2003) developed an enduring model whose sensitivity to local culture and historical legacies make it portable, permeable, and dynamic and substantially easier to situate and instantiate across a range of communities and contexts (a point I will address shortly). Thus, situating this book in *La Clase Mágica's* history is critical to understanding how the collective work featured here grows out of LCM's legacy and orienting principles.

A brief history. In 1996, faculty from the various campuses of the University of California created a network of Fifth Dimension–LCM models of afterschool/university/community partnerships, known as *UC Links*, which helped to create an innovative and more stable educational pipeline for youth from non-dominant communities across California. The Fifth Dimension–LCM model inspired the development of new innovations designed in response to the attacks on affirmative action and inequitable educational conditions for youth from non-dominant communities in California. In addition to the parent model developed by Michael Cole and colleagues (Cole et al., 2006), there was another related, but distinct model that was uniquely a bilingual, bicultural, and intergenerational approach to social action, called *La Clase Mágica*. It was LCM and Vásquez's (1996) contribution to the UC Latino Eligibility Report that provided the model and vision for the new educational innovation—an innovation targeting issues of diversity across the UC system, with particular focus on low-income and Latin@ youth.

Informed by cultural historical principles of learning and development, *La Clase Mágica* was organized around a different sensibility and pedagogical imagination that privileged the use of the cultural tools, particularly the linguistic tools, of its children and surrounding community. From the bilingual adventure guides used to mediate and level up children's play around new media technologies, to the formal inclusion of parents and community members in its day to day operation, *La Clase Mágica* uniquely combined the principles of a cultural historical approach to learning and development with a bilingual and bicultural tradition and sensibility. The model was and remains in and of the community and has created trajectories of possibility for its children and university participants.

It was *La Clase Mágica's* rich, respectful, and proleptic vision that made it the model that I aspired to re-create at UCLA. The UCLA team imported everything it could from LCM and these tools and practices became foundational to the development of another unique model grounded in expansive forms of learning (Engeström, 1987) and polycultural and polylingual approaches to education (Gutiérrez, Bien, and Selland, 2011). *Las Redes* (Networks) served as a kind of "change laboratory" (Engeström, 2004) in a longstanding partnership with an elementary school in a port-of-entry district in an unincorporated area of Los Angeles where it flourished for over fifteen years.[1]

We see LCM's utility and adaptability in the uptake of *La Clase Mágica* model internationally (see chapter 13, Macías Gómez-Estern and Vásquez's account of a Spanish instantiation) to the way this dynamic model can inform more robust policy formations (see chapter 4, Lopez and Valenzuela new epistemology for rethinking policy). This adaptability is key, as more robust notions of culture attend to both the regularity and variance in any cultural community, always mindful that culture is not a synonym for race and ethnicity (Gutiérrez and Rogoff, 2003). So the goal has never been to replicate, but to use LCM's principles to inform new instantiations and emerging design principles. Yet, attending to people's history of involvement in practices, including those enduring elements of culture—the cultural practices that give meaning and serve as resources for people and communities—remain important, if not central to leveraging everyday knowledge and expertise across all settings described in this volume.

In advancing the notion of "sacred sciences," *Generating Transworld Pedagogy: Reimagining La Clase Mágica* expands its theorizing of language, culture, and knowledge to include the knowledge and expertise that emerge from people's history of involvement in practices and the ecology of a lived culture (see chapter 2, Vásquez, Riojas Clark, and Flores). This critical bilingual/bicultural pedagogy for disciplinary learning science and mathematics is vividly taken up across the various ecological models that *La Clase Mágica* has inspired. Willey, LopezLeiva, Torres, and Khisty (see chapter 11) document how, *Los Rayos* afterschool mathematics project for elementary school supports Chican@ children's development of advanced mathematics. Biliteracy practices related to mathematical learning and dialogic mathematical problem solving help to create a rich ecology for mathematical learning that extends students mathematical repertoires. In the same vein, both chapters from colleagues Martinez-Roldan, and Ek and her colleagues Garcia and Garza illustrate the educational possibilities that emerge from leveraging youth's linguistic and sociocul-

tural histories (see chapters 9 and 10). In chapter 2, Vásquez et al. anchor
the text with a discussion of the youth's prior histories as critical tools for
teaching and learning.

As I commented several years ago, the Vygotskian (1978) notion of
"concept formation" is exceedingly relevant to Flores et al.'s argument, as
it helps us understand that the everyday and the scientific "grow into one
another." In my own work, I take a "syncretic approach" to the organization of everyday and scientific ideas (Gutiérrez, 2008; 2012). Within this
view, everyday knowledge is neither romanticized, nor are school-based
skills and knowledge privileged; instead, a syncretic approach recognizes
that expansive forms of learning involve the negotiation of the two. For
us, it involves the co-design of activity systems, which are organized
around an historicizing pedagogy that makes everyday genres and their
history of development and use in the community, the objects of reflection and analysis in ways that grounds students' repertoires of practice in
expansive forms of learning as it is stated-reinforced in chapters 1 and 14
(see Flores et al., and Clark et al., this volume).

The design of these expansive learning activity systems are iterative
and always under construction. Although the editors in this book describe their cultural work as design experiments (Collins et al., 2004), as I
argued several years ago at the American Education Research Association (AERA), the cultural work of *La Clase Mágica* is much more in the
tradition of formative experiments (Cole and Engeström, 2006,
Engeström, 2011) or what I term "social design experiments" (Gutiérrez,
2008; Gutiérrez and Vossoughi, 2010). As we have written,

> Social design experiments—cultural historical formations designed to
> promote transformative learning for adults and children—are orga-
> nized around expansive notions of learning and mediated praxis and
> provide new tools and practices for envisioning new pedagogical ar-
> rangements, especially for students from nondominant communities
> (Gutiérrez and Vossoughi, 2010, p. 100).

Of relevance, social design experiments are grounded in the histories of
the target communities and are not one-way, top-down interventions
with communities; at the same time, social design experiments are organized around robust forms of learning and theories of action, and employ
rigorous methods of inquiry. Vásquez's (2003) *La Clase Mágica* and its
constellation of sites (Flores et al., this volume), from my point of view,
are highly aligned with the principles and transformative aspects of social design experiments.

Finally, *Generating Transworld Pedagogy: Reimagining La Clase Mágica* is
about a series of social design experiments organized around a vision
and principles that bring together sociocultural histories, disciplinary
content, and new media to create new environments that both mediate
students' learning and engagement but also to help youth forge new,

relevant, and productive trajectories. This is a key feature of productive environments for learning in a globally connected world. Relatedly, researchers involved in the MacArthur Foundation's Connected Learning Research Network [CLRN] (Ito et al., 2012) have engaged in work to address the serious disconnect that youth experience, especially youth from non-dominant communities, as they move across practices and activity systems. Oriented toward addressing issues of inequality in education, the group of scholars in this volume, like the CLRN researchers, seek to leverage the potential of digital media to expand opportunity to learn in ways that are socioculturally embedded and relevant, interest-driven, and that augment educational, economic, and political opportunity (Ito et al., 2013, p. 1).

These are precisely the goals and vision embodied by all the projects designed within *Generating Transworld Pedagogy: Reimagining La Clase Mágica* experiment—an experiment that continues to show remarkable sustainability and consequence for the youth and adults who enter and learn in this innovative and culturally relevant system. The accounts detailed across the chapters in this volume are a testament to the powerful model at work and the ingenuity of educators, both nationally and internationally, to situate *La Clase Mágica* in new contexts to create new visions of education and the future.

NOTES

1. *Las Redes* was a fifteen-year collaboration with Moffett Elementary School, Lennox School District, and principal Joann Isken. Today, another instantiation, *El Pueblo Mágico*, is in its fourth year of innovation in Lafayette, Colorado, at Alicia Sánchez Elementary School.

REFERENCES

Cole, M. and the Distributed Literacy Consortium (2006). *The Fifth Dimension: An After-School Program Built on Diversity*. New York: Russell Sage Foundation.

Cole, M., and Engeström, Y. (1993). "A Cultural-Historical Approach to Distributed Cognition." In G. Salomon (ed.), *Distributed Cognitions: Psychology and Educational Considerations* (1–46). Cambridge, UK: Cambridge University Press.

——— (2006). "Cultural-Historical Approaches for Designing for Development." In J. Valsiner and A. Rosa (eds.), *The Cambridge Handbook of Sociocultural Psychology*. (484–507). Cambridge, UK: Cambridge University Press.

Collins, A., Joseph, D., and Bielaczyc, K. (2004). "Design Research: Theoretical and Methodological Issues." *Journal of the Learning Sciences*, 13(1), 15–42.

Engeström, Y. (1987). *Learning by Expanding: An Activity Theoretic Approach to Developmental Research*. Helsinki, Finland: Orienta-Konsultit.

——— (2004). "New Forms of Learning in Co-configuration Work." *Journal of Workplace Learning*, 16, 11–21.

——— (2011). "From Design Experiments to Formative Interventions." *Theory and Psychology*, 21(5), 598–628.

Gutiérrez, K. (2012). "Leveraging Horizontal and Everyday Practices: Toward a Theory of Connected Learning." Paper presented at the annual meeting of the Literacy Research Association, San Diego, CA, November 28, 2012.

——— (2008). "Developing a Sociocritical Literacy in the Third Space." *Reading Research Quarterly*, 43(2), 148–164.

Gutiérrez, K., Bien, A., and Selland, M. (2011). "Polylingual and Polycultural Learning Ecologies: Mediating Emergent Academic Literacies for Dual Language Learners." *Journal of Early Childhood Literacy*, 11(2), 232–261.

Gutiérrez, K. and Rogoff, B. (2003). "Cultural Ways of Learning: Individual Traits or Repertoires of Practice." *Educational Researcher*, 32(5), 19–25.

Gutiérrez, K. and Vossoughi, S. (2010). "Lifting off the Ground to Return Anew: Documenting and Designing for Equity and Transformation through Social Design Experiments." *Journal of Teacher Education*, 61(1-2), 100–117.

Ito, M., Gutiérrez, K., Livingstone, S., Penuel, W., Rhodes, J, Salen, K., Schor, J., Sefton-Green, J. and Watkins, C. (2013). *Connected Learning: An Agenda for Research and Design*. Irvine, CA: Digital Media and Learning Research Hub Reports on Connected Learning.

O'Connor, K. and Allen, A. (2010). "Learning as the Organizing of Social Futures." In W. Penuel and K. O'Connor (eds.), *Yearbook of the National Society for the Study of Education*, 108, (160–175). New York: Teachers College Press.

Vásquez, O. (1996). "A Model System of Institutional Linkages: Transforming the Educational Pipeline." In A. Hurtado, R. Figueroa, and E. E. García (eds.), *Strategic Intervention in Education: Expanding the Latina/Latino Pipeline*. University of California Latino Eligibility Study.

——— (2003). *La Clase Mágica: Imagining Optimal Possibilities in a Bilingual Community of Learners*. Mahwah, NJ: Lawrence Erlbaum.

Vygotsky, L. V. (1978). *Mind in Society: The Development of Higher Psychological Processes*. Cambridge, MA: Harvard University Press.

Preface

Generating Transworld Pedagogy: Reimagining La Clase Mágica forges multiple lines of theory and practice to address one of the greatest challenges to education in the twenty-first century — educating the increasing diversity in the classroom and society. It situates teacher preparation and transworld pedagogy as the focal point of a comprehensive approach to meet the social, cultural, technical, and ethical demands of a world in motion. This book builds on Flores, Sheets, and Clark's (2011) bilingual/bicultural transformative approach intersecting with Vásquez's (2003) technology-assisted pedagogy. It highlights the affordances of mobile devices and other forms of multi-media in facilitating a pedagogy that prepares youth as well as teacher candidates to negotiate their own cultural knowledge, history, and identity as well as those of the broader society as transworld citizens.

In this volume, we articulate our transworld pedagogy as a means for preparing teachers based on our five-year experience working with this research-based afterschool technology-driven pedagogy. Four theoretical concepts anchor *Generating Transworld Pedagogy: Reimagining La Clase Mágica* to provide a deeper understanding of what it takes to create the ideal learning and teaching conditions for bilingual learners: the dialectic method, Vygotskian notion of culture (1978), a bilingual/bicultural critical pedagogy, and the concept of the "sacred sciences" that we draw from indigenous native science (see chapter 2). We ground our pedagogy on the learner's critical intellectual capital for learning and teaching and build on a cultural-historical perspective that posits the learner's prior history as the basis for new learning and development (Vygotsky, 1978; Cole and Engestrom, 2006). Furthermore, we build on the sacred sciences passed down by our ancestors/*antepasados* to re-claim our space in this modern technological world. We find harmony in Vygotsky's (1978) ideas that the development of an individual occurs within the social world synchronizing with Frere's (1970) notion of praxis as evident in "bilingual/bicultural transformative pedagogy" (Flores, Sheets and Clark, 2011). Most importantly, these theories resonate with our cultural ways of being and thinking. We see the sacred sciences as the philosophical foundation of our positionality.

We make cross-disciplinary, cross-genre, and cross-culture knowledges the source of classroom learning and teaching and open our pedagogy to multiple languages and cultures in the U.S. classroom. Although we focus on Spanish-English bilingual learners of the Southwestern United States, we also present an international perspective, which we argue is the kind of education demanded by the socio- political, economic, and technical realities of the twenty-first century. *La Clase Mágica* (LCM) model, as evident in our volume, has a strong theoretical foundation, yet has the flexibility to be adapted to various contexts. Throughout the book, we connect and re-connect to prominent theories and the sacred sciences: the knowledges our ancestors generated in understanding the relationship of humankind to the earth and the cosmos. The intent of this approach is to articulate a pedagogical approach that prepares new transworld citizens with a strong foundation rooted in the home and group culture.

Of particular significance for *Generating Transworld Pedagogy: Reimagining La Clase Mágica* is its capacity to address the digital/technological divide that exists across ethnic and class lines. For many low-income Latinos, public classrooms are the only source of advanced technology. In schools serving a majority student population of color, while nearly 64 percent of instructional classrooms have Internet access, more often than not computers are used for low-cognitive demanding activities (Gorski, 2003; Gorski, 2009). The urgency of the ramifications of this widening digital gap is resulting in "digital deprivation" and even more acute "digital destitution" (Gordo, 2010) in low-income communities of color. Gorski (2009) calls for digital equity in which users are producing and creating knowledge. The use of mobile technology and other technologies within a laboratory of learning affords participants the opportunity to maximize their learning potential (see chapters 9, 10, and 11). Below, we outline the critical role that technology plays in enhancing engagement, expansive learning, and literacy development among participants in LCM and the need for further research.

BILINGUAL EDUCATION TEACHER CANDIDATES

Following Flores, Sheets, and Clark (2011), we refer to bilingual education teacher candidates as *aspirantes*. Bilingual education teacher candidates aspire to be role-models and change agents in their practice (Flores, Ek, and Sánchez, 2011). They recognize the need for social justice because of the historical schooling inequities prevalent in Latino communities. As role-models, they advocate for the linguistic and cultural capital of Latino students. As change agents, they are cognizant that they must engage in social change in order to transform schooling (Flores et al., 2011). While *aspirantes* are ideologically grounded, it is important for candidates to have opportunities to further gain political and ideological clarity (Bartolomé andTrueba, 2000). For example, in his talk to candidates, Milk (2012) appeals to them as future bilingual education teachers to become visionaries, pioneers, innovators, leaders, and *sabios* (wise):

Aspira (sus expectativas),
Inspirar (con su ejemplo para alcanzarla),
Respira (calmar las aguas porque siempre hay conflicto), y
Transpira (trabajar duro y luchar por justicia)[1]

LCM as a laboratory for learning gives *aspirantes* opportunities to gain the knowledge, skills, and experience to become culturally efficacious teachers. As *aspirantes*, they play a critical role in the development of the bilingual learners' capacity while encouraging them to realize their aspirations. Several researchers have highlighted the value of engaging teacher candidates in community-based service learning (Bollin, 2007; McDonald et al., 2011). Engaging *aspirantes* in LCM as an afterschool community based project provides them the unique opportunity for expansive learning that centers teaching on learners and families (Engeström, 2001; McDonald et al., 2011). Further, working with their protégé on a one-to-one basis, the *aspirante* is engaged in mediated praxis. According to Gutiérrez and Vossoughi (2010), they are:

> creating contexts where activity is guided by a mediated praxis aimed at the possible opens opportunities for equity-oriented and respectful learning to manifest concretely in the everyday social relations among human beings. Mediated praxis promotes expansive forms of learning in which individual and collective zones of proximal developments coalesce (p. 111).

To advance the field, our volume shares research that exemplifies mediated praxis and expansive learning for *aspirantes* as they engage with learners (see chapters 7 and 8).

BILINGUAL BICULTURAL LEARNERS

In this text, we recognize that bilingual learners are protégés, who are acquiring two languages within the social cultural contexts including the school and community. We see *protégés* as having potential and, as such, are taken under a guide's tutelage. As protégés, they bring their linguistic and cultural knowledge and ways of being to the learning setting, and then are guided through their development with the assistance of more expert others (Vygotsky, 1978). This shared experience of the dyad creates a harmonic balance in which they will carry on the legacy as our future leaders. At LCM, the protégés as well as the *aspirantes* are provided opportunities to acquire literacy, numeracy, and virtual learning and space to dialogue, create, and innovate. This is in direct contrast to using technology as tool of consumption or for the reproduction of schooling remedial practices (Gorski, 2003; Gorski, 2009). However, despite the potential for virtual learning, little research has explored its use among bilingual learners. Our volume reveals this potentiality for Latino children (see chapters 9–11).

FAMILIES' ENGAGEMENT

While there has been a preponderance of studies on college-educated parents' view of the important educational value of technology and computer usage (Ortiz, Green, and Lim, 2010), the same perception is held by low-income, ethnic minority families with exposure to technology (Rivera, 2008). Similarly, data on LCM focus groups indicate that low-income, Latino parents value their children's engagement with technology as well (see chapter 12). We argue that engaging families in LCM increases their confidence in technology and provides them the skills to assist their children in engaging in a mobile world. Our work brings to light these benefits for negotiating the exigencies of the twenty-first century.

We envision a world of permeable borders through which LCM transworld pedagogy provides teacher candidates as *aspirantes* and learners as protégés the opportunities to acquire digital, bilingual, and bicultural literacies. Through their use of technology as a tool for learning and development, they become innovators. At present, there is no other book that critically examines the intersection of teacher candidates–student learning within an informal learning context. Moreover, providing an understanding of the critical role families' play in promoting their children's digital literacy fulfills an important need.

Generating Transworld Pedagogy: Reimagining La Clase Mágica begins to fill this gap by presenting long-term research outcomes from a socially designed experiment. Using the epistemology of the sacred sciences, that encompass notions of spirituality, transcendence, evolution, and harmonic balance and synchronization, we have organized each of the chapters around four major parts: (1) embracing a transworld view, (2) transcending borders as transworld citizens, (3) enacting transworld pedagogy, and (4) evolving through innovation. Each of these parts suggest a spiral of expansive activity that generates transworld pedagogy blending in the past with the future.

Embracing a Transworld View

The chapters organized in the first part provide the conceptual and theoretical vision of transworld pedagogy (see chapters 1 and 2). This vision articulates the power of the broad system of knowledge from which the learner comes and how important it is to weave this wealth of knowledge and experiences into the learning context. We make connections to the distant past and see all knowledge as sacred especially that knowledge that has been generated across time in each of the different cultures that are represented in the classroom. Lastly, we capitalize on the success of *La Clase Mágica* in creating opportunities for transformative learning (see chapter 3).

Transcending Borders as Transworld Citizens

In the second part, we move beyond LCM's vision and conceptual, theoretical, and research underpinnings toward the transcendence of borders within the political arena, the local community, and the physical world. The chapters in this part examine the politics of educational policy issues in implementing a statewide LCM research initiative (see chapter 4), detail the process of creating a reciprocal collaborative university-school partnership grounded in community values (see chapter 5), and describe the development of a culturally relevant strategy for supporting a transworld pedagogy (see chapter 6). In these chapters, we see evidence of different types of discourse, the use of the sacred sciences in action, and the incorporation of culture.

Enacting Transworld Pedagogy

In the chapters for the third part, we provide evidence of the power of LCM's transworld pedagogy as praxis in action with the focus on *aspirantes*, protégés, and families. These chapters document the effective use of culturally mediated activities that advance teacher candidates' knowledge and competency using digital technology (see chapters 7 and 8); the intersection of Latino children's knowledge and expertise with technology in developing biliteracy, digital literacy, and numeracy (see chapters 9, 10, and 11); and demonstrate the use of technology to enhance families and communities' access to the digital world (see chapter 12). In each of these chapters, we see the weaving of the theoretical underpinnings of the dialogic process, culture, sacred sciences, and a bilingual/bicultural critical pedagogy.

Evolving through Innovation

Finally, the fourth part reflects an iterative process of progressive refinement towards harmony and balance. We reaffirm knowledge as relative, dynamic, and reflective of the sociocultural context, and as such, maintain LCM as relevant and adaptable to the changing needs of the community. For example, chapter 13 exhibits the magic of LCM and how its basic principles are formidable yet malleable tools for serving marginalized communities in an international context. The final chapter articulates how the wisdom of the sacred sciences and living in harmony parallel our post-modern critical theories, yet opens us to new profound ways of thinking that is critical for enacting our role as transworld citizens and incorporating transworld pedagogy.

NOTES

1. Aspires with expectations, inspires by example, respires to bring calm at times of conflict, perspires for social justice

REFERENCES

Bartolomé, L. I., and Trueba, E. T. (2000). "Beyond the Politics of Schools and the Rhetoric of Fashionable Pedagogies: The Significance of Teacher Ideology." In E. T. Trueba and L. I. Bartolomé (eds.), *Immigrant Voices: In Search of Educational Equity* (277-292). Lanham, MD: Rowman and Littlefield.

Bollin, G. G. (2007). "Preparing Teachers for Hispanic Immigrant Children: A Service Learning Approach." *Journal of Latinos and Education*, 6(2), 177–189.

Cole, M. and Engeström, Y. (2006). "Cultural-Historical Approaches to Designing for Development." In J. Valsiner and A. Rosa (eds.), *The Cambridge Handbook of Sociocultural Psychology*, 484-507. New York: Cambridge University Press.

Engeström, Y. (2001). "Expansive Learning at Work: Toward an Activity Theoretical Reconceptualization." *Journal of Education and Work*, 14, 133–156.

Flores, B. B., Ek, L., and Sánchez, P. (2011). "Bilingual Education Candidate Ideology: Descubriendo sus motives y creencias." In B. B. Flores, R. H. Sheets, and E. R Clark (eds.), *Teacher Preparation for Bilingual Student Populations: Educar para transformar* (40–58). New York: Routledge.

Flores, B. B., Sheets, R. H., Clark, E. R. (2011). *Teacher Preparation for Bilingual Student Populations: Educar para transformar*. New York: Routledge.

Freire, P. (1970) *Pedagogy of the Oppressed*. (M. Ramos, trans.), New York: Continuum.

Gordo, B. (2003). "Overcoming Digital Deprivation." *IT and Society*, 1(5), 166–180.

Gorski, P. C. (2008/2009). "Insisting on Digital Equity: Reframing the Dominant Discourse on Multicultural Education and Technology." *Urban Education*, 44, 348–364.

Gorski, P. C. (2003). "Privilege and Repression in the Digital Era: Rethinking the Sociopolitics of the Digital Divide." *Race, Gender and Class*, 10(4), 145–176.

Gutiérrez, K. D., and Vossoughi, S. (2010). "Lifting off the Ground to Return Anew: Mediated Praxis, Transformative Learning, and Social Design Experiments." *Journal of Teacher Education*, 61(1–2), 100–117. DOI: 10.1177/0022487109347877.

McDonald, M., Tyson, K., Brayko, K., Bowman, M., Delport, J., and Shimomura, F. (2011). "Innovation and Impact in Teacher Education: Community-Based Organizations as Field Placements for Preservice Teachers." *Teachers College Record*, 13(8), 1668–1700.

Milk, R. D. (2012, April 28). *Bienvenida a San Antonio: La cuna de educación bilingüe*. Bilingual Education Student Organization Leadership Institute, Our Lady of the Lake University, San Antonio, TX.

Ortiz, R.W., Green, T., and Lim, H. (2010). "Families and Home Computer Use: Exploring Parent Perceptions." *Urban Education*, 1–15.

Rivera, H. (2008). "Bridging the Technology Gap for Low-Income Spanish-Speaking Immigrant Families." *Association for the Advancement of Computing in Education Journal*, 16(3), 307–325.

Vásquez, O. A. (2003). *La Clase Mágica: Imagining Optimal Possibilities in a Bilingual Community of Learners*. Mahwah, NJ: Lawrence Erlbaum.

Vygotsky, L. S. (1978). *Mind in Society: The Development of Higher Psychological Processes*. Cambridge, MA: Harvard University Press.

Acknowledgements

Agradecemos el aliento, apoyo, y cariño de todos los que nos han respaldado en esta aventura intelectual y social. We wish to thank all who participated in making this book a reality, especially *a nuestras familias, colegas, y antepasados.* We give a special thank you to the Academy for Teacher Excellence at the University of Texas at San Antonio, who is responsible for actualizing and sustaining *La Clase Mágica* at UTSA for the last five years. Your dedication to educational equity enlivens our spirits to continue against all odds helping make the world a better place. *Estamos totalmente agradecidas por su trabajo.*

We are indebted to Edgewood ISD and Las Palmas Elementary for opening their doors and supporting our efforts. To all *La Clase Mágica* faculty, *aspirantes,* staff, children, *y padres de familia,* we thank you for the lessons we have learned from you. You have inspired us with your hard work and helped us gain important insights that could not have been visible without you. *Mil gracias,* Juan Diego Robledo, for your keen eyes in reviewing each chapter on multiple occasions. Thank you Kevin Wildberger, research assistant at UCSD, Elvia Rivera, Lauren Rodríguez, and Erika García, our UTSA work study students for checking bibliographic references and other tasks.

Gracias Mario Enrique Flores, *mi querido esposo y* Janelle, *mi preciosa hija,* for your love, warmth, smiles, patience, and always being my support system. *A mi familia* Bustos, especially my parents, Frances and Arturo, *gracias* for your love and support. *Le agradezco mucho a mi* Mama Julia, my maternal grandmother, whose *cuentos* and *dichos* are forever in my heart and memory—Belinda.

Yo les doy las gracias a mis padres, quien ya están con Diosito, for all the lessons and wisdom I brought to this book project. *A mi esposo,* Gary Lee Pooler, *agradezco mucho* your love and support and for understanding when my mind or body wandered away and became lost on this mission. I especially want to thank my son Rigel and his little Xochi Quetzal Elena for filling my heart with joy—Olga.

Mil gracias a mis colegas, Belinda *y* Olga, for a remarkable journey in defining our educational legacy. *A mi familia,* who has always been so supportive of all my endeavors, I acknowledge them with our work. *A nuestra casa y jardín,* Starpatch, that offers the space to be creative and productive, *gracias a* Hector for all that he does to keep it so, for my soul is continually nourished—Ellen.

I

Embracing a Transworld View

"Don't forget the teachings of the ancestors. In their paths we will find hope for the future." —Mayan Elder, 1997

Victor D. Montejo (1997), "The Pan-Mayan Movement, Mayans at the Doorway of the New Millenium." *Cultural Survival Quarterly* **21(2), 28.**

ONE

¡*Adelante! El Mundo Nuevo*: Educating the New Generation of the Twenty-First Century

Belinda Bustos Flores, Olga A. Vásquez, and Ellen Riojas Clark

WORKING TOWARD HARMONY

The prevalence of scientific thought among Latin American ancient peoples is evident in the scattered remains of many high cultures spread across the Americas. Their numerous architectural wonders such as the pyramids, astronomical observatories, and monolithic forms, as well as the countless progressions in mathematics, medicine, astronomy, and theology highlight a long tradition of science in the history of the Americas. These ancient contributions to the modern world include the use of zero, place value, and writing systems. The power of observation—the foundation of all scientific research and hallmark of Mesoamerica accomplishments—is readily evident in the ways they harnessed the physical world and the subsequent organization of social and civic life. The spiritual nature of the Mayan is epitomized in their knowledge of architecture, engineering, astronomy, and physics which is illuminated across the ancient cities of Tenochtitlan, Mitla, Chichén Itzá, and Tulum in Mexico. The visible prominence of these accomplishments made science a part of the everyday life of early Mesoamerican populations; albeit as sites of wonder.

In this book, we build on these scientific advancements of our *antepasados*/ancestors; in particular, we highlight the sacred sciences, i.e.,

3

knowledge of the laws of nature generated from living harmoniously with all living beings on earth and with the cosmos (Brayboy and Castagño, 2008, Fischer, 1999), in order to understand the relationship of these intellectual discoveries to everyday life. Through an exploration of the sacred sciences of our *antepasados,* we make visible what has been lost, obscured, or often not even considered as "official knowledge" (Apple, 2000) of the modern scientific and technological world. We seek to transform our ways of being and thinking:

> In the same way that the spirit of the *antepasados* was transformed, those who seek the growth and improvement of mankind, when they hear the lost voices of history that urges us to reconstruct ourselves as intelligent, respectful entities of the laws of the cosmic order, we will seek ways that ensure the evolution of the new generations in egalitarian conditions. (Lara, 2000, p. 7, translated by authors)

Hence, our goal for this chapter is threefold: First, we want to highlight the scientific thought and accomplishments of our *antepasados* (Fischer, 1999) as foundational of a new pedagogy for the twenty-first century. Second, we want to elucidate the disconnect between the scientific knowledge of our *antepasados* and the patrimony that informs present day educational practices. Third, we want to introduce *La Clase Mágica* as a catalyst for generating a research-based pedagogy of social change.

CONCEPTUAL RESONANCE: WHAT DO WE KNOW?

Unearthing the Conocimientos of Our Antepasados

We build on the long tradition of scientific explorations of Mesoamerica's indigenous people. In this book, we incorporate the method and the knowledge garnered from the interactions of everyday life. The connection among human beings, living things, and the cosmos was evident in the pre-Columbian indigenous peoples' approach to mathematics and in their depictions of numerical concepts. Lara (2013) posits:

> Through mathematics, one can understand the vision of the world, the laws of nature and of the human being from the origin of the universe; this also allow us to enjoy the harmonic message of the numbers. (p. 5, translated by authors)

For example, the concept of zero was depicted as a snail shell because of its spiral nature alluding to the idea of transcendence and its resemblance of movement toward the universe. The tips of our fingers, like the snail shell, and the Milky Way are also spirals that are symbolic of evolution and the cosmos. Mayan inventions such as the *Nepohualtzintzin,* a base twenty pre-Columbian mathematical tool, much like our modern computer, that was used to perform basic as well as advanced mathematical algorithms (Instituto Nacional de Astrofísica, Óptica, y Electrónica, 2004). Its development was not incidental, but intentional. Ancient Mayans used their whole body (fingers and toes) as their base and designed the *Nepohualtintzin* using the sacred number thirteen, which demonstrates the connection between humans and the cosmos. This is exemplified in the joints in the human body, the lunar cycles in a solar year, and the degrees the moon travels daily across the sky. The *Nepohualtintzin* was used in calculating and interpreting astronomical and gestational events. Mayan astronomical observations of celestial events, especially the movement of the planet Venus, led to the development of a complex and precise calendar system (Smiley, 1962; Fischer, 1999). The round calendar includes the Vague, a 360-day solar calendar guiding farming based on the seasons; and the Tzolkin, the sacred 260 day short calendar depicting the life cycles (Furner, Holbein, and Scullion, 2000). It also represents the human gestation period (Fischer, 1999; Scofield, 2004/2005). The long count calendar measures the five recurring cycles, such as the *Quinto Sol* (Smiley, 1962), which depicts the end of an epoch in 2012 (Sitler, 2006). Unlike Western thought which sees time in a linear fashion, the Mayans saw time as reoccurring cycles. As the Mayans prophesized, our enlightenment will occur during the next cycle:

> In the Sexto Sol, you will know what was hidden. The epoch of light will illuminate your being; it is your children who will travel the celestial skies. (Guochi cited by Lara, 2000, translated by authors)

In present day, practiced rituals of the Mayan and other indigenous groups maintain the harmony with the cosmos that transcends time and space (Fischer, 1999). Unbeknown to us, Mayan women have shared this sacred numerological knowledge in their weaving of sacred geometric numeric patterns in fabrics and in everyday clothing, such as *huiples* (Rosa and Orey, 2007; Clark, 2013). The Mayan mat pattern depicts the numbers one through nine as sacred values, which were used to express an understanding about life and the cosmos. The Mayan mat pattern is analogous with climbing a pyramid, mimicking the movement of a snake, "the numbers . . . progressed sequentially and zigzagged diagonally" (Rosa and Orey, 2007, p. 241). The patterning encapsulates a mathematical relation that emulates human action to the natural environment.

The use of the sacred sciences both generated and advanced ancient people's thinking and ways of life. For example, the Mayans between 800 BC and 1521 AD were ancient mariners who used star charts to traverse the Atlantic in large canoes to engage in trade and commerce (McKillop, 2010; National Oceanic Atmospheric Administration, 2011). During this epoch, Ecuadorian indigenous people had determined the center of the earth by studying the sun movements and using a wooden pole to examine the shadow casted during different points of time (Quisato Scientific Research Project, 2010), a precursor to the modern global positioning system. We recognize this intellectual history of knowledge and discoveries of our *antepasados* as critical resources to incorporate equally into our pedagogy alongside that of Western knowledge.

The Privileging of Multiple Knowledges

We recognize that our roots also trace back to the Old World and Western ideology that is based on reasoning and objectivity. Our education has made evident the cognitive prowess of European mariners who navigated the seas using rudimentary navigational maps based on the position of the sun and the stars. Later, the magnetic compasses and astrolabe or cross-staff were utilized. The power of these scientific tools led to the eventual discovery and conquest of the New World and the destruction of the native cultures. The Europeans had a distinct advantage in terms of military might and immunity to the diseases that they carried in their bodies that helped decimate entire populations (Rosa and Orey, 2007). Recognizing the power of the connection to history, culture, religion, and alliances, the Europeans systematically went about destroying any link to spiritual, material, and cultural power; a colonization occurred with destructive ramifications to the present day.

As a consequence, the means of oppression is not only economic, but also cultural as "the vanquished are dispossessed of the word, their expressiveness, their culture," (Freire, 2012, p. 138). Indigenous knowledge was not only lost, it was regarded as mystical and lacking in scientific underpinnings, privileging the knowledge held by the conquerors over all knowledge found in the New World. Indigenous knowledge was forever relegated as inadequate and as Foucault (1980) would concede, "buried and disguised in a functionalist coherence of formal systemisation" (p. 31). The blame, however, lies not only at the feet of conquerors but at the social organization of the ruling and elite classes of the indigenous, who did not the share their knowledge with all of their people. Only the privileged or elite were allowed to engage in formal study and given access to the sacred knowledge, making it vulnerable to the whims of war, disease, and other natural phenomena. The lesson learned from this history is that knowledge is a basic right beyond those who generate it and that it should be shared with all. Access to information and the distribution of knowledge is still determined by those in power and those with wealth. Limiting knowledge makes the people vulnerable and creates the conditions for subjugation, manipulation and utter destruction, ensuring those in power to remain in control (Foucault, 1980; Freire, 1990).

Countering Hegemony and the Status Quo

Our goal for this manuscript is to frame learning and teaching from a new perspective, one that unearths truths beyond what has been recorded and acknowledged as the only scientific certainty and make these available to all as pinnacles of new visions of history, knowledge, and reasoning. We mobilize the affordances of technology to new heights mediating accessibility to knowledge, communication, and power. We concur with Havel (1994) that our world "is the first civilization in the history of the human race that spans the entire globe and firmly binds together all human societies, submitting them to a common global destiny" (see Section: Science and Modern Civilization, paragraph 2, sentence 1). We have the ability to cross geographical terrain, cultural and linguistic barriers, as well as political structures with the click of our fingers to communicate with text, sound, and multimedia. The potentialities of telecommunication technologies make possible the ability to reach to the farthest points of modernity to people who have not had access to a telephone, mail, or the automobile and offer them the possibility of traveling across time and space. Even low-tech computers can make possible virtual voyages that take one out of RL (real life) and into the cosmos of virtual existence. Our fingertips have joined our minds in leading us to discover new knowledge, while also giving us opportunities to challenge or validate what we already know or believe.

We argue that all of these resources should be made available to all learners using culturally responsive educational programs ranging from classroom teaching methodologies to curriculum design (Moll and Gonzalez, 2004; Civil, 2007). Thus, we demonstrate throughout the ways in which we can incorporate learners' life experiences and cultural backgrounds as a sound pedagogical approach. If we are to ensure the viability of the survival of the earth vis-à-vis the tremendous demands we make upon it, we must include all learners.

Challenges to Countering Hegemony

In spite of the potentialities afforded by technological advances, access to information and the distribution of knowledge is determined by those in power. In the United States alone, this stance has resulted as a deterrent for higher education, health, employment, and the corporate board room. Paradoxically, these inequities exist in a country whose democratic ideals and scientific might should have both the moral authority and the power to resolve. Although the power differential is widespread across the United States, we are particularly concerned with Latinos, who constitute the numerical majority in many regions (Passel and Cohn, 2008). It is unconscionable that such a large segment of the society is denied access to the innovations that are demanded by the social realities of the twenty-first century.

We argue that inequality and exclusion exist, particularly in the absence of cultural and historical relevance within the learning environment. Regrettably, few examples of instructional technology initiatives make any reference to the cultural lives of its participant youth (Scott et al., 2010). In fact, few programs outside the *La Clase Mágica* network serve predominantly Latino learners (Vásquez, 2003; 2007; Vásquez et al., 2010). Software programs, for example, typically target a white, non-Latino, male, and English-speaking audience (Gorski, 2008/2009).

We acknowledge learners as historical beings, as is suggested by Freire (1990) and Vygotsky (1987), thus countering the practices that ignores their historical antecedents. As Freire (2012) poses:

> science and technology at the service of the former [oppressor] are used to reduce the oppressed to the status of "things"; at the service of the latter [revolutionary leaders], they are used to promote humanization. The oppressed must become Subjects of the process, however, lest they continue to be seen as mere objects of scientific interest. (p. 133)

Our new *pedagogía transmundial*/transworld pedagogy addresses the savage inequality in the participation of Latinos in the Science, Technology, Engineering, and Mathematics (STEM) areas curbing not only the U.S. leadership in an international arena, but also the right of a large sector of the population to build on a legacy of scientific accomplishments.

REPOSITIONING METHODOLOGY: BEYOND RELEVANCE TO THE SACRED SCIENCES

We offer *Generating Transworld Pedagogy: Reimagining* La Clase Mágica as an interstices of possibilities to help close the achievement, scientific, technological, and digital gaps that exist for Latinos today (Gordo, 2003; Gorski, 2003; 2008/2009). Its newly emerging *pedagogía transmundial/* transworld pedagogy arises from our epistemological understandings, as Anzaldúa (1990) proclaims:

> Theory, then, is a set of knowledges. Some of these knowledges have been kept from us—entry into some professions and academia denied us. Because we are not allowed to enter discourse, because we are often disqualified and excluded from it, because what passes for theory these days is forbidden territory for us, it is *vital* that we occupy theorizing space, that we not allow white men and women solely to occupy it. By bringing in our own approaches and methodologies, we transform that theorizing space. (p. xxv, emphasis in original)

La Clase Mágica's (LCM) interdisciplinary nature, its cultural, linguistic, and global relevance has all of the components to help us achieve our goals of linking our pedagogy to the sacred sciences. This aligns well with bilingual/bicultural critical pedagogy and sociocultural transformative perspectives, which requires the teacher (or the knowledgeable other) to activate prior learning, acknowledge and incorporate the cultural context in which learning occurs; and to validate the connections across disciplines guiding and engaging learners in authentic tasks (Flores, Sheets, and Clark, 2011). Given the nature of the authentic, problem-posing activities in the LCM's *Labrinto Mágico*/Magical Maze (see chapter 6), learners' motivation and self-efficacy are enhanced. Through dialogue, an interdisciplinary approach "prepares learners for work and citizenship by developing higher order cognitive skills such as problem-solving, critical thinking and the ability to employ multiple perspectives" (Lattuca, Voight, and Fath, 2004, p. 23). But also, through dialogue both the *aspirante* (bilingual teacher candidate) and protégé (child) learn from each other (Freire, 1990). Importantly, LCM's malleable structure makes it an ideal heuristic to test the viability of a new pedagogy to achieve harmony between a communal experience and the natural world through technology. Its cross-system structure has the potential to link extensive learning networks that achieve substantial educational reform, facilitating the establishment of digital literacy in the curriculum (Erstad, 2009).

In repositioning our methodology to link the past with the present in order to move toward the future, we use Vygotsky's (1987) notion that takes into account the child's intellectual history as foundational for learning and development. However, we reach beyond the everyday sociocultural practices of the learners' life-world to scaffold their development and extend to the group's history of accomplishments to build upon children's intellectual patrimony. That is, we go beyond ontogenesis to phylogenetic history of the group to re-interpret the idea of the historical child and we do what Vygotsky (1987) suggests: "the stone that the builders have disdained . . . [has] . . . become the foundational stone" (p. 91).

SYNCHRONIZING MULTIPLE WORLDS: FINDINGS AND CHALLENGES

Descubrimientos

Generating Transworld Pedagogy: Reimagining La Clase Mágica is anchored on sound research and practices as a transformational process; it is *praxis* (Freire, 1990). In California, for the last twenty-one years, *La Clase Mágica* (LCM) has become a proven practice of collaboration between communities and universities to provide new and innovative ways to support learning and development (Vásquez, 2003; Ek, Machado-Casas, Sánchez, and Alanís, 2010; Underwood, 2010). Longitudinal studies (Martínez Avidad, 2012) reveal that (1) 90 percent of former LCM child-participants, who partook three or more years, were enrolled or had already completed a college degree as early adults; (2) 32 percent of the middle school students, who served as Wizard Assistants (expert participants) had plans to pursue a graduate degree; (3) twenty undergraduate mentors indicated that their training and exposure to LCM led to graduate studies; and (4) seven of twenty undergraduate mentors became college faculty. Today, the University of California San Diego's (UCSD) research initiative includes five community-university partnerships, 120 UCSD undergraduates, approximately twenty to thirty community college students, and 120 bilingual children, ages four through thirteen, primarily from Latino and Native American backgrounds. As a research initiative, it has served as a "cultural laboratory" studying thinking and learning (Moll and Díaz, 1987), using the participants' culture and language as key intellectual tools for learning and development. These laboratories have been sites of experimentation and innovation that test the latest learning-teaching theories and practice. In particular, they have been useful in experimenting with designing optimal learning environments, curriculum, and technology-assisted pedagogy for diverse populations using their cultural and linguistic resources (Vásquez, 2007; Vásquez and Marcello, 2010). More recently, the experimentation has focused on incorporating global relevance through a transliteracy curricular initiative that focuses on five core literacies—digital, financial, environmental, health, and multicultural awareness—competencies privileged in our twenty-first century global society (Vásquez and Marcello, 2010).

Moreover, its practice of collaborative relations of exchange between communities and universities has given rise to new and innovative ways for supporting learning (Vásquez, 2003; Ek et al., 2010). As such, LCM has become a model for developing culturally responsive technological-based afterschool programs. For example, the Center for the Mathematics Education of Latinos at the University of Illinois at Chicago uses LCM as model for their afterschool program (see chapter 10). Gutiérrez has also launched *El Pueblo Mágico* in Colorado and *Las Redes* in Colorado using the social design principles that undergird LCM (see foreword; Gutiérrez, 2011; Gutiérrez and Vossoughi, 2010). More recently, Vásquez started a project in Bogota, Colombia, at the Politénico GranColombiano. Sites exist in Spain at the University of Sevilla, University of Pablo de Olavide, and the University of Barcelona among Gypsy populations (see chapter 13). Each context has created new activities specifically designed for its population and, as a result has flourished and served numerous diverse learners (see chapter 13).

The Academy for Teacher Excellence (ATE) at the University of Texas at San Antonio (UTSA) has also implemented *La Clase Mágica* (Vásquez, et al., 2010; Ek et al., 2010; Rico, Sánchez, Pallares-Weissling, 2012). Using an interdisciplinary community of researchers across various disciplines,

ATE has built a legacy of preparing *aspirantes* (see chapters 7 and 8) by using the latest mobile technology to engage children and parents (see chapters 9 and 12) and by developing a digitally-based maze (see chapter 6).

At UTSA's LCM, we have incorporated the use of mobile technology, developed interactive STEM task cards, and have created culturally-relevant digital *cuentos*/stories that reflect the local culture and mystical characters like the *Chupacabra* as the nemesis of *El Maga* (see chapter 6). Given the need for enhancing STEM literacy, LCM@UTSA provides learners opportunities to use abstract and perceptual skills that are crucial in the development of mathematical and scientific thinking (see chapter 8).

We have also found that to increase Latino participation in the STEM areas requires early exposure and engagement (Lee and Luykx, 2007; National Research Council, 1996, p. 22; Saracho and Spodek, 2008). In addition to field trips and career days, we have found that virtual experiences with scientists can be a possible avenue to increase exposure and interest in the STEM areas. Moreover, we consider the value of inclusive settings, which include children with varying ability and language levels, for promoting young children's STEM development (Moomaw and Davis, 2010), and access to technology (Gorski, 2008/2009).

La Clase Mágica provides bilingual learners opportunities to engage in informal learning while actively participating in interaction and joint decision-making with peers, teacher candidates, mentors, and others. As bilinguals who are bicultural, they can traverse the globe engaging in online activities in either or multiple languages. According to Gee:

> today's games encourage players to take an active role in creating—both physically and creatively—the worlds they play in. They also intermix instruction and demonstration, telling you how to do something, then letting you try the technique firsthand, so it sinks in. These learning methods, he said, are much more effective than the memorize-and-regurgitate style found in most classrooms. (as paraphrased by Morris, 2003)

In addition to games, we suggest that digital stories integrating culture representation—along with Alexander, Eaton, and Egan's (2010) learning principles that include narrative structure, imagination-heroic qualities, curiosity-exotic travel, role-playing into the content—holds the greatest educational potential.

RETHINKING RESONANCE: NEW CONCEPTUAL UNDERSTANDINGS

Generating Transworld Pedagogy: Reimagining La Clase Mágica continues to build on its previous success with a comprehensive approach that incorporates community-based learning across PreK–12 youth, *aspirantes*, faculty, families, and community members, while also enhancing opportunities for innovative research and practice. LCM researchers and practitioners from several national and international institutions have been experimenting to enhance this program with technology that captivates, encourages creativity, and invites discovery and inquiry in ways that mediate the acquisition of social and cognitive dispositions and skills. We present *una pedagogía transmundial* for preparing *aspirantes*—bilingual education teacher candidates—to develop optimal social and intellectual development situated within critical bilingual/bicultural education supported by cultural historical theories.

Our *pedagogía transmundial*/transworld pedagogy expands the scope of Western intellectual history and builds on the long tradition of scientific explorations of Mesoamerica's indigenous people. In our work, we incorporate the method and the knowledge garnered in the interactions of everyday life. For too long, our thinking has been influenced by what has been considered as scientific knowledge without taking into account the intellectual knowledge and discoveries of our *antepasados.* We propose the inclusion of the sacred sciences as essential to *una pedagogía transmundial.*

We lay out the rationale for establishing a link between our proposed *pedagogía transmundial* and the scientific advancements of our *antepasados* and include the sacred sciences, a philosophy interweaving mind, culture, and the unknown as an absolute whole that generates new epistemological understandings. In doing so, we are suggesting that cultural relevance is not enough to prepare new citizens for the realities of a highly technical world, but rather that they should also be critically attuned to the dynamics of the physical environment. We argue that the traditional distinction between every day and scientific thinking is not valid. In *una pedagogia transmundial*, we affirm that scientific knowledge is contained within the regularities of everyday living. As our *antepasados* did in linking the knowledge of astronomy to the building of temples, we reach beyond the physical manifestations of scientific accomplishment to the metaphysical realm that falls within the spiritual and the unknown to establish a fully grounded pedagogy that also re-cultivates a harmony with our planet. Living harmoniously requires that we do not make unsustainable demands on our planet and that we are in accord with our fellow human beings; this was the *cosmovisión* of our *antepasados.* This philosophical stance goes beyond an indigenous worldview to the survival of all humankind, as Havel (1994) elucidates in the following transcendent ideas:

> perhaps as old as humanity itself: that we are not at all just an accidental anomaly, the microscopic caprice of a tiny particle whirling in the endless depth of the universe. Instead, we are mysteriously connected to the entire universe, we are mirrored in it, just as the entire evolution

of the universe is mirrored in us (see Section: Two Transcendent Ideas, paragraph 3).

Hence, we are connected to our past, present, and future as human beings and our very existence is dependent on this understanding; this was also the Mayan's perspective on time. As Havel (1994) admonishes that we must transcend in this postmodern world:

> the abyss between rational and the spiritual, the external and the internal, the objective and the subjective, the technical and the moral, the universal and the unique, [which] constantly grows deeper. (see Section: When Nothing Is Certain, paragraph 3, sentence 4)

We take this into account in re-designing and re-conceptualizing *La Clase Mágica* (Vásquez, 2003) to meet the social, intellectual, technical, and environmental realities of the day. Thus, the sacred sciences become foundational to *una pedagogía transmundial* and its ideals. By incorporating the sacred sciences, we are ensuring that ancient knowledge is recognized, respected, and taken into account.

Situated within critical bilingual/bicultural pedagogy, we appropriate an interdisciplinary approach to learning and teaching (Boix-Mansilla, 2008; Boix-Mansilla and Gardner, 2003; Gardner and Boix-Mansilla, 1994; Lattuca, Voigt, and Fath, 2004). As we intersect the sciences, the arts, and mysticism, we apply Anzaldúa's (1999) cross genre, cross border organizing system to capture what we believe is the goal of the ideal pedagogy of a technological modern world: to live in harmony with self, the other, and our natural surroundings. Further, an interdisciplinary approach allows us to acknowledge the socio-cultural, historical, and political influences on education (Freire, 1990). We are proposing a transworld pedagogical model, *una pedagogía transmundial* that harnesses the advantages of new technologies of communication to open new channels of understanding for co-existence with our fellow human beings and our environment.

In sum, major interrelated long-term research outcomes will be shared in this book: (a) research-based theoretical principles for creating effective after-school educational activities that enhance student learning and for creating a system of learning networks that allow the experimentation of new ways of teaching and learning for preparing teacher candidates (see chapters 1–6), (b) the effective use of technology in advancing teacher candidates' knowledge and competency (see chapters 7 and 8); (c) the incorporation of Latino children's knowledge, familiarity, and the use of technology to develop biliteracy, digital literacy, and numeracy (see chapters 9, 10, and 11); (d) the enhancement of parents and communities' access to knowledge through technology (see chapter 12); and (f) the transportability of LCM within an international context (see chapter 13).

La Clase Mágica is a catalyst for transforming our thinking about new possibilities and opportunities for learning and teaching for the twenty-first century. As a result of this intellectual wave, a new paradigm for teacher preparation has surged as a *pedagogía transmundial*/transworld pedagogy.

¡ADELANTE!

REFERENCES

Alexander, G., Eaton, I., and Egan, K. (2010). "Cracking the Code of Electronic Games: Some Lessons for Educators." *Teachers College Record*, 112(7), 1830–1850.

Anzaldúa, G. (1990). *Making Face, Making Soul/Haciendo Caras: Creative and Critical Perspectives by Women of Color* (first ed.) San Francisco, CA: Aunt Lute Foundation Books.

——— (1999). *Borderlands/La Frontera: The New Mestiza* (second ed.) San Francisco, CA: Aunt Lute Foundation Books.

Apple. M. (2000). *Official Knowledge: Democratic Education in a Conservative Age* (second ed.) New York: Routledge.

Boix-Mansilla, V. (2008). "Integrative Learning: Setting the Stage for a Pedagogy of the Contemporary." *Peer Review*, 10(4), 31.

Boix-Mansilla, V. and Gardner, H. (2003) "Assessing Interdisciplinary Work at the Frontier: An Empirical Exploration of 'Symptoms' of Quality." Retrieved June 17, 2011 from www.Interdisciplines.org

Brayboy, B. M. J., and Castagño, A. E. (2008). "How Might Native Science Inform 'Informal Science Learning'?" *Cultural Studies of Science Education*, 3(3), 731–750.

Civil, M. (2007). "Building on Community Knowledge: An Avenue to Equity in Mathematics Education." In N. Nassir and P. Cobb (eds.), *Improving Access to Mathematics: Diversity and Equity in the Classroom* (105–117). New York: Teachers College Press.

Clark, E. R. (2013). *Claiming Cultural Spaces: Wearing Huiples a Fabric of Identity. Needle Arts Magazine: Embroiderers' Guild of America*, 44(3), 22–28.

Erstad, O. (2009). "'Learning Networks': Capacity Building for School Development and ICT." In R. Krumsvik (ed.), *Learning in the Network: Society and the Digitized School* (89–106). Nova Science Publishers.

Ek, L. D., Machado-Casas, M., Sánchez, P., and Alanís, I. (2010) "Crossing Cultural Borders: '*La Clase Mágica*' as a University-School Partnership." *Journal of School Leadership*, 20(6), 820–849.

Fischer, E. F. (1999). "Cultural Logic and Maya Identity: Rethinking Constructivism and Essentialism." *Current Anthropology*, 40(4), 473–499.

Flores, B. B., Sheets, R. H., Clark, E. R. (2011). *Teacher Preparation for Bilingual Student Populations: Educar para transformar*. New York, London: Routledge.

Foucault, M. (1980). *Power/Knowledge: Selected Interviews and Other Writings, 1972-1977*. (Gordon, C., ed. and trans.), New York: Pantheon.

Freire, P. (1990). *Pedagogy of the Oppressed*. New York: Continuum Press.

——— (2012). *Pedagogy of the Oppressed*. (Thirtieth anniv. ed.) New York: Continuum Press.

Furner, J., Holbein, M. D., and Scullion, K. J. (2000). "Taking an Internet Field Trip: Promoting Cultural and Historical Diversity through Mayan Mathematics." *TechTrends*, 44(6), 18–22. DOI: 10.1007/BF02763311.

Gardner, H., and Boix-Mansila, V. (1994). "Teaching for Understanding—Within and Across Disciplines." *Educational Leadership*, 51(5), 14-18.

Gordo, B. (2003). "Overcoming Digital Deprivation." *IT and Society*, 1(5), 166–180.

Gorski, P. C. (2008/2009). "Insisting on Digital Equity: Reframing the Dominant Discourse on Multicultural Education and Technology." *Urban Education*, 44, 348–364.

——— (2003). "Privilege and Repression in the Digital Era: Rethinking the Sociopolitics of the Digital Divide." *Race, Gender, and Class*, 10(4), 145–176.

Gutiérrez, K. D. (2011). "Teaching toward Possibility: Building Cultural Supports for Robust Learning." *PowerPlay: A Journal of Educational Justice*, 3(1), 22–37.

Gutiérrez, K. D. and Vossoughi, S. (2010). "Lifting off the Ground to Return Anew: Mediated Praxis, Transformative Learning, and Social Design Experiment." *Journal of Teacher Education*, 61(1-2), 100-117. DOI: 10.1177/0022487109347877.

Havel, V. (1994, July). "The Need for Transcendence in a Postmodern World." Speech presented at Independence Hall, July 4, 1994, Philadelphia, PA. Retrieved September 22, 2012 from http://www.worldtrans.org/whole/havelspeech.html.

Instituto Nacional de Astrofísica, Óptica, y Electrónica (2004). "Nepohualtzintzin: The PreHispanic Computer." Retrieved July 14, 2011 from http://www.inaoep.mx/iberamia2004/nepo_eng.htm.

Lara, E. G. (2000). *Computo relevante: Nepohualtzintzin*. Mexico, D.F.

———— (2013). *Nepohualtzitzin en el modelo matemático figurativo Náhuatl: Evidencia de su existencia a través de un retrato figurativo hablado en Náhuatal*. Mexico, D.F.

Lattuca, L. R., Voigt, L. J., and Fath, K. Q. (2004). "Does Interdisciplinarity Promote Learning? Theoretical Support and Researchable Questions." *The Review of Higher Education*, 28, 1, 23–48.

Lee, O., and Luykx, A. (2007). "Science Education and Student Diversity: Race/Ethnicity, Language, Culture, and Socioeconomic Status." In S. K. Abell and N. G. Lederman (eds.), *Handbook of Research in Science Education* (second ed.) (171-197). Mahwah, NJ: Lawrence Erlbaum.

Martínez Avidad, M. (2012). "Comunicación para el desarrollo y la inclusión social de minorías: La Clase Mágica, un modelo de intervención para el cambio social." Unpublished doctoral dissertation. University of Alicante, Alicante, Spain.

Moll, L. C., and Díaz, E. (1987). "Bilingual Communication Skills in the Classroom." Final Report, Laboratory of Comparative Human Cognition, University of California, San Diego, CA.

Moll L. C., and Gonzalez, N. (2004). "Engaging Life: A Funds of Knowledge Approach to Multicultural Education." In J. Banks and C. McGee Banks (eds.), *Handbook of Research on Multicultural Education*, (second ed.) (669-715). New York: Jossey-Bass.

Moomaw, S., and Davis, J. A. (2010). "STEM Comes to Preschool." *Young Children*, 26(5), 12–14, 16–18.

McKillop, H. (2010). "Ancient Maya Canoe Navigations and its Implications for Classic to Post-Classic Maya Economy and Sea Trade: A View from the South Coast of Belize." *Journal of Caribbean Archeology*, 3, 93-105. Retrieved August 30, 2010 from http://www.flmnh.ufl.edu/JCA/McKillop.pdf.

Morris, (2003, August 9). "Video Games as Teaching Tools? Junior's Grades Aren't Up to Snuff? Contact Prof. Lara Croft." *CNN Commentary*. Retrieved June 13, 2008 from http://money.cnn.com/2003/07/09/commentary/game_over/column_gaming/?cnn=yes.

National Oceanic and Atmospheric Administration. (2011). "NOAA and Partners Explore the Hidden World of the Maritime Maya: Ancient Port Site was Used Periodically between 800 BC and 1521 AD." Retrieved August 30, 2011 from http://researchmatters.noaa.gov/news/Pages/MayanMariners.aspx.

National Research Council. (1996). *National Science Education Standards*. Washington, DC: National Academy Press. Retrieved May 20, 2011 from http://www.nap.edu/openbook.php?record_id=4962.

Passel, J. S. and Cohn, D. (2008). *U.S. Population Projections: 2005-2050*. Pew Hispanic Center.

Quisato Scientific Research Project (2010). *Catepillo Mount*. Retrieved August 30, 2011 from http://www.quitsato.org/en/index.php?option=com_content%view=article&id=48&Itemid=58.

Rico, R., Sánchez, P., and Pallares-Weissling, A. (2012). "A Snapshot of Latina/o Bilingual Teacher Candidates and Their Use of iPads in an After-School Technology Program." *Journal of Bilingual Research and Instruction*, 14(1), 95–115.

Rosa, M. and Orey, D. C. 2007). "Pop: A Study of the Ethnomathematics of Globalization Using the Sacred Mayan Mat Pattern." In M. Atweh, A. C. Barton, M. Borba, N. Gough, C. Keitel, C. Vistro-Yu, and R. Vithal, *Internationalisation and Globalisation in Mathematics and Science Education*, section 2, 227–246. DOI:10.1-7/978-1-4020-5908-7_13.

Saracho, O. N., and Spodek, B. (2008). *Contemporary Perspectives on Science and Technology in Early Childhood Education*. Charlotte, NC: Information Age Publishing Inc.

Scofield, B. (2004/2005). "The Long and Short of the Mayan Calendar." The Mountain Astrologer.

Scott, K, Clark, K., Sheridan, K., Mruczek, C., and Hayes, E. (2010). "Engaging More Students from Underrepresented Groups in Technology: What Happens if We Don't?" Proceedings of Society for Information Technology and Teacher Education International Conference, 1269-1277. Chesapeake, VA: AACE.

Smiley, C. H. (1962). "The Mayan Calendar." *Astronomical Society of the Pacific Leaflets*, 8, 327–334.

Sitler, R. K. (2006). "The 2012 Phenomenon: New Age Appropriation of an Ancient Mayan Calendar." *Nova Religio: The Journal of Alternative and Emergent Religions*. Retrieved August 30, 2011 from http://michaelsheiser.com/PaleoBabble/2012%20Phenomenon%20in%20New%20Age.pdf

Underwood, C. and Parker, L. (2010). *University-Community Links to Higher Learning*. UC Links Annual Report, 2008–2009. Berkeley, CA: University of California, Berkeley.

Vásquez, O. A. (2003). *La Clase Mágica: Imagining Optimal Possibilities in a Bilingual Community of Learners*. Mahwah, NJ: Lawrence Erlbaum.

———(2007). "Technology Out of School: What Schools can Learn from Community-Based Technology." *Yearbook of the National Society for the Study of Education*, 106(2), 182–206.

Vásquez, O. A. and Marcello, A. (2010). "A Situated View at 'Scaling Up' in Culturally and Linguistically Diverse Communities: The Need for Mutual Adaptation." Paper submitted for publication to the *Revista de Educación of the Universidad Nacional Abierta y Distancia (UNAD) of Colombia*.

Vásquez, O. A., Razfar, A, Flores, B. B., Clark, E. R., and Claeys, L. (2010). Laboratories for Learning Collaborative Research-Based After-School Programs: A Research Policy Brief: *La Clase Mágica* Research Initiative. Retrieved August 30, 2011 from: http://ate.utsa.edu/Policy-Brief

Vygotsky, L. S. (1987). "Thinking and Speech." In R. Rieber and A. Carlton (eds.), *L.S. Vygotsky Collected Works* (Vol. 1, 39–285). New York: Plenum.

TWO

Una Pedagogía Transmundial/A Transworld Pedagogy: Anchoring Theory to the Sacred Sciences

Olga A. Vásquez, Ellen Riojas Clark, and Belinda Bustos Flores

WORKING TOWARD HARMONY

The Mexican axiom, *"cada cabeza es un mundo"* (every mind is a world), metaphorically encapsulates the pedagogy we propose in this chapter; a pedagogy that opens to multiple cultural worlds to offer new knowledge sources, exciting intellectual trajectories, and new possibilities for transformation. In this chapter, we seek to articulate a theory and practice that takes into account the intellectual capital of non-mainstream students as critical tools for teaching and learning. Theoretically, we conceive this worldview as the learner's "prior history" which cultural-historical theory posits as the springboard for new learning and development (Vygotsky, 1978; Cole and Engeström, 2006). We take to heart the importance that Vygotsky (1978) attributes to the particular social world in which the individual develops and then re-conceptualizes it as broader and replete with multiplicities and complexities. We extend the notion of a "bilingual/bicultural transformative pedagogy" (Flores, Sheets, and Clark, 2011) as foundational to this new pedagogical framework. Further, we weave in the theoretical and practical underpinnings of *La Clase Mágica* [LCM] (Vásquez, 2003) instantiated in an educational activity system linking a community and a higher education institution through an after-school technology-based program. We take these ideas beyond the local

17

and the material to re-vision what learners need to know in an increasingly diverse and complex "world in motion" as Inda and Rosaldo (2002) call the intersection of multiple languages, cultures, and knowledges coming together at any given moment in today's globalized world. Although we give special emphasis to Spanish-English bilingual learners of the United States, we propose a new pedagogy that aligns perfectly with the social realities of the twenty-first century and thus, relevant to all groups and all education.

Following Erikson's (1963) assertion that the nature of all teaching is an act of intercultural communication, we reassess our aims of education to "what is already going on . . . the resources and difficulties of the situation" (Dewey, 1916, p. 637). We take a perspective that sheds light on both the multivoicedness of the present conditions and the connections and interconnections that constitute identities. We reach back in time until we are in direct contact with the "collective heritage of human experience with the natural world" (Cajete, 2000, p. 3), what we are calling the "sacred sciences" and interweave the lessons learned across time into a new pedagogy. Hence, we aim to prepare learners to live in a world that demands the ability to move in and out of multiple perspectives and identities, while participating in the multiple cultural and imagined worlds that constitute life in the twenty-first century. We call this new pedagogy, *una pedagogía transmundial*, a transworld pedagogy that prepares learners to effectively assume the positionality of "boundary objects," which Star and Griesemer (1989) describe as the cognitive means to:

> Inhabit several intersecting worlds and satisfy the informational requirements of each of them . . . plastic enough to adapt to local needs and the constraints of the several parties employing them, yet robust enough to maintain a common identity across sites. (p. 393)

In ascribing to such pedagogy, we move away from privileging "official knowledge" rooted in the dominant culture and language (Apple, 1993), and infuse the pedagogic moment with culturally and ecologically relevant sources drawn from an assortment of accumulated knowledges, countless experiences, and the variety of worldviews present in schoolrooms worldwide. Rather than solely privileging one language and culture, we mobilize the community's "funds of knowledge" (Moll and González, 2004), both tacit and active and make these the foundation of our pedagogy for the development of the identity we want to inculcate: *un ciudadano transmundial*, a transworld citizen; a hybrid citizen who is both faithful to a cultural past and yet free to embrace multiple identities and ancestral trajectories (Anzaldúa, 1999).

We open the classroom to cross-disciplinarity, (Gardner, 1983), "cross-genre and cross borders" (Anzaldúa, 1989, p. 49) and thus, circumvent the exclusion of non-dominant languages or cultures, reflective of the current situation in educational contexts worldwide. We reconnect with prominent theories and formulations of learning and teaching and rearticulate more deeply the ways a learner's history as an individual member of a particular family, community, and society offers a reservoir of intellectual and cultural historical resources that can be used to inform an innovative pedagogy. As Latina educators and researchers, we draw on decades of scholarship and cultural experiences to propose a new pedagogical theory that is:

> much more readable but not any less rigorous, precisely because the "fit" between fact and theory, description and explanation, life and text is more immediate in terms of the political in which theory or explanation is written. (Torres, 2000, p. 124)

We define more clearly a pedagogical approach that strategically scaffolds a new view of rootedness in the local culture that reaches out to the many concentric cultures in which it is embedded — i.e., a view of belonging to both the local and global community that emanates from a repository of native and dominant knowledges and multiple roles a society has for its inhabitants. In the process of articulating such a pedagogy, we deploy the means we have sculpted through our long experiences in research and practice — i.e., critical pedagogy, information and communication technologies, and cultural and linguistic relevance — effective tools to encourage learners to objectify and reaffirm their multiple identities as they navigate the socio-cultural and -economic exigencies of the national doctrine.

While the experience of shifting in and out of the material and virtual worlds afforded by new information and communication technologies may be novel, these abilities align closely with the belief in spiritual and other extraordinary phenomena that situates nature and the supernatural, often within the same thought. Latinos, as well as other groups, share a wealth of experience in "brokering, boundary interactions and boundary practices, and boundary zones" (Akkerman and Bakker, 2011, p.134) as Anzaldúa's depicts in her struggles to harness the complexities embedded in the many identities she occupied. Skillfully, Anzaldúa weaves in the social and cognitive complications that she endured as she moved in and out of these distinct identities, an experience attributed to life in Latino communities. Anzaldúa argues that this new conscious has to:

> shift out of habitual formations; from convergent thinking, analytical reasoning that tends to use rationality to move toward a single goal (a Western mode), to divergent thinking, characterized by movement away from set patterns and goals and toward a more whole perspective, one that includes rather than excludes. (1999, p. 79)

We recognize the pivotal role that these social and cognitive resources play in life on the borderlands/*fronteras* and thus, make them foundational to a transworld mindset we want to endorse. Given the sociopolitical, economic, and technical realities of communities and societies today, it is critical for learners to embrace their cultural ways of being so as not to lose to their bearings as they form new ways of being in the world. Chapters 8, 9, and 10 illustrate multiple resources that bilingual learners bring to the learning setting and the ways that this new pedagogy facilitates the acquisition of new knowledge and skills to successfully assume new roles and expectations increasingly demanded by an ever changing world.

CONCEPTUAL RESONANCE: WHAT DO WE KNOW?

We know from almost twenty-five years of independently experimenting with culturally relevant curriculum and a bilingual/bicultural critical pedagogy that incorporating the linguistic and cultural capital of learners helps prepare youth to "look at the past only as a means of understanding more clearly what and who they are so that they can more wisely build the future" (Freire, 1970, p. 72). Our contention is that "the learner is in a state of readiness, willing and able to move to the next level of development with expert support" (Vásquez, 2005, p. 324) and that his or her community's cultural and linguistic resources are critical tools for intellectual development (Moll, 1990; Vásquez, 2003). We also know that the world has changed dramatically in the last 20 years and that the wired classroom of today has become a "space of flows" (Castells, 1989)—in which "the material organization of time-sharing social practices work through flows" (p. 147). That is, the students are rooted in cultures, languages, knowledges, and histories that could very well form the basis for interrelating across time and space within a digital world. In a world where time and space dynamically intersect, learners need not only what is essential in the local communities, but also what is vital to navigate the world at large.

Regrettably, in spite of this tremendous complexity of today's world, educational systems and teachers continue to compel their students to trade in their precious cultural capital for a dominant one that is ostensibly more powerful in the marketplace (Cummins, 1996; Walsh, 1991; Nieto, 1994). Adopting the canonical language and culture has never ensured the participation of all. Learners of today need more knowledge and skills to negotiate the multiplicities brought about by the continuous movement of people, ideas, economics, cultures, and technologies worldwide. In today's world, it is a liability to solely align to one culture and language.

Surveying the accumulated knowledge we have gained through our separate research and practice over the last several decades and through implementing *La Clase Mágica* in both California and Texas, four theoretical concepts—Vygotsky's dialectic method, his notion of culture, a bilingual/bicultural critical pedagogy, and our recent unearthing of the notion of "sacred sciences"—frame the vision of the pedagogy we propose. Together these ideas fundamentally structure the perspective we take in attempting to advance learners' development in accordance with the new digitally based social reality of the second decade of the twenty-first century. These theoretical concepts also shed light on the tasks and resources that learners must acquire in order to easily navigate the intersection of time and space that digital media makes possible, and ultimately bolster and makes relevant their cultural and linguistic capital. Given the displacement that learners experience in a world that increasingly separates them from their knowledges and traditions, we add the concept of the "sacred sciences" as a means to ground one's sense of self as a cultural being.

The Dialectical Method

In guiding human behavior under these conditions and for that matter, introducing new realms of possibilities, we must first consider the landscape of cultural development that Vygotsky's dialectical method makes visible. According to this perspective, the social world plays a vital role in learning and development, particularly in the ways that a child develops into a skilled participant of his or her cultural world. Known as Vygotsky's dialectical method, which proposes that higher intellectual functions—i.e., those ways of knowing and acting in the world that a developing child acquires as a member of a particular group—appear twice . . . first in the social, later, on the individual level; first, between people (interpsychological), and then *inside* the child (intrapsychological) (1978, p. 57).

Through numerous routine arrangements and interactions with members of their social group, children learn who they are, what is expected of them and how and what language is used for each particular occasion. According to Valsiner (1987), "all higher psychological functions are internalized relationships of the social kind, and constitute the social structure of personality" (p. 67). That is, through their participation in the daily life of the social group, children become "skilled practitioners in the specific cognitive activities of their communities" (Rogoff, 1991, p. 351).

As educators and researchers who ascribe to the multiplicities made visible in Anzaldúa's (1999) work, Vygotsky's perspective introduces an implied uniformity of the social world which put us in a quandary—that of the child or that of the dominant society? The important contribution the dialectical method makes, however, is that it centers our attention on the vital role social processes play in the cultural development of the child. It also recognizes the value of the cognitive and cultural capital learners bring to the social setting and to relate these to intellectual competencies they need to skillfully participate in the complex and multi-dimensional world of the twenty-first century.

Vygotsky's Notion of Culture

Vygotsky's idea that the starting point of the pedagogical enterprise is to understand the sociocultural conditions in which higher intellectual functions develop, only takes us so far. It answers the questions: What do we have to work with? And, to what extent does it help us reveal the point at which learners clash with the broader social environment? It does not tell us where we go from here or what learning environment would facilitate more readily the acquisition of the tools learners need to navigate new sociocultural conditions. Vygotsky's notion of culture provides us an entry point to imagine the kind of conditions that foster the development of knowledge and skills to operate not only within the sociocultural conditions of the world of today, but also those we can imagine for the future. Like Vygotsky, we conceive culture as:

> the socially structured ways in which society organizes the kinds of tasks that the growing child faces and the kinds of tools, both mental and physical, that the young child is provided to master those tasks. (quoted in Luria, 1979, p. 44)

This perspective on culture, entreats us to ask a series of questions such as: What kind of culture do practitioners and researchers need to organize to promote the kind of learning that is required for the social conditions of today? Or, for that matter, the future? And, at the practical level, it leads us to ask how can we organize a new social practice involving the knowledge and skills the young need to become expert participants of a new social world? That is, what type of cultural experience can we provide learners to prepare them to meet the demands of a technologically based multilingual/multicultural world? And, finally, what kind of cultural capital must learners have to navigate the new world order as legitimate participants (Lave and Wenger, 1991). The chapters in this volume provide ample examples of the culture and cultural capital learners must possess in order to be dynamic and productive actors in the new world realities.

These questions challenge education that historically excluded those not considered to be part of the mainstream and, as such, have been made to leave their language and culture at the classroom door. In effect, they have been told that "their ways of being" are not valued in the classroom and to leave these at the door. Additionally, these questions also signal the exact point where to begin exploring the cultural resources students bring. Ample research on the effectiveness of culturally relevant educational experiences ranging from classroom teaching methodologies and curriculum design (Bergeron, 2008; Ware, 2006; Moll and Gonzalez,

2004; Civil, 2007) to community-based health and educational programs (Tarlow and Mahoney, 2005; Finucane and McMullen, 2008; Vincent, et al., 2006; Vásquez, 2003) support our contention that beginning with students' life experiences and cultural background is a sound and tested pedagogical approach. It is at this point that Vygotsky's notion of culture provides the guiding principle for socially and theoretically inscribing an entire system of artifacts (tools and symbols imbued with sociocultural meaning), interactional routines, and learning activities with the intellectual tools for understanding and navigating multiple languages, cultures, knowledges, and technologies that represents the social realities.

Critical Bilingual/Bicultural Pedagogy

While Vygotsky's notions lead us to consider the possibility of creating an idioculture (Cole, 1996; Fine, 1979) for the promotion of optimal learning, the notion of a critical bilingual/bicultural pedagogy establishes a link to culture, cognition, and language. Essentially, it recognizes the power of language and language choice in knowledge construction, identity formation, and a social, cultural, historical, and political consciousness among teachers and learners alike (Flores et al., 2011; Darder, 1991; 1997). Bilingual/bicultural critical pedagogy unleashes the promise that teachers bring to the learning context as Díaz-Soto (2011) asserts:

> Most of our [teacher] candidates come to us with idealism and joy for their chosen profession. It is up to us to harness these elements and ensure that children and families are the beneficiaries of an education that is transformative and liberating. (p. 242)

A bilingual/bicultural critical pedagogy is actualized in the daily life of the classroom as students come to know who they are and where they are going. This type of critical pedagogy counters the assimilationist function of schooling and the banking approach to learning through six basic tenets that we have generated over time: (1) the formation of identity and *concientización*, (2) authentic democratic dialogic participation, (3) cultural knowledge of the home and community, (4) interdisciplinary inquiry and problem-posing/solving knowledge construction,(5) authentic, linguistically and culturally relevant projects and tasks developed using multiple literacies and technologies, and (6) transformative and liberating social action. The goals and objectives of the interactions and system of artifacts of *La Clase Mágica's* transworld pedagogy align closely with these tenets of this kind of critical pedagogy (Flores et al., 2011; Vásquez, 2003):

Sacred Sciences

Science, and particularly, a science that is sacred and social (Kuhn, 1996) is a critical component of our objective to prepare learners for a world that is typified by multiplicities as well as vulnerabilities brought about by the neglect of attention to local culture and local environment. In including the scared sciences in our theorizing, we argue, that science is not the sole purview of credentialed white men who seek "pure" knowledge in sterile laboratories. Rather, we hold that the Western conception of science is narrow and untenable when defined as:

> a knowledge or a system of knowledge covering general truths or the operation of general laws especially as obtained and tested through the scientific method and concerned with the physical world and its phenomena. (Merriam-Webster, 2012)

Instead, we build on the ideas of native sciences as subscribed by indigenous scholars such as Cajete, (2000); Bang and Medin (2010); Brayboy and Castagño (2008) and view science as knowledge that:

> includes ideas of constant motion and flux, existence consisting of energy waves, interrelationships, all things being animate, space/place renewal and all things being imbued with spirit. (Little Bear in the foreword to Cajete, 2000)

It is a perspective that goes beyond the confines of modern science to embrace the spirituality of nature. Science does not belong to a select few but rather forms the mystery of everyday life in which all humans are immersed. All human action is imbued with the potential for achieving new conceptual understandings of self and its relation to all life in its multiple dimensions. It is our task as teachers and guides to illuminate those points of crossing where knowledge is instinctive, and at that point facilitate its discovery. In the sacred role of teacher, we must personify living in harmony through the love, respect, relevance, reciprocity, and responsibility to all in the past, the present, and in the future. Like Anzaldúa, we seek understanding beyond the material technology to spirituality, to the site of reciprocal relations between culture and nature. We seek a unique pedagogy grounded on the epistemology—*cosmovisión* of the indigenous and sift through all that we have come to know on our own and have been taught to inform the core of our pedagogy. We recognize how the universal principles of the Mayan civilization also come to underscore such understanding, showing us how the physical laws of creation were used to sustain the world.

This view of sacred sciences resonates well with new meditational tools that Pontecorvo (quoted in González and Moll, 2002) calls the:

> semiotic systems pertaining to different languages and to various scientific fields; these are procedures, thought methodologies, and cultural objects that have to be appropriated, practices of discourse and reasoning that have to be developed, and play or study practices that have to be exercised (p. 364).

We use these new concepts to reinforce and ground the sociotransformative theoretical framework of the *pedagogía transmundial*.

Ultimately, we seek to unearth ways of knowing that come from a people's long history of traditions and relations to the natural environment and privilege them as valuable resources for teaching and learning. We incorporate into our pedagogy, a view of science as active; one that draws on the groundbreaking achievements by early indigenous groups of the Americas, which were:

> "discovered" only centuries later by "normal science" in the areas of constitutions and governance, military tactics, agriculture and agronomy, cosmology, long distance navigation, architecture, engineering, medicine including even neurosurgery, unified monetary systems for long distance trade, preservatives for foods, mathematics and symbolic logic, flora and fauna management and breeding, effective education and pedagogy, law and constitutions, meteorology, immunology. (Craven, 2012, see section Classical and Neoclassical Paradigms of "Science," paragraph 3, last sentence)

We further ground the cultural relevance of *una pedagogía transmundial* in communal sources that are rooted in a spiritual orientation, experiential insights, and a relational methodology to all life knowledges (Hart, 2010), which are often instantiated in the stories and everyday practices of a people.

REPOSITIONING METHODOLOGY AT THE ROOT OF THE SACRED SCIENCES

Building on Optimal Possibilities

The dialectical method, the idea of culture as the tasks and resources a society offers its young, and the linking of bilingualism/biculturalism to power have been the backbone of the *La Clase Mágica* (Vásquez, 2003) and its offspring, *La Clase Mágica's* transworld pedagogy now weaving the sacred with the natural sciences. In both interpretations, an educational activity system (in-school or out) is linked to a university undergraduate field-based courses to experiment with the design of the ideal pedagogical conditions to enhance learning and development of bilingual learners. Following Vygotsky's urging that it is not enough to learn about psychological functions, but that we must also intervene (Vygotsky, 1978), *La Clase Mágica* has made a difference in the academic achievement of diverse learners in K–12 and their equitable representation in higher education (Martínez Avidad, 2012). It accomplishes this goal by reflecting the learners' background experiences as critical intellectual tools, adding an inter-generational approach to its pedagogy, and a social-action community-based approach to its goals and objectives—i.e., working directly with community members to address local inequality in education (Vásquez, 2003; Vásquez, Guarrasi, and Carr, 2012).

In focusing on the future development of learners, *La Clase Mágica's* transworld pedagogy poses knowledge as socially constructed, learning as an active process and knowledge as constructed from experience (Dewey, 1916; Vygotsky, 1978). It mobilizes a system of artifacts inscribed with a specific kind of learner, worker, and citizen fully prepared to effectively negotiate a globalized world as bilingual/bicultural active learners and thinkers.

Under this framework, our experimentation has focused on designing an activity system of adult-child interaction routines—i.e., the tasks and the resources to accomplish them—of a constructed culture known as the "culture of optimal learning" (Vásquez, 2007, p. 199). Our end goal has been to enculturate children to the demands of a bilingual/bicultural world rapidly changing as a result of globalization. In this book, we extend our focus to *aspirantes*, undergraduate students preparing for a teaching career in bilingual/bicultural settings. As such, we refocus the research lens on how the constructed culture of *La Clase Mágica's* transworld pedagogy affords *aspirantes* the opportunity to be producers of culture as they, in Dewey's terms (1916), "survey the present state of experience of pupils, form a tentative plan of treatment, keep the plan constantly in view and yet modify it as conditions develop" (p. 101). In the process, they learn how to engage their protégés (bilingual learners) through theoretically informed interactions that scaffold their progress through their zone of proximal development to achieve their future development (Vygotsky, 1978). Importantly, they learn to deploy the learners' own primary language and culture—and other cultural elements such as information and communication technology as instrumental tools for solving the tasks set by a new vision of the culture of optimal learning. Ultimately, they come to understand that these tools not only promote cognitive development and digital literacy, they also guide participation in the values and practices of a unique cultural community that is conceptualized outside of school activities (Rogoff, 1995). That is, they learn the competencies and dispositions that the learner will face vis-à-vis the social realities of a fluid world (Vásquez, 2007).

The experienced success in LCM on how best to design learning environments to meet the needs of cultural communities is evident in California (Underwood et al., 2000; Vásquez and Marcello, 2010), nationally (Ek, Machado-Casas, Sánchez, and Alanís, 2010; Arreguín-Anderson, 2011; Martínez-Roldán and Smagorinsky, 2011; Rico, Sánchez, and Pallares-Weissling, 2012), and internationally (Lalueza, Crespo, Luque, and Padrós 2011; Lamas and Lalueza, 2012). This leads us to not only continue with this line of thinking but to ground it even deeper in the collective memory of the respective group's social history and its interrelations with the local environment. To accomplish this, we extend our theorizing of knowledge, culture, and language to the notion of the "sacred sciences," those knowledges that come from a long history of interaction with tradition and the ecological environment of a lived culture.

Together, all four theoretical concepts—the dialectic method, Vygotsky's notion of culture, a bilingual/bicultural critical pedagogy, and the sacred sciences form the building blocks of our *pedagogía transmundial/* transworld pedagogy. Together, they weave a life in harmony with self, the other, and our natural surroundings into a pedagogy that addresses the social realities of a technical modern world that both connects and deterritorializes us simultaneously in time and space. These conditions make it more critical for learners to acquire and mobilize an "interliteracy" that Moll (2011) argues:

> helps students garner and combine valuable funds of knowledge from their multiple environments for personal or academic use; that is, biliteracy serves to expand, one could say, the students' cultural and intellectual geographies in a transnational world. (p. 156)

These conditions also call for the means to access those knowledges of the mainstream world with legitimate participation rights and privileges; a mainstream, we argue, given the social realities of today, is increasingly more multicultural and multilingual. We contend that the new system of activity within the classroom will provide the tools for learners to navigate the geographies of a transnational world. As bilingual/bicultural beings centered in the sacred sciences, they will be able to read many worlds without losing their sense of self vis-à-vis the hegemonic forces of the culture in power.

The inclusion of the sacred sciences rearticulates Vygotsky's focus on sociocultural context and social history within a much larger framework that spans time and space to the very essence of life and our indelible relation to our cultural and natural ecology. Additionally, we employ the methodology of design experiment to organize the environment and continually tweak it, to embody the depth and breadth of a new worldview. We consider Gutiérrez and Vossoughi's (2010) notion of social design experiment that allows the researcher to "make visible the practices, meanings, and contradictions that often become invisible to those closest to the action" (p. 101); further, "organized around equity-oriented and robust learning principles, social design experiments are oriented toward transformative ends through mutual relations of change" (p. 101). Through an ongoing process of "progressive refinement" (Collins et al., 2004, p. 18), we scrutinize and refine our pedagogical goals and instructional objectives until we achieve the ideal learning conditions and optimal outcomes for the moment and the specific learner. Our objective is not to simply seek a state in which "all the bugs are worked out" as Collins and colleagues (2004) suggest, but rather believe that continuous revision is the natural state of any educational enterprise that seeks to meet the ever-changing needs and resources of cosmic transworld citizens and an interconnected and interdependent society.

RETHINKING RESONANCE: NEW CONCEPTUAL UNDERSTANDINGS

Arguelles (2007) describes resonance as reverbaerations between us and reality or matter. He describes the different overtones and "keys to different coexisting dimensions—the different dimensions of reality that coexist" (p. 72). If everything is in resonance, ultimately, everything is in a condition of harmony. There are different shifts, different waves, and particular cycles that dissolve and others that begin, but basically, there is a harmonic structure to all reality. As we make clear throughout, we interact with the world as we mentioned above—we resonate with our environment.

Through our *pedagogía transmundial,* we establish a connection and respect for what makes us whole. We go beyond what Aikenhead (1996) suggests:

> (1) make border crossings explicit for students, (2) facilitate these border crossings, (3) validate students' personally and culturally constructed ways of knowing about nature, and (4) teach the knowledge, skills, and values of Western Science and technology in the context of societal roles. (pg. 18)

Further, we make visible the numerous multiple resources—both social and cultural—brought in by all learners. Using *El Maga* (see chapter 7, 8, and 14), the mystical digital being that serves as the conduit between past, present, and future, we explore new epistemological understanding of the sacred sciences. With *El Maga's* guidance, we explore the interstices of informal life and illuminate the complexities of knowledge held within time and space. It is in these spaces that *aspirantes* must situate themselves as cultural brokers to perceive multiple ways of knowing and weave these into a deeper understanding of a complex whole. Through this process, *aspirantes* awaken and develop their personal and professional identities and beliefs. They also strengthen their bilingualism, critical reflective thinking, and cultural efficacy that help *aspirantes* recognize their inherent responsibilities for deconstructing the borderlands that exist between home and school.

SYNCHRONIZING MULTIPLE WORLDS: FINDINGS AND CHALLENGES

The challenge, then, for a *pedagogía transmundial* is to go beyond the Western worldview and embrace the epistemological potentialities of the sacred sciences to carry out our intellectual work. Unearthing the sacredness of knowledge and the cultivation of a spiritual vision becomes a new methodology in the formation of *aspirantes*. In incorporating the sacred sciences into our pedagogical approach, we not only reach back to the "pioneering achievements" of our *antepasados*, we also look forward in time to address the unsustainable ecological footprints we are leaving for our descendants. The depth of this methodology is echoed by Maximilliano García, a Makuna *capitán* (tribal leader) and Colombian education leader of the Amazon, who underscores the need to first understand self and community as a means to navigate Western knowledge and language (Vásquez, Valbuena, Hernández, Montoya, and García, 2013). *Capitán* García poses the ability of the Makuna learner to identify "a noise in the jungle that is unrelated to the local ecology and then describe it in the Makuna language" as the criteria for assessing the foundation of their own local education (personal communication, September 11, 2011). What *Capitán* García is proposing is a well-grounded Makuna epistemology that supports a strong cultural identity required to deliberately and productively navigate the outside world without losing one's identity, language, and epistemological connection to one's traditions and ecology.

In summary, this chapter provides a new pedagogical framework based on the theoretical concepts we have presented. It also illustrates the ways this *pedagogía transmundial* has been put into practice beyond the training of the *aspirantes* to the design of theoretically informed adult-child interactions, optimal learning environments and instructional materials, the use of digital technology, and the strategic involvement of multiple participant groups, such as parents and administrators. We have developed this transworld pedagogy to address the underrepresentation of language, culture, and power for we are confident of its broader applications worldwide.

REFERENCES

Aikenhead, G. S. (1996). "Science Education: Border Crossing into the Subculture of Science." *Studies in Science Education*, 26, 1–52.

Akkerman, S. F., and Bakker, A. (2011). "Boundary Crossing and Boundary Objects." *Review of Educational Research*, 81(2), 132–169.

Anzaldúa, G.E. (Spring, 1989). "Border Crossings." *Trivia: Journal of Ideas*, New Amherst, MA.

———— (1999). *Borderlands/La Frontera: The New Mestiza* (second ed.) San Francisco, CA: Aunt Lute Foundation Books.

Apple, M. W. (1993). "What Post-Modernists Forget: Cultural Capital and Official Knowledge." *Curriculum Studies*, 1(3), 301–316.

Arguelles, J. (2007). "The Mayan Factor: Path Beyond Technology." In G. Braden, P. Russell, D., Pinchbeck, J. R., Macy, J. M., Jenkins, and others. *Mystery of 2012: Predictions, Prophecies, and Possibilities* (63–76). Boulder, CO: Sound True.

Arreguín-Anderson, M. G. (2011). "Mobile Learning in Bilingual Environments: A Case Study of Preservice Teachers' Cognitive and Linguistic Engagement through Cell Phone Technologies in a Science Methods Course." *Journal of Border Educational Research*, 10, 70–84.

Bang, M., and Medin, D. (2010). "Cultural Processes in Science Education: Supporting the Navigation of Multiple Epistemologies." *Science Education*, 94(6), 1008–1026.

Bergeron, B. S. (2008). "Enacting a Culturally Responsive Curriculum in a Novice Teacher's Classroom: Encountering Disequilibrium." *Urban Education*, 43(1), 4–28.

Brayboy, B. M. J., and Castagño, A. E. (2008). "How Might Native Science Inform 'Informal Science Learning'?" *Cultural Studies of Science Education*, 3(3), 731–750.

Castells, M. (1989). *The Informational City: Information Technology, Economic Restructuring, and the Urban-Regional Process.* Oxford: Blackwell.

Cajete, G. (2000). *Native Science: Natural Laws of Interdependence.* Santa Fe, NM: Clear Light Publishers.

Civil, M. (2007). "Building on Community Knowledge: An Avenue to Equity in Mathematics Education." In N. Nassir and P. Cobb (eds.), *Improving Access to Mathematics: Diversity and Equity in the Classroom* (105-117). New York: Teachers College Press.

Cole, M. (1996). *Cultural Psychology: A Once and Future Discipline.* Cambridge: Harvard University Press.

Cole, M. and Engeström, Y. (2006). "Cultural-Historical Approaches to Designing for Development." In J. Valsiner and A. Rosa (eds.), *The Cambridge Handbook of Sociocultural Psychology*, 484-507. New York: Cambridge University Press.

Collins, A., Joseph, D., and Bielaczyc, K. (2004). "Design Research: Theoretical and Methodological Issues." *Journal of the Learning Sciences*, 13(1), 15–42.

Craven, J. (2012). "Indigenous Epistemology and Science: Some Parallels and Contrasts with Neoclassical Theory (NT), Chaos Theory (CT) and Dialectical-Historical Materialism (DHM)." Presented at the 16th Congress of the IUAES, Kunming, China, July 26-31, 2012.

Cummins, J. (1996). *Negotiating Identities: Education for Empowerment in a Diverse Society.* Ontario, CA: California Association for Bilingual Education.

Darder, A. (1991). *Culture and Power in the Classroom: A Critical Foundation for Bicultural Education.* Westport, CT: Bergin and Garvey.

———— (1997). "Creating the Conditions for Cultural Democracy in the Classroom." In A. Darder, R. D. Torres, H. Gutiérrez, (eds.), *Latinos and Education: A Critical Reader* (331–350). New York: Routledge.

Dewey, J. (1916). *Democracy and Education: An Introduction to the Philosophy of Education.* New York: Free Press.

Díaz-Soto, L. (2011). "Afterword: Implementing a Critical Bilingual/Bicultural Pedagogy." In B.B. Flores, R. H. Sheets, E. R. Clark, *Teacher Preparation for Bilingual Student Populations: Educar para transformar* (239–242). New York: Routledge.

Erikson, E. H. (1963). *Childhood and Society*, (second ed.). New York: W.W. Norton.

Ek, L. D., Machado-Casas, M., Sánchez, P., and Alanís, I. (2010) "Crossing Cultural Borders: *La Clase Mágica* as a University-School Partnership." *Journal of School Leadership*, 20(6), 820–849.

Fine, G. A. (1979). "Small Groups and Culture Creation: The Idioculture of Little League Baseball Teams." *American Sociological Review*, 44(5), 73–745.

Finucane, M. L., and McMullen, C. K. (2008). "Making Diabetes Self-Management Education Culturally Relevant for Filipino Americans in Hawaii." *The Diabetes Educator*, 34(5), 841–853.

Flores, B. B., Sheets, R. H., Clark, E. R. (2011). *Teacher Preparation for Bilingual Student Populations: Educar para transformar.* New York, London: Routledge.

Freire, P. (1970) *Pedagogy of the Oppressed.* (M. Ramos, trans.) New York: Continuum.

Gardner, H. (1983). *Frames of Mind: Theory of Multiple Intelligences.* Philadelphia, PA: Basic Books.

González, N., and Moll, L. C. (2002). *Cruzando el puente*: Building Bridges to Funds of Knowledge. *Educational Policy*, 16(4), 623–641.

Gutiérrez, K. D. and Vossoughi, S. (2010). "Lifting off the Ground to Return Anew: Mediated Praxis, Transformative Learning, and Social Design Experiment." *Journal of Teacher Education*, 61(1–2), 100–117. DOI: 10.1177/0022487109347877.

Hart, M. A. (2010). "Indigenous Worldviews, Knowledge, and Research: The Development of an Indigenous Research Paradigm." *Journal of Indigenous Voices in Social Work*, 1(1), 1–16.

Inda, J. and Rosaldo, R. (2002). "Introduction: A World in Motion." In J. X. Inda and R. Rosaldo (eds.), *The Anthropology of Globalization: A Reader* (1–34). Oxford: Blackwell.

Kuhn, T. S. (1996). *The Structure of Scientific Revolutions*. Chicago: University of Chicago Press.

Lalueza, J. L., Crespo, I., Luque, M. J., and Padrós M. (2011). "Projecte shere rom: Fent de l'escola una experiència significativa en entorns multicultural I en risc d'exclusió social." *Barcelona Educación*, 74, 6–7.

Lamas, M., and Lalueza, J. L. (2012). "Apropiación de un modelo colaborativo en escuelas multiculturales con alumnado en situación de exclusión social." *Cultural y Educación*, 24(2), 177–191.

Lave, J., and Wenger, E. (1991). *Situated Learning: Legitimate Peripheral Participation*. New York: Cambridge University Press.

Luria, A. R. (1979). *Vygotsky, in the Making of Mind*. Cambridge, MA: Harvard University Press.

Martínez Avidad, M. (2012). "Comunicación para el desarrollo y la inclusión social de minorías: La Clase Mágica, un modelo de intervención para el cambio social." Unpublished doctoral dissertation. University of Alicante. Alicante, Spain.

Martínez-Roldán, C. M., and Smagorinsky, P. (2011). "Computer-Mediated Learning and Young Latino/a Students' Developing Expertise." In P. R. Portes and S. Salas (eds.), *Vygotsky in Twenty-First Century Society: Advances in Cultural Historical Theory and Praxis with Non-Dominant Communities* (162–179). New York: Peter Lang.

Merriam-Webster (2012). "Science." Retrieved June 17, 2012 from http://www.merriam-webster.com/medical/science.

Moll, L. C. (1990). "Introduction." In L. C. Moll (ed.), *Vygotsky and Education: Instructional Implications and Applications of Sociohistorical Psychology* (1–27). New York: Cambridge University Press.

——— (2011). "Only Life Educates: Immigrant Families, the Cultivation of Biliteracy, and the Mobility of Knowledge." In P. R. Portes, and S. Salas (eds.), *Vygotsky in Twenty-First Century Society: Advances in Cultural Historical Theory and Praxis with Non-Dominant Communities* (152–161). New York: Peter Lang.

Moll, L. C. and Gonzalez, N. (2004). "Engaging Life: A Funds of Knowledge Approach to Multicultural Education." In J. Banks and C. McGee Banks (eds.), *Handbook of Research on Multicultural Education*, (Second ed.) (669–715). New York: Jossey-Bass.

Nieto, S. (1994). "Lessons from Students on Creating a Chance to Dream." *Harvard Educational Review*, 64(4), 392–427.

Rico, R., Sánchez, P., and Pallares-Weissling, A. (2012). "A Snapshot of Latina/o Bilingual Teacher Candidates and their Use of iPads in an After-School Technology Program." *Journal of Bilingual Research and Instruction*, 14(1), 95–115.

Rogoff, B. (1991). "Social Interaction as Apprenticeship in Thinking: Guidance and Participation in Spatial Planning." In L. B. Resnick, J. M. Levine, and S. D. Teasley (eds.), *Perspectives on Socially Shared Cognition* (349–364). Washington, DC: American Psychological Association.

——— (1995). "Observing Sociocultural Activity on Three Planes: Participatory Appropriation, Guided Participation, and Apprenticeship." In J. V. Wertsch, P. del Rio, and A. Alvarez (eds.), *Sociocultural Studies of Mind* (139–164). Cambridge, UK: Cambridge University Press. Reprinted (2008) in K. Hall and P. Murphy (eds.), *Pedagogy and Practice: Culture and Identities*. London: Sage.

Star, S. L., and Griesemer, J. R. (1989). "Institutional Ecology, Translations, and Boundary Objects: Amateurs and Professionals in Berkeley's Museum of Vertebrate Zoology, 1907–1939." *Social Studies of Science*, 19(3), 387–420.

Tarlow, B. J., and Mahoney, D. F. (2005) "Parity in Computer-Based Health Education: Designing Culturally Relevant Alzheimer's Disease Information." *Health Informatics Journal*, 11(3), 211–224.

Torres, H. A. (2000). "In context: Gloria Anzaldúa's *Borderlands/La frontera: The New Mestiza*." In H. Augenbraum and M. F. Olmos (eds.), *U.S. Latino Literature: A Critical Guide for Students and Teachers*, (123-133). Westwood, CT: Greenwood Press.

Underwood, C., Welsh, M., Gauvain, M., and Duffy, S. (2000). "Learning at the Edges: Challenges to the Sustainability of Service Learning in Higher Education." *Journal of Language and Learning Across the Disciplines*, 4(3), 7–26.

Valsiner, J. (1987). *Culture and the Development of Children's Action*. Chichester, UK: Wiley.

Vásquez, O. A. (2003). *La Clase Mágica: Imagining Optimal Possibilities in a Bilingual Community of Learners*. Mahwah, NJ: Lawrence Erlbaum.

———(2005). "Social Action and the Politics of Collaboration." In P. Pedraza and M. Rivera (eds.) *Educating Latino Youth: An Agenda for Transcending Myths and Unveiling Possibilities*, (321–343). Mahwah, NJ: Laurence Erlbaum.

——— (2007). "Technology out of School: What Schools Can Learn from Community Based Technology." *Yearbook of the National Society for the Study of Education*, 106(2), 182–206.

Vásquez, O. A., Guarrasi, I and Carr, R. (2012). "Designing Curriculum and Building Minds: Developing Readiness for Science-Related Skills and Dispositions." Final Report to the Rokenbok Foundation.

Vásquez, O. A. and Marcello, A. (2010). "A Situated View at 'Scaling Up' in Culturally and Linguistically Diverse Communities: The Need for Mutual Adaptation." Paper submitted for publication to the *Revista de Educación of the Universidad Nacional Abierta y Distancia (UNAD) of Colombia*.

Vásquez, O. A., Valbuena, W. S. Hernandez, J. C., Montoya, A., and García, M. (2013). Presentation at the DIME conference, Jerusalem, Israel.

Vincent, D., Clark, L., Zimmer, L. M., and Sanchez. J. (2006). "Using Focus Groups to Develop a Culturally Competent Diabetes Self-Management Program for Mexican Americans." *Diabetes Educator*, 32(1) 89–97.

Vygotsky, L. S. (1978). *Mind in Society: The Development of Higher Psychological Processes*. Cambridge, MA: Harvard University Press.

Walsh, C. E. (1991). *Pedagogy and the Struggle for Voice: Issues of Language, Power, and Schooling for Puerto Ricans*. New York: Bergin and Garvey.

Ware, F. (2006). "Warm Demander Pedagogy: Culturally Responsive Teaching that Supports a Culture of Achievement for African American Students." *Urban Education*, 41(4), 427–456.

THREE

La Clase Mágica: Creating Opportunities for Transformative Learning

Mayra Martínez Avidad

WORKING TOWARD HARMONY

This chapter focuses on the important role interpersonal communication plays in educational contexts, not just as an intrinsic element of cognitive development among children, but also as an indispensable mechanism for achieving social justice. Two research studies conducted at the University of California, San Diego provide compelling evidence of the critical role that strategically designed adult-child dialogic interactions play in transformative learning. The first study focused on the long-term effects that *La Clase Mágica* (LCM) had on the life choices of four participant groups four or more years after they left the program: Latino elementary school-aged youth, undergraduate students enrolled in the associated practicum course, Mexican origin immigrant women who served as site coordinators, and graduate and undergraduate researchers who had been members of the research team. The second study examined the effects that participation in LCM-related activities—the course and the afterschool site—had on the perceptions that undergraduate students presently enrolled in the practicum course had about immigrants and Latinos. These studies provide the basis for arguing that social interaction as dialogic learning in action promotes social change, which is the bedrock of LCM's goals to affect change in the social and academic advancement of language minority groups.

La Clase Mágica's pedagogical approach is closely related to the notion of "dialogic learning" drawn from prominent theories advocating human communication and interaction as the engine of social change. Freire's theory (1970), for example, asserts that the role of the teacher as a purveyor of knowledge would greatly improve if teacher and learner were to "discover the world" (p. 81) together. This position emphasizes the importance of horizontal communication in educational contexts, not only as a determining factor in learning but also as a necessary element of social justice. Cultural psychology has also sought to demonstrate the ways in which social activity as a shared practice evokes symbolic interchange that affects individual behaviors (Cole 1998). According to this theoretical perspective, culture is not only received, but is also socially constructed through mediated and joint activity (Bruner, 1988). These theories assume that reality is comprised of meanings derived from communicative interactions among people and that these communicative interactions (dialogue) also alter the meanings that transform reality. Moreover, also relevant is Allport's (1954) proposal that prejudices that influence negative attitudes towards a group can be reduced through positive contact with the group. This contact must, however, be produced in favorable conditions, including (1) cooperation between the two groups, (2) common goals, (3) equal status, and (4) support of an authority (p. 280-281). LCM's founding principles align closely with Allport's proposal. In the first place, inter-group contact is structured around cooperative activities;[1] second, *La Clase Magica's* philosophy of leveling the hierarchy preserves the equal status of participants from different social and class backgrounds.[2]

Creatively combining these two approaches, critical pedagogy and cultural psychology, provide powerful evidence that horizontal communication between adults and child participants facilitates the co-construction of meaning and patterns of behavior. As a result, a specialized ideoculture (Fine, 1987) is created, as exemplified in *La Clase Mágica*, in which dialogue has the capacity to transform an unequal and unjust society. The assertion that social interaction promotes social change has interdisciplinary breathe, according to Elboj and colleagues (2002):

> This is a learning that changes in its relationship to its social context and also changes the context (Vygotsky), which is based on communicative action (Habermas), relies on the ability of human agency to fight against the reproduction of systems (Giddens), assumes that the end of the industrial society radicalizes the risk, but has the ability to overcome it with a new type of human relations and political activities (Castells) that are centered on a pedagogy of dialogue and hope (Freire). (original citation, p. 74)

Consider for example, the fact that critical pedagogy has struggled since its inception to develop the awareness of social justice in the educator (oppressor) as the mediator of social change in the learner (oppressed). To strike harmonic balance between the educator and the learner, however, requires a heightened awareness. This awareness is critical to changing the perceptions people have toward underrepresented groups and influences the reduction of discriminatory conduct. It also has implications for responding to social support that underrepresented communities require for participation in the larger societal context. According to Freire (1970), critical pedagogy, communication, and dialogue are the center of the educational enterprise. Dialogue, from this perspective, is the principle means by which humans come to understand the world. Furthermore, as Freire (1997) and Habermas (1981) contend, dialogue in social relations can in any context be oriented towards inclusion of different social agents, or conversely towards the imposition and/or inhibition of the rules of interaction (Prieto and Duque, 2009). Thus, the construction and re-construction of meaning is highly dependent on the orientation of the interaction. For example, vertical interaction maintains social control, promotes adaptation of the dominant patterns and leads to standardization and conformity; conversely, horizontal communication sets the individuals on an equal plane and serves as a tool for social change or innovation (Moscovici, 1985).

This premise suggests that egalitarian communication and dialogue and the validation of the arguments provided by each partner (Habermas, 1981) can create intergroup solidarity and cohesion. By extension, optimal conditions of intergroup contact can lead to an appreciation of the other at a practical, emotional, and cognitive level, as well as cultural appreciation. The use of communicative strategies in educational contexts to facilitate social inclusion of underrepresented groups is clearly one of the most important implications of LCM.

A case in point, strategically structured interactions, organized between undergraduate students (*amigos*/friends) at USCD and *aspirantes* at LCM@UTSA[3] (see chapters 7 and 8) with children from low income communities, are not only expected to promoted learning and development, but are also expected to provoke social change by exhorting social influence capable of transformation. It is precisely this dialogical moment where dominant and ethnic groups can begin to work together to rectify unequal distribution of resources embedded in power and status inequities.

In contrast to the transmission model of instruction, inflexible curriculum, and stifling dependence of the students on their teachers, the founding principles of *La Clase Mágica* are centered on the idea of dialogic transformative learning around strategically designed interactions leading child participants to their optimal development. These educational activities encourage reflection, critique, and interpersonal communication, as joint mediated activity, between participants with different sociocultural backgrounds—i.e., Asian or White American undergraduates and Spanish-English bilingual children of Mexican origin—all contributing to the construction of knowledge. The findings of the two LCM studies confirm that negotiated knowledge and co-constructed behavior achieves social cohesion and intergroup solidarity. That is, the bicultural bilingual context of *La Clase Mágica* sets the conditions for shared mediated activity that lead to greater intergroup understanding (Gallego and Vasquez, 2011).

These studies also show that the same can be true for the social relations between undergraduate students, faculty, research staff, and community members who in a context of collaboration toward shared goals, accomplish bonds of friendship, tolerance, and social justice that promote the social inclusion of the Latino youth and their community. The children's relationship with UCSD students in fact, had long-lasting positive influence on all participants long after they had left the project. The follow-up study conducted years after participation revealed that on numerous occasions, child participants who had advanced to Wizard Assistants—i.e., experts—as young adults reported that performing the same tasks and responsibilities as the university students, made them feel capable and important just like their older peers. They also reported that this sense of personal empowerment had influenced their decisions to pursue admissions to higher education. The university students, too, reported benefitting from the experience, personally and academically; they learned about education, human development, and community service. As one former UCSD undergraduate student reported, "Overall, going to an immigrant community made the immigrant population come to life in my eyes." She continues: "They are no longer numbers of immigrants but children, peers, friends."

CONCEPTUAL RESONANCE: WHAT DO WE KNOW?

Cultural and economic capital, vital to social mobility, are strongly related and enhanced by education. By introducing educational opportunities, *La Clase Mágica* seeks to enhance the cultural capital of Latino youth and by extension, the Latino community, expecting that it will contribute to the expansion of the community's economic capital, creating the pathway towards social inclusion.

This was indicated by the findings of the Impact Study that showed that 90 percent of college-age former child participants were, in fact, enrolled in university courses or had already completed their diplomas. This percentage represents a positive progression towards eradicating education gaps among Latinos. It stands in contrast to recent data that shows that while the number of Latinos enrolling in college has increased, a gap in the number enrolling and obtaining a U.S. four-year college degree continues to exist in comparison to other groups (Fry and

Taylor, 2013). The college-going rates of former participants attests to the achievement of *La Clase Mágica's* social action goals in promoting educational inclusion and intergroup communication that expand the social opportunities of the Latino community.

The attainment of social capital from Bourdieu's (1983) lens is "the sum of the current or potential resources connected to a more or less institutionalized long-lasting network of relationships of mutual knowledge and recognition which is more or less institutionalized" (p. 240). This also lends support to the assertion that communication and human interaction are sources of power. The findings of both studies referenced in this chapter show that adult-child interactions between representatives of unequal status groups contribute to an increase in the social capital of both groups. In the case of the Latino participants, LCM serves as a bridge to interaction with U.S. mainstream society, and for the undergraduate students, as a means for the re-evaluation of the Latino community. Specifically, *La Clase Mágica* is the source of three types of social capital: bonding, bridging and binking (Woolock, 2001). Bonding refers to the existing relationships between those who are close (such as family members) which in the context of *La Clase Mágica* refers to the interaction between parents working as program coordinators and their children who participate in the program. Participating parents have ample opportunity to obeserve and acquire the scaffolding techniques that the undergraduate use with their children, such as prompting children with mnemonic probes, questions, examples, references and elaborations that focus the children's attention, builds their vocabulary and supports literacy and language development (Vásquez, 2003). Thus, parent-child interactions strengthen relationships and support children's academic success.

The bridging aspect of social capital, on the other hand, is instantiated in many the relationships that LCM site coordinators established with child participants at each of the centers. Within a common space, these interactions open up the opportunity to preserve language and culture—in this case, Spanish and Mexican origin culture, a feature that reinforces the feeling of belonging, a sense of community, and a strong Latino identity (see Gallego and Vasquez, 2011 for elaboration).

Additionally, *La Clase Mágica* contributes to the linking aspect of social capital generated in relationships between people of unequal power status, leading to establishment of relationships with those who are completely outside of the community (Woolcock, 2001, pp. 13–14). This type of social capital is enacted in intimate and sustained interactions are difficult to attain across geographical isolation and social exclusion, as is often the case for Latinos in the greater society. However, in bringing together students and researchers from the University of California, San Diego and children and their families from low-income immigrant communities, *La Clase Mágica*, provides the opportunities for authentic and reciprocal relationships that make possible the acquisition of social capital.

These interactions cultivate a college-going culture, academic language and knowledge as well as the aspiration to pursue higher education as supported by the Impact study findings that show that child participants enrolled in higher education in greater numbers than reported in the general society.

Coleman (1988) extends Bourdieu's definition of social capital to include obligations and expectations, channels of information, and social norms. In LCM, these axioms are exemplified in the reciprocal relations of exchange between the undergraduates and child participants that establish social norms for productive adult-child interactions, the responsible and productive uses of digital media and the bi-directional relations of exchange that not only prompted children's development, but also helped generate expectations of cooperation and mutual aid. In many cases, UCSD students serve to demystify the college experience by sharing about their daily lives at the university, how to qualify for college, and how to obtain financial support for their education. Reinforcing a college-going culture among the children and the parents was particularly evident when SD, a child participant, spoke about the influence that the college students had exerted:

> I remember that the students who would come to UCSD would tell me that I should go to college because it would be very important for me. Olga also counseled me regarding which subjects I should chose to go to college. My experience in LCM was one of those things that influenced me to go to college. (interview, March 5, 2005)

Reciprocity was evident in the social interactions as these helped the undergraduate students acquire an understanding of the culture of *La Clase Mágica* as well as Mexican cultural history and values (Vásquez, 2003). Through these close relationships with the children they acquired a more accurate account of the realities and aspirations of Mexican origin communities and individuals, the inclusion of the intellectual and cultural resources of the learner as an essential part of their learning and the social construction of different perceptions of this population.[4] The presence of the Spanish language and Mexican cultural artifacts woven into the learning activities and learning ecology, enhanced the child participants' ethnic consciousness and cultural identity as well as allowed the undergraduates to practice their Spanish and learn about Mexican cultural history and values.

Importantly, the study on the undergraduates enrolled in the practicum course revealed significant changes in the undergraduates' attitudes and opinions towards the Latino community. There was a significant decrease in undergraduate students' beliefs that "immigrants took jobs away from Americans." Their short ten-week practicum experience at the sites produced a significant attitudinal change on their views of immigration policies. For example, there was a significant decrease in the number of college students who believed that the U.S. government should spend more to impede undocumented immigration.

While social interactions provide a medium for LCM's transformative pedagogy digital technology, or more specifically a technology-driven pedagogy provides means the preparation of the learner to meet the greater goals and expectations to engage as competent and active participants of a globalized and technology-meditated world of today. As is suggested by Gutiérrez et al. (2009), "Increased transnational migration, new diasporic communities, and the proliferation of media technologies have resulted in a variety of intercultural activities in which a range of linguistic practices become available to members of nondominant communities (Gutiérrez, 2008b)" (original citation, p. 215). *La Clase Mágica*, for example, provides participating children the opportunity to explore emerging digital technologies that contribute to the development of digital literacy as well as other twenty-first century competencies[5] (see chapters 9, 10, and 11). Financial literacy is one such globally relevant competency promoted at *La Clase Mágica* helping children make astute financial decisions that include the value of understanding the equivalence of foreign currency to the U.S dollar, the implications of staying within a specified budget, and of the importance of saving for the future.

LCM makes clear that mastering the use of technologies is vital for entering the labor market and for participation in the virtual sphere. This is supported by Castells (2009), who argues that mastery of digital technology allows different social groups to use their influence to change and transform the society. Through information and communication technologies, communities are able to appropriate their right to a voice and have a say in the public sphere.[6] The counter-hegemonic capabilities of virtual communication networks (Atton, 2002; 2004; Couldry and Curran 2003) are examples of the advocacy aspect of technology. That is, navigating the Internet, is not simply a personal pastime but also "about the means of expression of the citizens, a space similar to the notion public sphere conceptualized by Habermas (1989), in which citizens freely exchange opinions, ideas and other forms of expression" (Martínez Avidad, 2011, p. 279). In other words, digital literacy promoted at *La Clase Mágica* as the means by which Latino youth and adults can voice their own views on reality and share views according to their interests (see chapters 12 and 13).[7]

REPOSITIONING METHODOLOGY: LINKING TO THE SACRED SCIENCES

La Clase Mágica counters hegemonic forms of traditional experimental sterile settings in that it is a laboratory for learning, a social designed experiment situated within a non-dominant, underrepresented community's context (Gutiérrez and Vossoughi, 2010). Moreover, as Gutiérrez, Morales, and Martinez (2009) elaborate, "social design experiments, organized around equity-oriented principles and expansive forms of learning, are oriented toward transformative ends through mutual relations of exchange among participants" (p. 236). Every norm and principle promoted by *La Clase Mágica* is aimed at creating the most favorable context for mutual understanding and inter-group cohesion. This context recreates the necessary mechanisms, according to Pettigrew (1998)[8] for inter-group contact to produce positive effects. Among these is the "learning about the exclusion groups," a main objective of the program and the vehicle by which it counters the misconceived and stereotypical views sometimes held by the students of different ethnicities toward the Latino community. Reciprocal collaboration based on shared objectives creates bonding among participants that help reduce the fear and suspicion often present in people when dealing with immigrants and minorities. As Pettigrew (1998) contends, these experiences result in experiences that incite a reappraisal of the group which includes a review of one's own individual beliefs about the excluded group. This mechanism is important because it often includes the questioning of social practices that benefit one group over another (McClelland and Linnander, 2006). Other possible forms of social support include (1) organizational support—i.e., resources that encourage coordinated political action—i.e., acts of activism, protests, associations in organizations working for the cause and (2) institutional support that provides space and other resources for community to exercise their political, academic, business, or social actions (Stansfeld, 2006; see chapters 12 and 13). These are, in short, active initiatives of solidarity that the dominant group can make available to underrepresented groups and that greatly improve the chances of social inclusion, as exemplified among the Gypsy community in Sevilla, Spain (see chapter 13).

Furthermore, human interaction and communication are at the core of the liberalization process involving a critical understanding of the contextual reality (Freire, 1970). From this perspective, real communication is genuinely reflective and practical in nature. The dialogic exchange that occurs within LCM, for example, allows the Latino community to use its ancestral knowledge and history to transform Western mainstream thinking. This appears to be especially true among UCSD Latino college students. An undergraduate female related if she had learned anything through her participation in the project it was that, "I have become more aware (from LCM's experience) how much this community needs their fellow Latinos to reach out and be there for them to help them in the often bumpy road to success and wealth." Another Latina student shared her epiphany that:

> Working with these children has allowed me to realize that many immigrant families still don't have the same benefits that Americans do,

no matter how long they've been here. Immigrant families that don't have a strong English language skills also are a great disadvantage. They don't have all the resources (i.e., computers at home) which affects the kids greatly.

The findings of the two "effect" studies provide ample evidence of the efforts of *La Clase Mágica* to eliminate inequality in the partnering community. However, the solution to deeply disrupt social structures cannot rest solely on the shoulders of the underrepresented community. Involving students from more affluent communities provides an opportunity for members of the mainstream society to bare some of the burden, for developing different perspectives vis-à-vis minority communities and possibly distributing the need for social change widely.

The findings also demonstrated that behavior directed toward correcting inequalities suffered by the immigrant community was evident for both groups. Latinos, in the sample reported a renewed consciousness about the need to participate in actions that improved the situation of the community; in their interviews more than half of the adult Latinos reported that they now actively participate in volunteer activities within the community. This impact was evident in the UCSD research staff's self-reports as they were interviewed years after their participation in the project. Many were or had actively participated in organizations that worked towards rectifying educational disparities and finding new multicultural formulas for inclusion.

SYNCHRONIZING MULTIPLE WORLDS: FINDINGS AND CHALLENGES

According to the study findings, awareness of social justice was present among all participants in *La Clase Mágica*. Although the developmental progress of Latino youth has been typically highlighted in other studies (Vásquez, 2003), the two studies showed that the undergraduate students—the young adults—were the ones who gained the most from their relationships with the community. These UCSD university students, who came from families of different ethnic, cultural, and economic backgrounds learned a great deal about the tremendous challenges facing the Latino immigrant community in the U.S. society. The survey of the undergraduate students' enrolled in the practicum course, for example, revealed that 70 percent of respondents admitted that the contact with the community expanded their knowledge about the community and influenced a shift in their perceptions about the Mexican American community. This was the case of K. R., who acknowledged that before his experience in LCM, he used to unconsciously "criminalize Latinos."

In getting to know the community better and more intimately, undergraduate students were able to rectify many of the misconceptions that had led to their negative evaluations and/or prejudice towards the community in the first place—the stereotyping of "Latinos as lazy people, who have little interest in learning English, in educating themselves or integrating into U. S. American society." Such misconceptions of the community were often replaced by a set of real and positive attributes that contribute to the formation of a more positive perception of the community:

> My first notion of the site was filled with nervousness because I felt uncomfortable to enter a class room of the Latino community. From previous knowledge and experiences in high school, I noticed how the Latino community stuck together and have usually given me a bad impression of them since there were rumors going around that many were part of gangs. I entered the classroom for the same on a Wednesday morning and all my fears were erased. These three- to five-year-old children had no predestined life and are just children eager to learn. (interview, February 13, 2005)

Moreover, members of the research and implementation team, who took part in the design of this social action project, had an affirmative experience. Perhaps because of their professional training and experience, from the onset, these individuals were the most sensitive to the problems of the Latino community; nevertheless, as a result of their participation, recommitted to social justice. Researching the efficacy of the project to meet its intended goals and designing tasks that aimed to improve the lives of Latino immigrants made them even more aware of the need for mobilization, inspiring them to take part, in solidarity, in initiatives that favor the Latino cause. The data shows that 65 percent of former college student employees were at the time of the interviews participating as volunteers in organizations involved in political activism or taking or teaching courses related to social citizenship that improved the well-being of Latinos in this country.

Thus, the *concientización* that members of the research team experienced at *La Clase Mágica* resulted in a long-term commitment to pursue higher education as professors in universities that serve low-income and/or minority students. In some cases, their research was devoted to issues related to the problems of social and academic integration of ethnic minorities. Self-reports indicate that their participation in *La Clase Mágica* also encouraged them to participate in activities that implicitly, if not directly, supported the Latino community. Many reported that they had become involved in activist organizations that advocated or provided aid to low income Latinos. For example, several volunteered providing free bilingual legal advice to individuals not able to afford it.

Interestingly, as some former members of the research team began their academic careers at other universities in the United States or the world, they showed an interest in implementing various aspects of *La*

Clase Mágica to help other underrepresented communities (Relaño Pastor, 2005; see chapter 13). The interviews of university researchers also revealed that a great percentage of them retained their social justice inclinations long after they participated in the project.

The two LCM studies provide ample evidence that joint mediated activity between the Latino and university communities gives rise to an ideoculture that develops and promotes new meanings around productive communication and the bonding that occurs between members of the academy and children from low-income, immigrant communities (see chapters 9–12 for further evidence). Communication mediated through a specialized context of interaction involving theoretically and ideologically inspired tools, goals and objectives, program norms, encourages the development of a collective identity and affinity, as well as ties of interdependencies, friendship, unconditional acceptance, and shared meanings. This ecological context creates/maximizes benefits for the Latino community that go beyond mere cognitive development and academic outcome.

The challenge now is to identify other systems of rules, goals, norms, and artifacts that increase the further development of other positive responses by participants who do not belong to the Latino community, such as the White U.S. mainstream community. This new objective must, therefore, optimize the optimal learning context where the White U.S. community assumes the responsibility for the advancement and social inclusion of the Latino community. This position is, as argued by Freire (1970), the foundation of critical pedagogy but also a central aspect of the concept of culture which Vygotsky (1978) viewed as a system of knowledge, beliefs, and shared behaviors which new members must acquire through their interactions with others more capable and knowledgeable others, such as parents and teachers and in the case of *La Clase Mágica*, the *amiga/os* (friends) and *aspirantes* (see chapters 7 and 8) who together engineer a new social reality.

RETHINKING RESONANCE: NEW CONCEPTUAL UNDERSTANDINGS

The results of two of the studies presented in this chapter support the contention that *La Clase Mágica* fosters cognitive, emotional, and critical skill acquisition, as well as facilitates the productive inclusion of the Latino community in the information society. Both investigations showed the tremendous impact that intergroup communication and dialogue has on learning, intergroup relations and social integration. They illustrate the ways that communication within a non-hierarchical structure produces a series of changes among participants that improves the quality of life of Latinos and reformulates the views that representatives of more advantaged communities have of Latinos and immigrants. Finally, these studies show that *La Clase Mágica* is moving towards the goals of reducing ethnic, gender, and economic inequalities through its efforts to provide Latino communities educational resources and institutional support (Stanton-Salazar, et. al, 1996; Elboj, Puigdellívol, Soler, and Valls, 2002). Further revealed is that *La Clase Mágica* at UCSD offers of the type of norms and expectation embedded in interactions that serve as instruments of social change and innovation. As García Saiz and Gil (1999) argue:

> Innovation can be defined as a process of social influence whose source is generally a minority whose goal is to try to introduce or develop new ideas, ways of thinking or behavior or change, established ideas, traditional attitudes, old ways of thinking or behavior. (p. 264)

Also evident in the studies is that interactional principles governing *La Clase Mágica* increased social acceptance and intergroup cohesion. Its bilingual bicultural environment, with a notable presence of Mexican culture elements, awakened in the university students' respect with a better understanding of not only Mexican culture, but of other cultures as well. Another interesting finding of the Impact Study was that long-term participant children reported that *La Clase Mágica* made it possible for them to feel comfortable in cross-group relationships at work and in their social lives. University students, on the other hand, reported that their work in LCM had an enormously enriched their personal experience which, in addition, contributed to their academic and professional goals in significant ways. This meaningful and positive experience with the Latino community contributed to cultivating positive attitudes toward Latino immigrants as Allport (1954) found.

In all, in rousing a reaction to injustice and channeling responses to overcome such situations through self-affirmation and commitment, *La Clase Mágica* achieves its goals of social action. These studies allow us to conclude that social activity and shared *La Clase Mágica* practice provokes symbolic exchange that modifies the beliefs of individuals, causing changes in behavior and the social environment. In fact, although the normal conditions under which intergroup communication occurs in all types of partnerships, these also help the child participants to feel comfortable in a world that typically excludes their language, intellectual history, and knowledge. Thus, *La Clase Mágica* provides the heuristic to test optimal conditions for intergroup communication that can serve as instruments of innovation and transformation towards a more just and egalitarian society. In short, it clearly revealed the promise of transformation that was an impetus behind implementing LCM's transworld pedagogical model at the University of Texas at San Antonio for the preparation of teachers. As research-based evidence, these two studies support LCM@UTSA efforts to bring about social change in both the mainstream and minority populations.

NOTES

1. Students from both groups work together in the use of technology, perform tasks in a cooperative manner, and share different types of activities. Similarly, UCSD researchers cooperate in finding new ways that help children of the community to acquire skills in the use of technology and achieve optimum academic development

2. The equality of roles is promoted in various ways, for example by referring to university students as *amigos* (which helps Latino children not to perceive them as a higher authority) or use the help and greater experience of the *wizard assistants* in many of the activities taking place in the community centers.

3. LCM@UTSA: abbreviated name for La Clase Mágica at the University of Texas at San Antonio.

4. In many cases, the exclusion of the minority languages in schools affects the motivation for learning and provokes anxiety and inhibition among learners. Aspects such as fear or linguistic ridicule can provoke the rejection of the culture of origin or lack of identification with any other cultures that triggers negative emotional processes (Díaz-Aguado, 2005).

5. Recently, *La Clase Mágica* integrated skills and competencies thought to be the defining characteristics twenty-first century workers and citizens (Váquez and Marchello, 2010. The program has established a system of "hubs of innovation" focused on developing five key competencies, including: digital literacy, financial literacy, health and nutrition, environmental stewardship, and language and culture.

6. The Internet has become a tool of citizen and political empowerment by making of the subjects the issuers and producers of information themselves (Castells, 2009).

7. Through local technological communities have managed, in fact, not only to meet specific demands, but at times, completely transform the political system into a democratic regime.

8. Pettigrew proposes four mechanisms necessary for contact to produce its effects (a) learn about the minority group (b) behavior change (c) generation of affective ties, and (d) *in-group reappraisal* or re-evaluation of the in-group. Thus, key factors are identified with causing a change in attitudes, both in the learning process, as well as in the friendship between the groups. On the importance of friendships between groups, Pettigrew is the first to suggest that feelings can be more susceptible to contact than their own beliefs.

REFERENCES

Allport, G. (1954). *The Nature of Prejudice*. Addison-Wesley.

Atton, C. (2002). *Alternative Media*. London: Sage.

——— (2004). *An Alternative Internet*. Edinburgh: Edinburgh University Press.

Bourdieu, P. (1983). "Forms of Capital." In J. C. Richards (ed.), *Handbook of Theory and Research for the Sociology of Education*, (241–258). New York: Greenwood Press.

Bruner, J. (1988). *Desarrollo cognitivo y educación. Selección de textos e introducción de Jesús Palacios*. Madrid: Morata.

Castells, M. (2009). *Comunicación y poder*. Madrid: Alianza Editorial.

Cole, M. (1998) *Cultural Psychology: A Once and Future Discipline*. Cambridge, MA: Harvard University Press.

Coleman, J. C. (1988). "Social Capital in the Creation of Human Capital." *American Journal of Sociology*, 94, 95–120.

Couldry, N., and Curran, J. (2003). "The Paradox of Media Power." In N. Couldry and J. Curran, (eds.), *Contesting Media Power: Alternative Media in Networked World*. (3–15). Lanham, MD: Rowman and Littlefield.

Díaz-Aguado, M. J. (2005) *Aprendizaje cooperativo. Hacia una nueva síntesis entre la eficacia docente y la educación en valores*. Madrid: Santillana.

Elboj, C., Puigdellivol, I., Soler, M., and Valls, R. (2002). *Comunidades de aprendizaje. Transformar la educación.* Barcelona: Editorial Graó, de IRIF, S.L.

Fine, G, A. (1987). *With the Boys: Little League Baseball and Preadolescent Culture.* Chicago: The University of Chicago Press.

Freire, P. (1970). *Pedagogía del oprimido.* Madrid: Siglo XXI.

――― (1997). *A la sombra de este árbol.* Esplugues de Llobregat, Spain: El Roure.

Fry, R. and Taylor, P. (2013). "Hispanic High School Graduates Pass Whites in Rate of College Enrollment: High School Drop-Out Rate at Record Low". PEW Research Hispanic Trends Project. Retrieved September 1, 2013 from http://www.pewhispanic.org/2013/05/09/hispanic-high-school-graduates-pass-whites-in-rate-of-college-enrollment.

Gallego, M., and Vásquez, O. A (2011). "Praxis in Dis-Coordination." In P. Portes, P. and S. Salas (eds.), *Vygotsky in the Twenty-First Century: Cultural Historical Theory and Research in Non-Dominant Communities* (214–228). New York: Peter Lang Publishing.

García Sáiz, M. y Gil, F. (1999). "Procesos de influencia social." In F. Gil y C. M. Alcover (coords.), *Introducción a la psicología de los grupos* (251-279). Madrid: Alianza.

Giddens, A. (1984). *The Constitution of Society.* Cambridge, MA: Polity Press.

Gutiérrez, K. D., Morales, P. Z., and Martínez, D. C. (2009). "Re-Mediating Literacy: Culture, Difference, and Learning for Students from Nondominant Communities." *Review of Research in Education, 33,* 212–245. DOI: 10.3102/0091732X08328267.

Gutiérrez, K. D. and Vossoughi, S. (2010). "Lifting off the Ground to Return Anew: Mediated Praxis, Transformative Learning, and Social Design Experiments." *Journal of Teacher Education,* 61(1–2) 100–117. DOI: 10.1177/0022487109347877.

Habermas, J. (1981) "Teoría de la acción comunicativa. Volumen I: Racionalidad de la acción y racionalización rocial y Volumen II: Crítica de la razón funcionalista." Madrid: Taurus.

――― (1989). *The Structural Transformation of the Public Sphere.* Cambridge, MA: MIT Press.

Martínez Avidad, M. (2012). "Comunicación para el desarrollo y la inclusión social de minorías: La Clase Mágica, un modelo de intervención para el cambio social." Unpublished doctoral dissertation, Universidad Complutense de Madrid, Spain.

Martínez Avidad, M. (2011). "Redes alternativas de comunicación, *framing* y la construcción del poder político." *Obets, Revista de Ciencias Sociales,* 6(2), 269–291.

McClelland, K. and Linnander, E. (2006). "The Role of Contact and Information in Racial Attitude Change among White College Students." *Sociological Inquiry,* 76, 81–115.

Moscovici, S. (1985). "Social Influence and Conformity." In G. Lindzey and E. Aronson (eds.), *Handbook of Social Psychology,* 2, (347–412), New York: McGraw-Hill.

Pettigrew, T. (1998). "Intergroup Contact Theory." *Annual Review of Psychology,* 49, 65–85

Prieto, O. and Duque, E. (2009). "El aprendizaje dialógico y sus aportaciones a la teoría de la educación. Teoría de la educación." *Educación y Cultura en la Sociedad de la Información,* 10(3), 7-30. Universidad de Salamanca, Spain.

Relaño Pastor, A, M. (2005). "La negociación de la elección lingüística y su respuesta ideológica en La Clase Mágica." In Franzé, A; Jociles, M.I; Martín, B; Poveda, D. y Sama, S. (coords). *Actas de la I Reunión Científica Internacional sobre Etnografía y Educación.* Valencia, Spain: Editorial Germanía.

Stansfeld, S. A. (2006). "Social Support and Social Cohesion." In M. Marmot and R. G. Wilkingson (eds.), *Social Determinants of Health* (155–178). Oxford: Oxford University Press.

Stanton-Salazar, R., Vásquez, O.A., and Mehan, H. (1996). "Engineering Success through Institutional Support." In A. Hurtado, R. Figueroa, E. Garcia (eds.), *Strategic Interventions in Education: Expanding the Latina/Latino Pipeline.* (100–137). University of Santa Cruz, CA.

Vásquez, O. A. (2003). *La Clase Mágica: Imagining Optimal Possibilities in a Bilingual Community of Learners.* Mahwah, NJ: Lawrence Erlbaum.

Vásquez, O. A. and Marcello, A. (2010). "Una mirada contextualizada del uso de practicas de innovación en communidades cultural y linguistacmente diversas: La necesidad de adaptación mutua." *Revista de Educación of the Universidad Nacional Abierta y Distancia (UNAD) of Colombia.*

Vygotksy, L. S. (1978). *Mind in Society: Development of Higher Psychological Processes.* Cambridge, MA: Harvard University Press.

Woolock, M. (2001). "The Place of Social Capital in Understanding Social and Economic Outcomes." Isuma, Canada: *Canadian Journal of Policy Research*, 2(1), 1–17.

II

Transcending Borders as Transworld Citizens

"Where shall we obtain the fragrance which intoxicates our souls? We do not yet know the various flower-songs with which we may rejoice the Cause of All, however desirous we are; thou my friend, would that thou bring to my instrument various flowers, that thou shouldst clothe it in brilliant oco flowers, that thou shouldst offer them, and lift thy voice in a new and worthy song to rejoice the Cause of All."

Anonymous (1890). Ancient Nahuatl Poetry, Containing the Nahuatl Text of XXVII Ancient Mexican Poems. *Briton's Library of Aboriginal American Literature, Number VII.* Translated by D. G. Brinton (Original work circa 1400-1800).

FOUR

Resisting Epistemological Exclusion: Inserting *La Clase Mágica* into State-Level Policy Discourses

Patricia D. López and Angela Valenzuela

WORKING TOWARD HARMONY

Concerned with the notion that "access to information and the distribution of knowledge is still determined by those in power and those with wealth," (see chapter 1), this chapter centers on the politics of education policy and the limits and possibilities of research-based initiatives in informing political debates at the state level. The goal of this chapter is twofold: first, we will provide an example of the politics involved in the education of emergent bilingual[1] students in the state of Texas; and second, we will provide an example of the concept of engaged policy as praxis and its potential to bring together, rather than close off, political actors.

By drawing from primary and secondary sources, as well as participant observation, we will excavate the policy process as it pertains to the complexity of the political contexts that Texas' emergent bilingual youth ultimately get caught up in this struggle. Guiding our analysis is the theoretical and methodological concept of policy archeology (Scheurich, 1994), together with the work of the Texas Center for Education Policy (TCEP), that facilitated the coming together of researchers, policymakers, educators, and community entities to insert *La Clase Mágica* (LCM) into state-level policy discourses in light of the state's negligence in serving the educational needs of emergent bilingual youth. What this two-year effort reveals is that in the Texas context, and elsewhere, the politics of

51

whose knowledge counts (Scheurich and Young, 1989) contributes to the continued marginalization of emergent bilingual youth.

In the state of Texas, emergent bilingual students are the fastest growing subgroup, accounting for 17 percent (or 831,812) of all public school students, 91 percent (or 757,392) of whom are primarily of Mexican origin[2] (TEA, 2011). While emergent bilingual students have an attendance rate just above the state average (96.5 percent versus 95.6 percent, respectively), they are less likely to meet exit-level performance requirements on the state's standardized assessment—63 percent compared to the state average of 92 percent (TEA, 2011, 2010–2011 data). These same students also have the lowest graduation and college-going rates (Johnson, 2010). Absent from these figures are the large number of students that are no longer in the system altogether (see Valenzuela et al., 2006), and are left to negotiate the global economy without a high school diploma at a time that an advanced education is the de facto criterion for any hope for attaining middle class status in the twenty-first century.

Under our current era of high-stakes testing and accountability policies, battling the educational rights of these students has been waged in the courts in two significant cases: one, regarding the use of high-stakes exit exams (*GI Forum et al. v. Texas Education Agency et al., 87 F. Supp.2d 667* [*W. D. Tex.* 2000]) and the more recent case surrounding the state's failure to adequately monitor emerging bilingual learners' educational progress and the inadequacy of programs serving their educational needs (*USA and LULAC GI-Forum v. Texas* 2008). While the courts erred on the side of emergent bilingual students and the claim that access to a quality education are being obstructed, the state was granted an appeal.

At a time when Texas fails to adequately provide its growing emergent bilingual population a quality education, programs like *La Clase Mágica* would appear to be one desirable solution. Rather, research shows (Valenzuela, 2004; Cervantes-Soon and Valenzuela, 2011), that political factors outweigh research evidence, even when couched in terms of official "outcomes-based" discourse. When made aware of the potentiality of LCM in 2008, the political will and support to address bilingual learners was evident among select state political leaders and community entities alike. However, this effort failed alongside many other bills focused on addressing the education of emerging bilingual children and youth.

CONCEPTUAL RESONANCE: POLICY AS PROCESS

According to Wedel, Shore, Feldman, and Lantrop (2005), an understanding of the cultural and philosophical underpinnings of policy help us to unmask the disenabling discourses, mobilizing metaphors, and underlying ideologies at play. Dating back to sixteenth century France, the term policy, or *"policie,"* a verb, meant "to policy; to organize and regulate the internal order of," and "how policy aids the state in shaping, controlling, and regulating" (Wedel et al., 2005, p. 35). When used as an adjective modifying a noun like "policy proposal" or "policy agenda," policy connotes "elegancy, refinement, culture, and civilization" (Wedel et al., 2005, p. 35). Today, the concept of policy is "laden with often quite contradictory meanings . . . that can be coded and decoded to convey very ambiguous messages" (Wedel et al., 2005, p. 36). Because policies can govern and regulate the conditions of our daily livelihoods and entire existences, a critical task for those studying policy is to expose the political aspects that infiltrate policy processes that consequently cast people and problems in ways that actively frame and (re)create marginalizing categories and definitions of individuals.

In the context of knowledge utilization, Levinson and Sutton (2001) note the importance of "bring[ing] the insights of the sociology of knowledge to bear upon policy processes" (p. 7), with a focus on "how research can be designed and undertaken so that researchers and policymakers construct knowledge together" (p. 7; see also Apter, 1974; Böhme and Stehr, 1986; Eismon, 1981; Korr-Cetina and Mulkay, 1983). In most cases, this approach builds upon work that focuses on how policies are formulated within governmental agencies (Levinson and Sutton, 2001). How research is used, if at all, is found to be applied selectively and after the fact, in such a way to justify political decisions that have already been decided. In response, scholars argue that, "before research knowledge can substantially inform policy processes, the cultures of policy formation must be reformed" (Levinson and Sutton, 2001, p. 7; see also López, 2012; López, Valenzuela, and Garcia, 2011). This process, in part, can begin with researchers examining policy issues by uncovering instances where the politics of policymaking is "masked . . . under the cloak of neutrality" (Wedel et al., 2005, p. 34; also see López, 2012; Shore and Wright, 1997). Such an examination begins by unraveling the assumptions embedded in policy debates, which are often more political than empirical (see López, 2012).

Responding to critical theorists' call for the analyses of educational policies to move beyond a focus on outcomes, and official accounts of state-level policymaking, the concept of "engaged policy" emerged (see López, 2012, for elaboration; see also Foley and Valenzuela, 2005 for an early articulation). This theoretical concept rests on the notion that multiple people embody policy, and that the knowledge generated from research can in some instances, function as a catalyst for political action and social change. Engaged policy also argues that polices are comprised of a dynamic ecology (see Weaver-Hightower, 2008, for similar argument). Policies are alive, continuously evolving, and multidimensional. In tangible terms, policies have lives—sometimes dirty and corrupt, and other times noble and humane. Policies also have friends—some you'd take home to mama and others you wouldn't dare. Finally, policies have histories. In order to really understand policy, it is important for researchers to consider engaging its genealogy, its friends, and its constituencies across different contexts.

REPOSITIONING METHODOLOGY: BEYOND RELEVANCE TO THE SACRED SCIENCES

This chapter will draw from qualitative techniques, specifically participant observation, informal conversations, and written correspondences from October 2008 to June 2009. The data generated from direct participation will be complimented by primary source data collected from public hearings, policy texts, public forums, and stakeholder meeting discussions. Together, these data provide a textual representation of the politics involved in the process of inserting LCM into state-level policy debates in the form of House Bill 4122. Had this bill become law, this legislation would have provided emergent bilingual children in both Austin and San Antonio with access to an effective, research-based, culturally relevant, technologically-rich, and a community-based after-school program.

From a theoretical perspective, the methodological approach of policy archeology is concerned with interrogating the social construction of policy and the actors and discourses that give shape to it (Scheurich, 1994). Drawing from the work of Foucault, policy archeology investigates:

> the conditions necessary for the appearance of a [social problem], the historical conditions required if one is to "say anything" about it, the conditions necessary if it [the social problem] is to exist in relation to other objects. (Foucault, 1972, p. 44; as cited in Scheurich, 1994)

Policy archeology reminds us that issues (and actors) have histories, and that, "to avoid an archeology of policy actors is to see only that policy problems are constructions without fully understanding the conditions of their construction" (Gale, 2001, p. 389). Accordingly, both this critical, socio-historical approach and engaged policy remind us to step back and critically examine the various factors and events that occur prior to a concrete text product, or outcome.

Policy archeology also helps us to reconceptualize policy, generally, by putting into question conventional approaches to understanding educational issues by centering on those processes that occur across the following, namely the social problem, social regularities, policy solutions, and policy studies arenas. Because the scope of this chapter is focused on the process of inserting LCM into state policymaking, we focus on the social problem and social regularities arenas (see Scott 1998, for a comprehensive argument about the regulatory state).

According to Scheurich (1994), the social problem arena is focused on the social construction of education issues and specific social problems within education. Guiding the inquiry for this arena is the notion that "social problems are social constructions" (Foucault, 1972, p. 27; as cited in Scheurich, 1994). Examining the social construction process consists of understanding how the social problem manifests itself and becomes nameable and describable. In this arena, such questions as the following arise: By what process or processes did a particular issue or problem emerge; and by what process does an issue or social problem result variously in the reactive "gaze" of the state and of society? The social problem arena further asks how the social invisibility of subaltern individuals and groups subsequently connects to decision-making visibility (see López et al., 2011, for example). The dynamics of the latter factor, in the context of state-level policymaking, is of primary interest herein.

Social regularities are patterns of knowledge that permeate policy processes. Regularities are informed by values, beliefs, norms, and ways of knowing that are constructed and conveyed through social interaction. At the core of the social regularities arena is the concern for how individuals approach education issues and social problems that by extension inform policy processes. The rules that individuals and groups subscribe to are also construed as guiding political actors' orientations towards issues at the same time that they inform their respective actions. The social regularities arena is guided by the following four intersecting assumptions: (1) regularities and social orders are continuous and are not intentionally or consciously created by any one individual or group; (2) social regularities play a role in informing the conditions within which social problems and policy solutions are constructed; (3) regularities are historical and change over time; and (4) regularities operate below the surface where political actors' subjectivities may or may not be self-consciously aware. The next section brings to light these regularities in the context of the attempted passage of House Bill 4122, alongside the various pieces of legislation that sought to address the needs of emergent bilingual students in the state of Texas.

Inserting La Clase Mágica *into State-Level Policy Discourses*

On July 24, 2008, the state of Texas witnessed a monumental legal decision concerning the civil rights of secondary English learners [EL] (MALDEF, 2008). United States District Judge William James Justice ruled that that Texas Education Agency (TEA) failed to adequately meet the educational needs of the state's more than 140,000 Latino/a secondary students (MALDEF, 2008). Among those failings mentioned in the opinion are the following: poor evaluation of such programs, the lack of effective monitoring of secondary students enrolled in ESL programs, low test scores and graduation rates, and high dropout rates (MALDEF, 2008; Alonzo, 2008). This court ruling has placed national attention on the fact that secondary emergent bilingual youth labeled "Limited English Proficient" in the state of Texas are "much more likely to drop out of high school and to be kept back or retained in class" than their white counterparts, and that these students are "much less likely to be afforded opportunities for advanced placement classes even though such classes could be offered" to these students (*USA and LULAC GI-Forum v. Texas*, 2008, p. 9).

Following Judge Justice's opinion, the Texas state legislature began holding interim hearings to identify "best practices and programs for students targeted to improve the academic success of limited English-proficient students" (Texas Senate Committee on Education, 2008). On October 20, 2008, the Texas Center for Education Policy (TCEP) provided testimony to the Texas Senate Public Education Committee citing the longitudinal success of *La Clase Mágica* as a viable, research-based initiative (López, 2008). Prior to testimony, the authors had been working for over six months to develop a university-community-school partnership as one of the first programmatic initiatives housed within Valenzuela's Associate Vice Presidency portfolio, the same office within which TCEP was situated. These efforts consisted of developing a constituency for LCM and securing local-level partnership agreements—first, in Austin, and subsequently, in San Antonio with the help of faculty researchers from the Academy for Teacher Excellence (ATE) at University of Texas at San Antonio (UTSA).

During the same legislative session that TCEP sought to insert LCM into state-level policy conversations, the Center was simultaneously playing a key role in the debate on House Bill 3—Texas' omnibus legislation that today is referred to as the State of Texas Assessment and Academic Readiness (STAAR) system (see López et al., 2011; and López, 2012). House Bill 3 transitions the state's system to one that will develop college and workforce measures of readiness. In the lower grades, STAAR removes students' access to Spanish assessment in the sixth grade. At the high-school level, STAAR increases the number of all-English, exit-level high school exams from four to twelve and uses these same tests to determine 15 percent of students' grades. Among some of the positive changes that were made by HB 3 are the elimination of high-stakes testing for all third-grade students, requiring the grade placement committee (GPC) to include the bilingual education teacher during the review of those students participating in a bilingual education program, and requiring that those students who do not pass the state assessment and are promoted by the GPC to be given a qualified teacher in the following academic year, increasing these students' chances of success.

SYNCHRONIZING MULTIPLE WORLDS: FINDINGS AND CHALLENGES

When considering the state of education for emergent bilingual students in Texas in an environment of high-stakes testing and accountability policies, it is important to acknowledge the historical use of testing. According to Baker and Stites (1991), "standardized examinations were born out of the struggle for control of the state between bureaucratic and aristocratic power bases" (p. 139). This approach has deep roots in the Confucian ideology of education, which argued for a standardized metric to identify talent and "men with sufficient talent and moral character" who would "maintain order in the state" (Baker and Stites, 1991, p. 139).

With regards to the United States, the post-Enlightenment era embraced the ideological commitment to merit by acknowledging and rewarding innate qualities of individuals and institutionalized these social regularities into the country's educational system. What follows is a historic focus on individual-level differences and an investment in methods that ostensibly measure levels of intelligence, initially through mental testing (Lemann, 1999). These social regularities remain deeply entrenched in the ideological orientations of multiple political actors at all levels, as this chapter demonstrates.

Social Regularities and Emergent Bilingual Students

In 2001, based largely upon the Texas-style accountability framework, the No Child Left Behind Act (NCLB) created a national accountability structure that reigns over today's educational landscape. This standards-based system places an added focus on the outcomes of ELs—an element that was not present in the initial articulations of Texas' system of accountability. The politics of how the state addresses its fastest growing demographic provides the context in which LCM would enter the policy arena.

From a political standpoint, Latino/a critical race theories in the field of education help us to see some of the ways in which social regularities, such as color blindness, are deeply entrenched and institutionalized in policy discourses; not only by the dominant group, but by people of color. This view perpetuates an idea of racism as being "an individual and irrational act in a world that is otherwise neutral, rational, and just" (López, 2003, p. 69; see also Crenshaw, Gotanda, Peller, and Thomas, 1995). In this framing, regularities are minimized to individual, rather than "social and/or civilizational construct[s]" (López, 2003, p. 69), thereby absolving the state, and relevant political actors' role in marginality (see also López, 2012; López et al., 2011; Valenzuela, 2004).

Emergent bilingual students are positioned to have to negotiate multiple regularities. Among those regularities are issues of race, ethnicity, class, gender, achievement, documentation status, regional location, and language. A social regulatory that is under-researched in the context of emergent bilingual students is professionalism, or the proliferation of political actors' management of the citizenry as a means to, "produce the disciplined, productive citizen" (Scheurich, 1994, p. 307). Professionalism builds on a panoptical-style of governance that expands the reach of the state into all aspects of peoples' lives, bringing all human actions under its gaze. This construct associates the happiness, productivity, and the wellbeing of individuals with those behaviors that reinforce the desired social order of the dominant group (Foucault, 1972, as cited in Scheurich, 1994). Because there is no room to delineate all of the social regularities that emergent bilingual students must negotiate, we will focus on the intersecting factors of language and professionalism.

Language as a Social Regularity

In the context of NCLB, Callahan (2006) explains how the Act's focus on literacy as a primary measure of achievement has produced cumulative effects for emergent bilingual students. Specifically, achieving literacy for these students involves measuring their grade level proficiency under Title I and English proficiency under Title III. These policies have, in effect, narrowly constructed literacy in a way that divorces the interactive and communicative aspects of language. This process begins by privileging the English language and defining educational achievement based on an all-English standardized test performance. These acts are compounded by fiscal pressures that tie access to funding to student's progress towards acquiring English, where everything else becomes secondary. These policies perpetuate long-standing exclusionary practices that relegate the needs of emergent bilingual students to the margins of cross-cutting policy streams. Intertwined with the social regularity of language is achievement, or socially constructed merit, which further assigns the assets and needs of the already marginal, emergent bilingual learners to the periphery.

The social regularity of achievement in the current era of accountability and assessment policies are primarily an outgrowth of the standards movement; although for emergent bilingual learners, a long history of regulatory systems that place them at the periphery exists (Vega, 1979; Blanton, 2004). Under current systems, the process for defining success and failure centers on outcomes, standardized curricula, and all-English assessments (i.e., test performance). These policies are increasingly formalized through federal and state mandates, and are also appropriated and sometimes exacerbated at local levels by way of informal policies (see for example, García and Menken, 2010, 249–261). The latter point is one we will elaborate more on in the following section.

During the Senate Public Education interim hearings, the sole expert witness ushered in by Senator Florence Shapiro, Chair of the Committee on Public School Education, was the Center for Research on the Educational Achievement and Teaching of English Language Learners (CREATE). During their testimony, CREATE would stay clear of advising the state on the benefits of providing resources for bilingual education. Rather, when asked by Senator Shapiro what methods work best for emergent bilingual students, specifically noting English immersion, dual language, and bilingual education as prevailing options, CREATE responded that there is "no one-size-fits-all approach" that can be identified, thereby redirecting the conversation away from the issue of language. This local-control-friendly notion played into the hands of conservative leadership with ideological commitments to English-only and local (non-state-supported) approaches for addressing the needs of emergent bilingual students.

CREATE would further argue that a focus on the language of instruction continues to dominate the discourse when speaking about emergent bilingual youth, calling this a distraction from the more important issue, which is how students are being instructed. Specifically, CREATE stressed the importance of identifying methods to "incorporate English language as an enhancement, with respect to improving outcomes," and that focusing on vocabulary concepts and strategic enhancers in English (i.e., phonics) have been shown to produce optimal outcomes for students. Touting phonics as the embodiment of "principles of effective instruction," and focused on developing the English language, CREATE constructed a context where they were able to deemphasize bilingual education, albeit within bilingual education contexts, without structuring the phonics program out of opportunities to be integrated into bilingual classrooms.

CREATE's advocacy found expression in Senate Bill 1460, a piece of legislation sponsored by Florence Shapiro and filed during the 2009, 81st legislative session. The bill was also scheduled for a hearing on the same day as SB 2002, one of the three bills in the bilingual policy packet. These dynamics are addressed below in the subsequent paragraphs.

Following CREATE's testimony, the Texas Association for Bilingual Education (TABE) followed by arguing, in contrast, that attention *must* be given to the language of instruction and that focusing solely on reading and learning vocabulary does not lead to literacy. Understanding that phonetic instruction has an ideological constituency in the state and that debating on this premise would not be enough, TABE took a fiscal imperative approach in their response, telling the committee: "You get what you pay for." TABE supported its testimony by discussing the economic development and human capital imperatives of bilingual education, at the same time that they challenged the myth that quickly transitioning emergent bilingual students into English is in their best interest:

when you do that [rush students into English], you get initial success but in the later grades like sixth and eighth, they start doing bad. So in the best intentions in trying to help these children assimilate into the classroom and learn, you really actually are hurting them, and they test badly, and then when they test badly in the later grades, what's the solution? "Let's give them more English," so you push them to the edge and in the fifth and eighth grade you push them more over the edge, and then they drop out, and then they become that strain upon society and they don't achieve that economic development or get to participate in that very viability of what we've been talking about.

Referring to empirical research that showed the positive impact that teaching in the native language had on emergent bilingual students, investing in literacy and the multitude of resources that together embody a fully-funded, bilingual education program is what research shows will lead to these youth performing just as well academically, if not better, than their monolingual peers. TABE's testimony ended by stating, "One thing is clear. The more instruction in the native language the better they do . . . when you do that [provide bilingual instruction] you increase their proficiency, their ability to achieve at academic grade level, and that is from empirical evidence." If outcomes are in fact the focus of policies, attempts to invest in what produces them should be appealing. Rather, these efforts fall on deaf ears when they come into conflict with opposing ideological commitments together with interests that stand to profit from their own proposals.

During the same interim charge hearing, TCEP followed TABE's lead in showing empirical data on the success of emergent bilingual students involved in LCM, a biliteracy program with twenty years of data (López, 2008). Among the findings on the success of LCM, TCEP showed that 90 percent of the students who participated were enrolled in or had already completed a college degree (Vásquez, 2003). In the case of those students who served as wizard assistants (secondary-level participants), 32 percent had plans to pursue graduate education (Vásquez, 2003). For many, the most common, influential factor that expanded their academic success was their exposure to working side-by-side with university students. In the case of undergraduate mentors, follow-up interviews revealed how their exposure to LCM encouraged them to pursue graduate studies. As a matter of fact, seven of the former university mentors interviewed went on to become faculty members of colleges and universities across the United States, all referring to their experiences with LCM as influential in their career choices. Awestruck by the outcomes of LCM, Senator Shapiro's response was that the program should be considered as a statewide effort.

Following TCEP's testimony, the legislative director to San Antonio Senator Leticia Van de Putte rushed down the hall to ask for more information regarding LCM. Weeks later, the TCEP research team joined faculty and researchers from the ATE at University of Texas at San Antonio at a presentation at the Texas State Capitol. This meeting was followed up with a joint research brief and multiple meetings that culminated into the co-construction of House Bill 4122 (HB 4122), a piece of legislation that would provide emergent bilingual students in both Austin and San Antonio with access to LCM. This piece of legislation would accompany two other bills, Senate Bill 548 and Senate Bill 2002 — both co-authored by Senators Van de Putte and Zaffirini, respectively — in a policy packet aimed at addressing the diverse needs of the state's growing emergent bilingual students. The politics of the 81st legislative session would respond to the three bills in similar ways, highlighting the politics of whose knowledge drives policy discourses for emergent bilingual students in the Texas state legislature.

Professionalism and the Role of Educators as Political Actors

Another significant detail that is important in understanding the sustainability of language and professionalism as social regularities in the context of Texas-style policymaking is the role of educators as political actors. Professionalism allows us to consider that "while governing bodies might play a role in developing and codifying policies, they do not operate in a vacuum" (López, 2012, p. 158).

During testimony on Senate Bill 2002, one of the three bills in the bilingual policy packet, teachers played a key role in preventing the bill from getting out of committee, and set the tone for the other two (i.e., SB 548 and HB 4122). The advocacy of select educators would add yet another layer to the complexities involved in understanding the politics of inserting LCM into the legislative arena. Both LCM and the bilingual education agenda, generally, would come in direct conflict with Senator Shapiro's investment in SB 1460, the phonics constituency, and a sector of teachers.

Attempting to address the capacities of teachers to instruct emergent bilingual students, SB 2002 was a piece of legislation that came directly out of William Wayne Justice's court opinion. Supporting this bill was a coalition of civil rights groups, research organizations, and the Texas Association for Bilingual Education. This coalition clashed with select groups of educators that were opposed to having their required professional development hours prescribed in order to ensure that the capacities of Texas teachers were enabling them to better serve the state's fastest growing demographic in a consistent manner. Many key members of the coalition supporting the bilingual policy packet were also being stretched thinly due to their attention being diverted to deal with anti-immigrant legislation.

Among the complaints expressed by select educators opposing the bilingual education bills was the argument that emergent bilingual students were not the majority of students, and in some instances, were a small minority, in many Texas classrooms. The notion that making changes to instructional approaches for "a few" emergent bilingual students was simply ridiculed by these educators who testified, giving opponents on the Senate Education Committee enough leverage to claim that the proposals were not worth supporting. This was further compounded with other statewide organizations'—specifically teacher organizations'—decision to support SB 1460 due to the fact that it had a stronger chance of passing. Even if many of these organizations did not support the language in SB 1460, helping the legislation progress meant there could be opportunities to amend and fold in those elements of their respective agendas into the final iteration of the bill.

RETHINKING RESONANCE: NEW CONCEPTUAL UNDERSTANDINGS

At the end of the 81st Session of the Texas State Legislature, none of the bills in the bilingual education policy packet would find their way into statute. Nor would the goals of these bills find expression in House Bill 3, the state's new system of accountability and college readiness. Our findings demonstrate the dire need to increase communities' awareness of policies and regulatory processes, both governmental and non-governmental entities and persons. While HB 4122 was able to benefit from the pro-bilingual constituency mobilized around SB 548 and SB 2002, it also meant that its fate would hinge on the outcomes of those two pieces of legislation as a result of the political context within which they were situated.

Based on our participant observations of the policymaking process, we argue that researchers must be mindful of the larger political context into which policy suggestions enter. For example, while the pro-bilingual education policy packet agendas were all research-based proposals that had a select statewide constituency, these efforts were having to simultaneously take on the philosophical tenets that many policy actors, state elected officials, and educators, alike, continue to hold in their understanding of language, success, failure, and outcomes. Because so much of what it means to be educationally successful relies on reductive measures like standardized test scores and school ratings, it is easy to lose sight of how these very outcomes are so deeply internally referential. That is, these are the artifacts of regulatory processes that differentially situate students within the larger system of accountability.

What is also important to understand is that the authors, as the primary researchers associated with HB 4122, were simultaneously involved in the political debate on House Bill 3, the state's omnibus legislation that overhauled public education. At the center of our arguments in the HB 3 debate were the criticisms that the state's growing EL population were either left unaddressed entirely, or were an afterthought, attended to with superficial and/or programmatic solutions (López et al., 2011). During the final stages, efforts to insert the policy packet into HB 3 amendments were met with contempt, and our involvement in the highly contentious political debate on HB 3, generally, also meant that HB 4122 took a political hit. That is, our fingerprints on HB 3 "tainted" HB 4122 by association—a process that makes sense for a regulatory state that rationalizes and normalizes existing social relations of dominance and subordination.

Rather than harmonic balance, we find disjuncture between those who create policy, those who engage in policy processes, and those who are recipients of policies. For advocates, a lesson here is that research and researchers must be prepared to enter highly political debates, ideally with a cadre of supporters, because expertise alone is insufficient. Significant court challenges notwithstanding, for ELL youth in Texas, their instructional needs are again sacrificed at the altar of shorthand formulas masquerading as "accountability" where only certain forms of language, knowledge, and control require a narrowing of vision.

NOTES

1. The authors will use the term "emergent bilingual" when referring to students who speak a language other than English and are acquiring English in school. We choose this term rather than Limited English Proficient (LEP) or English language learners (ELL) because these terms reflect there linguistic situation as a problem rather as a resource, as García, Kleifgen and Falchi (2008) characterize students' language diversities; as resources for an increasingly globalized world. However, the latter terms will be used when citing or referencing state and national data systems, policy language or research that does not extend the same perspectives.
2. According to the 2010 census data, Mexican-origin Latino's comprise 85 percent of the 9.5 million Latino/as in the state (Ennis, Ríos-Vargas, and Albert, 2011).

REFERENCES

Alonzo, R. (2008, July 31). "Alonzo: Bilingual Education Task Force Now Needed." *Rio Grande Guardian*, feature story. Retrieved July 31, 2008, from http://www.riograndeguardian.com/features_story.asp?story_no=1.

Apter, D. (1974). "The Role of the New Scientific Elite and Scientific Ideology in Modernization." In S. P. Restivol and C. R. Vanderpool (eds.), *Comparative Studies in Science and Society* (398–408). Columbus, OH: Merrill.

Baker, E. L, and Stites, R. (1991). "Trends in Testing in the USA." In S. H. Fuhrman and B. Malen (eds.), *The Politics of Curriculum and Testing* (139–157). New York: Falmer Press.

Blanton, C. K. (2004). *The Strange Career of Bilingual Education in Texas, 1836–1981*. College Station, TX: Texas A&M University Press.

Böhme, G. and Stehr, N. (1986). "The Growing Impact of Scientific Knowledge on Social Relations." In G. Böhme and N. Stehr (eds.), *The Knowledge Society* (7–30). Dordrecht, Netherlands: D. Rekiel.

Callahan, R. (2006). "The Intersection of Accountability and Language: Can Reading Intervention Replace English Language Development?" *Bilingual Research Journal*, 30(1), 1–21.

Cervantes-Soon, C., and Valenzuela, A. (2011). "Subtractive Legislative Policy: The Plight of Texas Bilingual Learners." In B. B. Flores, R. H. Sheets, and E. R. Clark, (eds.), *Teacher Preparation for Bilingual Student Populations: Educar para transformar,* (191–204). New York: Routledge.

Crenshaw, K., Gotanda, N., Peller, G., and Thomas, K. *Critical Race Theory: The Key Writings that Formed the Movement.* New York: New Press.

Eismon, T. O. (1981). "Scientific Life in India and African Universities: A Comparative Study of Peripherality in Science." *Comparative Education Review,* 164–182.

Ennis, S. R., Ríos-Vargas, M., and Albert, N. G. (2011). *The Hispanic Population: 2010.* Washington, DC: U.S. Department of Commerce, Economic and Statistics Administration.

Foley, D. E., and Valenzuela, A. (2005). "Critical Ethnography: The Politics of Collaboration." In N. K. Denzin and Y. Lincoln (eds.), *The Handbook of Qualitative Research* (third ed.). (217–234). Beverly Hills, CA: Sage Publications.

Foucault, M. (1972). *The Archeology of Knowledge and the Discourse of Language.* New York: Pantheon Books.

Gale, T. (2001). "Critical Policy Sociology: Historiography, Archeology, and Genealogy as Method of Policy Analysis." *Journal of Education Policy,* 16(5), 379–393.

García, O. and Menken, K. (2010). "Stirring the Onion: Educators and the Dynamics of Education Policies (Looking Ahead)." In K. Menken and O. García (eds.), *Negotiating Language Policies in Schools: Educators as Policymakers,* (249–261). New York: Routledge.

García, O., Kleifgen, J., and Falchi, L. (2008). "From English Language Learners to Emergent Bilinguals." Research Review Series Monograph, Campaign for Educational Equity, Teachers College, New York: Columbia University.

GI Forum et al. v. Texas Education Agency et al., 87 F. Supp.2d 667 (W. D. Tex. 2000).

Johnson, R. L. (2010). *Texas Public School Attrition Study, 2009–2010.* San Antonio, TX: Intercultural Development Research Association.

Korr-Cetina, K. and Mulkay, M. (eds.), (1983). *Science Observed: Perspectives on the Social Study of Science.* London: Sage.

Lemann, N. (1999). *The Big Test: The Secret History of the American Meritocracy.* New York: Farrar, Strauss and Giroux.

Levinson, B.A. and Sutton, M. (2001). "Policy as/in Practice: Developing a Sociocultural Approach to the Study of Educational Policy." In M. Sutton and B.A. Levinson, (eds.), *Policy as Practice: Toward a Comparative Sociocultural Analysis of Educational Policy,* (1–22). Westport, CN: Ablex Publishing.

López, G. R. (2003). "The (Racially Neutral) Politics of Education: A Critical Race Theory Perspective." *Educational Administration Quarterly,* 39(1): 68–94.

Lopez, P. D. (2008). Testimony to the Senate Committee on Education. *Interim charge: Review to make recommendations regarding best practices for programs targeted to improve the academic success of limited English-proficient students,* Hearing, October 20, 2008. Retrieved November 15, 2012 at: www.senate.state.tx.us/avarchive/?yr=2008.

——— (2012). *The Process of Becoming: The Political Construction of Texas' Lone STAAR System of Accountability and College Readiness.* Unpublished Dissertation Manuscript. University of Texas, Austin, TX.

López, P. D., Valenzuela, A., and Garcia, E. (2011). "The Critical Ethnography for Public Policy." In B. A. Levinson and M. Pollock (eds.), *Companion to the Anthropology of Education,* (547–563). Maiden, MA: Wiley-Blackwell Press.

Mexican American Legal Defense and Educational Fund (MALDEF). (2011, December 13). *MALDEF Lawsuit: Texas' School Funding System Unlawfully Shortchanges Many Districts and Students, Including Low-Income and English Language Learners.* San Antonio, TX: MALDEF. Retrieved January 2, 2012 from: www.maldef.org/news/releases/tx_school_funding/

———— (2008, July 25). *Major Ruling in Case for Texas English Language Learner Students: Dismal Failure for Secondary Programs Violates Civil Rights of English Language Learners*. San Antonio, TX: MALDEF. Retrieved December 5, 2011 from www.maldef.org/news/releases/us_texas_072508/index.html

Scheurich, J. J. (1994). "Policy Archeology: A New Policy Studies Methodology." *Journal of Education Policy*, 9(4), 297–316.

Scheurich, J. J. and Young, M. D. (1989). "Coloring Epistemologies: Are Our Research Epistemologies Racially Biased?" *Educational Researcher*, 26(4), 4–16.

Scott, J. C. (1998). *Seeing Like a State: How Certain Schemes to Improve the Human Condition have Failed*. New Haven, CT: Yale University Press.

Shore, C., and Wright, S. (1997). *Anthropology of Public Policy: Critical Perspectives on Governance and Power*. London: Routledge.

Texas Education Agency (TEA). (2011). *Enrollment in Texas Public Schools, 2010–2011*. Austin, TX: Texas Education Agency. Retrieved November 20, 2011 from: www.tea.state.tx.us/acctres/Enroll_2010-11.pdf

United States of America and LULAC GI-Forum v. State of Texas, No. :71-CV-5281-WWJ (District Court for the Eastern District of Texas July 24, 2008), Retrieved December 5, 2011 from www.maldef.org/.../us_v_texas_memorandum_opinion_2008.pdf

Valenzuela, A. (1999). *Subtractive Schooling: U.S.-Mexican Youth and the Politics of Caring*. Albany, NY: State University of New York Press.

———— (2004). "Introduction: The Accountability Debate in Texas: Continuing the Conversation." In A. Valenzuela (ed.), *Leaving Children Behind: How 'Texas-style' Accountability Fails Latino Youth*, (1–32). Albany, NY: State University of New York Press.

Valenzuela, A., Fuller, E. J., and Vasquez Heilig, J. (2006). "The Disappearance of High School English Language Learners from Texas High Schools." *Williams Institute Journal*, 1, 170–200.

Vásquez, O.A. (2003). *La Clase Mágica: Imagining Optimal Possibilities in a Bilingual Community of Learners*. Mahwah, NJ: Lawrence Erlbaum.

Vega, J. E. (1979). "The Enactment of Bilingual Education Legislation in Texas, 1969-1973." In R. V. Padilla (ed.), *Bilingual Education and Public Policy in the United States* (109–135). Ypsilanti, MI: Eastern Michigan University Department of Foreign Languages and Bilingual Study.

Weaver-Hightower, M. B. (2008). "An Ecology Metaphor for Educational Policy: A Call to Complexity." *Educational Researcher*, 37(3), 153–167.

Wedel, J. R., Shore, C., Feldman, G., and Lantrop. S. (2005). "Toward an Anthropology of Public Policy." *Annals of the American Academy of Political and Social Science*, 600, 30–51.

FIVE

Unearthing Sacred Knowledge: *Enlazándonos con la comunidad*

Lorena Claeys and Henrietta Muñoz

WORKING TOWARD HARMONY

Learning from our *antepasados* is a sacred practice in many cultures, especially to those who are native to this continent. From Lara (2004), we gain insights about the term *tekio*, a vibrant communal collaboration that was central to community activity in our Pre-Columbian cultures:

> *En la visión indígena, únicamente tiene significado lo que representa unión o asociación, porque así es la evolución natural. Esto ha quedado de manifiesto en la unión de familias que conforman la red de naciones comunales a lo largo del continente, donde se comparten raíces y conocimientos. La cooperación entusiasta, conocida como tekio, es una práctica de trabajo comunitario que, por fortuna, conservamos, y en algunas comunidades todavía se espera con ansia y regocijo.* (Lara, 2004, p. 10)[1]

These types of collaborative efforts have existed since the time our *antepasados* would gather in *centros ceremoniales* to undertake religious, social, marketing, and trading affairs. For centuries, in order to assist entire *Náhuatl* villages in some parts of Mexico, the local native men and women have been gathering and organizing themselves in cooperative groups to realize collective works. An example of this work is when men in the fields helped each other sow and harvest during the corn season and then the crop was shared among the people in the village. Another example is when women would gather during the village festivities to prepare corn tortillas for the entire community to enjoy. This same type of *tekio* tradition has emerged in the implementation of an afterschool program known as *La Clase Mágica* (LCM). LCM is a communal initiative engaging a university, a teacher preparation program, a youth and community initiative, and an elementary school in a collaborative partnership.

Setting

We believe that the implementation of LCM at Las Palmas Elementary School in Edgewood Independent School District (EISD) in San Antonio, Texas was a natural *tekio*-like collaboration since its inception. For instance, since all partnership stakeholders shared common goals, in addition to sharing similar ethnic, cultural, and linguistic identities to various degrees (e.g., Latino mayor, superintendent, principal, university scholars, teacher candidates, children, parents, and community representatives), the "engine" of LCM worked together quite naturally to meet those goals. LCM's natural *tekio* provides a closer connection to the sacred practice of sharing knowledge through enhanced connections and communications among all involved.

Community Profile

Edgewood ISD (EISD), located in the west side of San Antonio, is one of the ten poorest school districts in the state of Texas based on property tax structure. It is a district embedded in the heart of the barrio with a large Latino community (93 percent) that is young, low-income, and who have less than a 9th grade education (U.S. Census Bureau, 2010). The EISD Latino student enrollment (92 percent) is considered economically disadvantaged, 19 percent are English learners, and 71 percent are classified at-risk (Texas Academic Excellence Indicator System, Texas Education Agency, 2011). Despite these figures, those involved with LCM see that the EISD community is rich in history and among its greatest assets are the families who carry on the legacy of community and collaborative work. The historical legacy of the EISD community includes the birthplace of heroic community advocates, military veterans, and the struggle for financial equity in poor school districts as evident in *Rodriguez vs. Texas*, 1976 (Montejano, 2010).

In essence, just like our ancestors engaged in a *tekio*-like collaborative to help entire communities (Montemayor, 2007), LCM partners have built a reciprocal collaboration to provide rich informal learning experiences to all involved. The mutuality of LCM's partnership provides equal benefits to all collaborators, addressing a local need by engaging children and their parents, teacher candidates referred to as *aspirantes,* and university faculty in a bicultural-bilingual magical world complemented with the latest in mobile technology. In this collaborative, our unity stems from the common goals immersed in a common culture, but also from our cosmic link to the sacred sciences providing the foundation needed for the ancient Pre-Columbian *tekio* to meet, greet, and integrate with the modern technology used to help create the magical world of LCM in an effective and highly successful manner.

Collaborative Partnership

The EISD community has all the characteristics of a *tekio*-like collaborative, where members of a community invest time and effort, in addition to material resources. making it an ideal environment to implement *La Clase Mágica* (LCM). From the onset, it was also prudent to engage in a partnership with the Academy for Teacher Excellence (ATE) at the University of Texas at San Antonio (UTSA), Making Connections Partnership (MCP), and Las Palmas Elementary School to collaboratively and enthusiastically implement LCM, as a reciprocal collaboration of partners working together to solve educational challenges, build capacity of the partners, and serve the Latino community.

The Academy for Teacher Excellence (ATE), established in 2003, serves as a center for the College of Education and Human Development at UTSA, school districts, and community stakeholders. ATE has been the vanguard of development and research of innovative demonstration projects that promote the growth of culturally efficacious teachers, mentors, and university faculty. In addition to teachers having strong content, pedagogical, and technological-pedagogical knowledge, cultural efficaciousness means holding a strong ethnic identity, demonstrating self-determination, employing critical reflection, exhibiting positive efficacy, revealing sociocultural competence, and engaging in transformative practices (Flores, Clark, Claeys, and Villarreal, 2007), These characteristics, along with the sensitivity and understanding that connects every person who shares the same cultural and linguistic affinities, sets-up the opportunity to understand and incorporate the practice of sharing knowledge as a sacred science into research and practice. Thus, the sacred science principle embraces the conception of knowledge generated by coexisting harmoniously with all living things using numerology to understand the world (see chapters 1 and 2).

Another important component of the LCM groundwork in San Antonio, Texas is the Making Connections Partnership (MCP), a neighborhood-based initiative funded by the Annie E. Casey Foundation, aimed at improving the lives of children in the Edgewood community. This collaborative effort brings together residents, non-profit organizations, faith-based entities, and government in creative ways to achieve neighborhood transformation through family and child development. EISD, already working very closely with the MCP initiative on piloting, implementing, evaluating, and scaling groundbreaking programs had the experience and practice to strengthen and continue a collaborative relationship with a local university. Thus, partnering and aligning with ATE's efforts and mission of preparing culturally efficacious *aspirantes* and with working in a community appeared like a natural connection.

CONCEPTUAL RESONANCE: WHAT WE KNOW?

La Clase Mágica (LCM) is a research-based program. Its collaborative nature, innovativeness, and inventiveness requires a partner school district to not only have a deep understanding of how the program works, but to have a commitment to join scholars from universities and communities in a collaborative undertaking that assembles the blending of resources towards the goal of educational equity (Vásquez, 2003; Vásquez and Marcello, 2009). LCM has also demonstrated to be extremely successful in Latino communities where it has effectively deflected high student attrition and promoted a college-going culture, thereby, increasing college going rates (Vásquez, 2003; Collins, Vásquez, and Bliesner, 2011). Much of this success has been attributed to the efforts of a school-community-university partnership focusing on developing an optimal learning environment to meet the diverse needs of a community through culturally relevant technology-based pedagogy. The success of the LCM depends heavily on a school district partnership that understands the underlying principles behind LCM, communication, and reciprocal collaboration. Fundamentally, LCM embraces the sacred sciences by promoting the potential of technology to engage young students in the learning and dialogic process, and fostering the magic of a community-oriented curriculum to connect children, parents, and educators outside the structured formal educational setting.

Another key component in any collaboration is communicating and sharing of ideas. It is important to note that the sacred sciences have been communicated and documented by our *antepasados* who created and utilized the art of "rock-carvings" or petroglyphs as basic communication tools (Carr and Nevin, 2012). Thus, communication in a collaborative environment for thoughtful and important matters has been considered a sacred practice. Archeologists have documented this critical practice by unearthing its nature and underpinnings from prehistoric sites where our *antepasados* lived, played, and worked (Carr and Nevin, 2012). Even though the exact meaning of most petroglyphs is unknown to us, archeologists agree that carving symbols served as a means to communicate and propagate important information. One example is the similar communication documented in petroglyphs not only in the American continent, but also across the world among ancient groups, which included information pertaining to good hunting grounds and astronomical significance to indicate annual equinox and solstices, for instance, to guide the planting cycles. Another prehistoric illustration is the Mayan codex, which depicts the communication of the sacred sciences through the craft of weaving and wearing clothing made by the native women. Consequently, petroglyphs and codices tell a story, share information, and provide a foundation on how modern communication has emerged and evolved over time, specifically in the spectrum of communal collaborative efforts. LCM, like petroglyphs and the Mayan codex, provides opportunities for everyone involved to learn new linguistic, cultural, mathematical, scientific, and technological knowledge and skills by weaving these into our past, present, and future.

The LCM initiative effectively links communication for collaboration to the cultural elements derived from the sacred sciences and cultural practices that have evolved overtime (see chapters 1 and 2). Learning of the sacred science begins at home, in the community, and continues throughout children's formative years in a Pre-kindergarten through higher education (P-20) environment, in particular in the LCM partnership. This partnership brings together resources to achieve optimal learning. We argue that responsibility for effective learning rests not only on the learners' ability to control what and how to learn, but also on the support afforded by families and communities. Recognition, validation, integration of sacred sciences, funds of knowledge, and a trusting relationship among LCM stakeholders are the foundation and impetus for this critical collaborative work. Further, this formulation for collaborative work generates the integration of community into the formal and informal learning environments. Thus, members within the community have opportunities to engage in an effective problem solving process. Tapping the communication that exists among children, family, and community members is critical for the success, sustainability, and expansion of LCM. Therefore, it is imperative to engage all involved and committed participants in ongoing dialogues to strategically document, develop, and execute action plans to collaboratively seek funding to continue implementing and begin expanding LCM across the school district and eventually the city.

The importance of creating a strong relationship is clearly stated in the Making Connections (MCP) website:

> Residents in the West Side know what their neighborhoods need. They know what it takes to create change. One way that residents create transformation is by working in community-based organizations that advocate on behalf of neighborhood residents. Through these organizations, residents develop strong relationships with one another and links to vital information or resources. We call this social networking, and it is the lifeblood of *Making Connection Partnership*. (Making Connections~San Antonio, 2012)

MCP utilized Open Space Technology (OST) to provide opportunities for the community residents to engage in critical dialogue, leadership development, and to determine its needs and wants (Owen, 2008). In this process of open circle communication to problem solve, Open Space Technology has been conceptualized as:

> one way to enable all kinds of people, in any kind of organization, to create inspired meetings and events. Over the last twenty-plus years, it has also become clear that opening space, as an intentional leadership practice, can create inspired organizations, where ordinary people work together to create extraordinary results with regularity. In Open Space meetings, events and organizations, participants create and manage their own agenda of parallel working sessions around a central theme of strategic importance. (Herman, 1998, paragraphs 1 and 2)

Over time, OST has been appropriated for use in a variety of setting with successful outcomes.

In essence, this OST process parallels our *antepasados* use of central open space, what we might know as the town square or *centros ceremoniales*, to provide space for conversation, reflection, and moving to decision making and furthering their thinking together. Out of these MCP community gatherings, given the openness and safe environments for participating members to voice their needs and desires, emerged an expressed need for more effective educational strategies and after-school programming.

Comparable to the documented systemic and independent barriers, which obstruct the quality of public education and prevent school-age children from academic achievement to pursue a college education (Collins, Vásquez, and Bliesner, 2011), some of the concerns voiced by the EISD community indicated the need for additional culturally sensitive resources to be made available to students and families. They expressed a desire for their children to have access to a curriculum relevant to their cultural and linguistic backgrounds, while at the same time recognizing the need for their children to develop twenty-first century literacy and technology skills in order for the children to be college and career ready. The parents themselves also voiced a desire to learn how to use and have access to technology. Parents felt that the acquisition of technology skills would allow them to become better informed and to be able to provide additional support for their children. It is not unusual for families to feel ignored by the educational community (Delgado-Gaitán, 2012); however, the OST format provided a safe space for families to voice their concerns and needs. Shortly thereafter, MCP received a proposal from the university to consider the implementation of LCM. Thus, when stakeholders from the university, MCP, and Las Palmas Elementary School gathered to discuss the possible implementation of LCM, there was a natural fit between this initiative and the documented community needs and desires.

REPOSITIONING METHODOLOGY: LINKING TO THE SACRED SCIENCES

We employed participatory action research (PAR), as an epistemological stance situated in Freirian principles, which calls for researchers and participants to engage in collaborative and self-reflective inquiry in forming partnership that leads to transformative change (Baum, MacDougal, and Smith, 2006; Chevalier, and Buckles, 2013; Torre and Ayala, 2009). The reflective process of PAR is "directly linked to action, influenced by understanding of history, culture, and local context and embedded in social relationships." (Baum et al., 2006, p. 854)

Data sources included meeting notes, multiple iterations of reflecting, planning, acting, and observing; triangulation and member checking were used to develop a comprehensive summary of the development of a school-community-university partnership in the establishment of LCM as a *tekio*-like collaboration. In reflecting and dialoguing, we found ourselves *entremundos* in which we encountered *choques* as we attempted to incorporate the sacred sciences as a research lens. As Torre and Ayala (2009) proclaim: "Within a PAR framework, *choques* emphasize the importance of incorporating conflict and disjuncture that arise in the research as potential analytical resources" (p. 390). Specifically, PAR helped us understand the partnership through the notion of the sacred sciences that erupts from our ancestral languages, ceremonial customs, and traditions, using the lens of *compadrazgo and confianza.*

Compadrazgo or co-god/parenting in the Latino community is a system of fictive kinship, the notion of having co-parents and/or taking a village to raise a child (Marshall, 1998; Mendoza Ontiveros, 2010). We use *compadrazgo* within the LCM school-community-university partnership to stress that: (1) educating a child requires the involvement and collaboration of many; (2) school is the second most important home of the child because its impact will determine the child's future; and (3) the school must work closely with parents and the community in the education of a child.

Although researchers argue that *compadrazgo* is being destroyed by the urbanization of our world (Kemper, 1982), in the westside of San Antonio, this practice of *compadrazgo* is thriving. For example, the LCM is *compadrazgo* in action—born out the common cultural heritage of the school-community-university partnership ensuring mutuality and respect for the betterment of humanity. This *tekio*-collaborative work represents the cosmic world of the sacred sciences.

As a research lens, pairing the cultural tradition of *compadrazgo* with the shared value of *confianza* (mutual trust) as "the single most important mediator in social relationship" (Vélez-Ibáñez, 1983 p. 136), we see that LCM is much more than just an afterschool program. In LCM, *compadrazgo* is also a collaborative practice where *confianza* is the critical element for fruitful partnerships. As Flores and Claeys (2010/2011) assert, the following practices maximize synergy: (1) building relationships and dialoguing across partners, (2) communicating information and coordinating outreach, and (3) networking and leveraging resources. Equally complementary is Torre and Ayala's (2009) acknowledgement of the mutual respect and benefit for collaborative work:

> A PAR for social justice must assume multiplicity and hybridity among its participants, if the goal of meaningful liberatory action is to take place. The more a research collective values, grows and builds on the strengths of collective members' various selves, relationships and histories, opportunities for participation increase and windows for action open.

LCM partnership provides opportunities for collaboratively unearthing the communal knowledge of the sacred sciences, creating opportunities for sharing this knowledge, and thereby, garnering it for the new generation of the twenty-first century.

SYNCHRONIZING MULTIPLE WORLDS: FINDINGS AND CHALLENGES

Compadrazgo

Initially, LCM in San Antonio was designed to be implemented at the MCP~The Neighborhood Place community center where many other communal activities take place. While actualizing the plan, one of the major challenges that emerged was transportation of children to MCP, which meant a delay in the programming start date. Thus, MCP, working in collaboration with the university and the EISD, felt compelled to bring this work to a neighborhood school; thereby establishing that schools are spaces where parents, faculty and the community bring the concept of *compadrazgo*/communal responsibility into fruition. Everyone involved at the school, community, and university made a commitment to support and nurture the implementation of LCM.

Paralleling the successful LCM legacy (Vázquez, 2003), UTSA faculty and ATE administrators engaged in critical dialogue and reflection with Latino school leaders to make adaptations, modifications, and innovative creations to adopt the curriculum and implement an enhanced LCM at Las Palmas based on the local context and specific identified community needs (Ek, Machado-Casas, Sánchez, and Alanís, 2010). In contrast to Vásquez's model, the LCM at Las Palmas included an afterschool program that introduced mobile devices to deliver cultural and relevant activities, along with the adaptation to the local context of the *Laberinto Mágico* (see chapter 6).

Compadrazgo coupled with *Confianza*

Listening to the community's needs allowed the community members and school administrators to feel *confianza*/mutual trust with the university representatives. Consequently, as a result of this reciprocity, LCM children, their parents, and bilingual education *aspirantes* have been able to enjoy the fruits of a *tekio*-like collaborative for over five years (see chapters 6–9 and 12). *La Clase Mágica* at UTSA has served as a mechanism to bring together individuals from the university, the school district, and community organization into a unique partnership where all parties are working together on similar initiatives. By working together in partnership, we avoid diffusing efforts and together are able to make a concentrated impact.

A mutual desire to work with and serve children was instrumental in originating the conversations among entities that eventually joined forces to implement LCM and establish a relationship for a long lasting school-community-university partnership. The practice of collaboration and cooperation as a way of life has a long tradition in the sacred sciences, mapping for us today the way Latinos can work together for the greater benefit of a community. Reflection upon the establishment of a specific school-community-university partnership that builds on the sacred sciences as funds of knowledge, reveals existing community *compadrazgo* for the common good and *confianza* as mutual trust. To support this relationship, we note that *respeto* and *conocimientos* are the sociocultural tenets of a sustainable critical partnership. To elaborate on these tenets, we offer the following reflections:

Reciprocity *con respeto*

We have found that reciprocity *con respeto* is central to any collaborative endeavor. Valdés (1996) speaks to the importance of *respeto* when working with ethnic minority families and communities. For example, the high interest in and commitment to LCM's success shared by all partners (Making Connections Partnership, Las Palmas, university faculty, and *aspirantes*) has provided the impetus for the smooth implementation of LCM, garnering the support of the community, and a mutual desire for the sustainability of LCM.

A significant lesson learned, at the onset of the project, is the mutual reciprocal benefit afforded by the community and the university. Parental *apoyo, confianza y respeto* (support, trust, and respect) must be established at the onset with scholars and all others engaged in order for the implementation of institutional support and instructional resources to be effective (Vásquez, 2003). Reciprocity, as indicated by Vélez-Ibáñez (1988), exemplifies "an attempt to establish a social relationship on an enduring basis. Whether symmetrical or asymmetrical, the exchange expresses and symbolizes human social interdependence" (p. 142). Thus, "reciprocal practices that establish serious obligations based on the assumption of *confianza* (mutual trust), which is reestablished or confirmed with each exchange and leads to the development of long-term relationships" (Moll, et al., 2005, p. 74) are essential. The continuous commitment and active participation of children and parents, in addition to university faculty and *aspirantes'* dedication to LCM over the years have contributed to the successful implementation of LCM. Specifically, the reciprocal collaboration *con respeto* is demonstrated when university personnel and representatives of the community initiative engage in the process of procuring the community's sacred knowledge. In doing so, they discovered pathways that lead to mutual benefits including the transformation of all involved, including *aspirantes'* cultural efficaciousness, through an informal learning setting and increasing access to mobile devices for both children and parents (see chapters 6–9 and 12). The unity of this partnership is evident in the work and passion demonstrated through visible actions where all involved have developed a unified sense of purpose.

Conocimientos

We have also found that in order to unearth, rediscover, and promote the sacred sciences buried in the community, it is important for all representatives of the partnership to recognize, value, and integrate children's *conocimientos*—the funds of knowledge in their everyday practices. Researchers indicate that learners are a reflection of cultural and linguistic communities faced with historical, social, and political struggles, whose valuable experiences enrich the school context (Delgado-Gaitán, 2001; 2012; Moll et al., 2005; Yosso, 2005). In addition, the collaborative engagement of parents and children, from the perspective of sharing their *conocimiento*/knowledge with each other has been crucial to the implementation and sustainability of LCM. Parents are able to see directly how sharing *conocimientos* benefits their children and themselves. The rich communal knowledge that informs the ongoing development and enhancement of culturally relevant LCM activities, has contributed to the curriculum, bringing forth the sacred sciences within LCM. The active engagement, support, and contributions of LCM parents in the informal learning process (see chapter 12) have ensured the sustainability of LCM. Both children and parents benefit from developmentally appropriate, well-planned, culturally relevant activities that reflect the sociocultural context of the school and community at large. The active participation of children and parents with *aspirantes* and teacher educators/scholars to establish a reciprocal learning environment has had a significant effect for transforming practice.

RETHINKING RESONANCE: NEW CONCEPTUAL
UNDERSTANDINGS

LCM as an intergenerational approach has provided a truly working *te-kio*-like collaboration that promises to address educational equity in the public school system and facilitate entrance to the digital world. In a *tekio*-like collaborative comprised of multiple stakeholders working together to create sustainable efforts all in the name of the common good, *confianza* and *compadrazgo* are the new conceptual understandings. The principle that worked for us included listening first to the needs and desires of the community; then leveraging the work of a long-term community organization and a committed local university to establish *confianza* in validating the notion of *compadrazgo*. These practices draw on the teachings and knowledge of our *antepasados*, which help us rediscover their richness and sacredness. Thus, by following these practices, we are providing a trajectory for children, parents, *aspirantes*, and all involved to become bicultural, bilingual, and technologically efficacious members of a community.

Our experience of engaging Las Palmas and in connection with the Annie E. Casey Foundation's local initiative, Making Connections Partnership (MCP), in the implementation of LCM taught us the following lessons:

- A school district, when engaged since the initial exploration and planning phases, is more likely to become a willing and collaborating partner;
- A mutual sense of ownership of a project since its conception is vital to its success; and
- A commitment founded on effective principles of collaboration and reciprocity *con respeto* has greater chances for sustainability overtime.

While efforts for establishing a school-community-university collaboration have been realized through the implementation of an innovative after-school program, we are faced with a *choque* between the needs of the researchers and the needs of the community. Academics are caught at a crossroads between institutional recognition of research productivity versus community engagement. This threatens the collaborative partnership and the researchers alike. Moreover, the lack of initial local funding further threatens the sustainability of LCM beyond external grant funding. As a result, ongoing conversation, critical reflection, and forecasting among stakeholders is imperative in seeking external support valued by academia and to leverage local financial and human resources to sustain LCM at Las Palmas and expand to other sites to serve as laboratories for collaborative learning and research.

In sum, the following implications provide insight on how a university teacher preparation program, a youth and community initiative, and a school district built a trusting relationship to expand the way our *antepasados* lived by working to create and establish a successful *tekio*-like collaborative to sustain LCM or similar afterschool programs:

- *Establishing a partnership with a university teacher preparation program, a youth and community initiative, and a school district.* The experiences of *compadrazgo* by families and community members, and the value of the community's funds of knowledge by schools and the university, and the *confianza* gained by a community initiative proved the right mix for the successful implementation of LCM.
- *Engaging stakeholders to dialogue with each other as a tekio-like collaborative.* The community initiative, Making Connections Partnership, had established the *confianza* with the community and the university personnel had the wherewithal to value *confianza* and build upon the existing relationships to establish a school-community-university partnership.
- *Nurturing an effective partnership effort.* Effective communication for collaboration must include the cultural elements derived from sacred sciences and build upon the cultural aspects and values of a community.
- *Providing opportunities to close the digital gap while fostering biculturalism and bilingualism.* It is imperative for children and parents to recognize their bilingualism and biculturalism as a resource for the community's success in a global world. Therefore, LCM is a magical world that provides a space for all involved to use their bilingualism and biculturalism along with technological tools, such as mobile devices, to engage in creative and innovative learning opportunities.
- *Creating community-based learning opportunities and transworld pedagogy for becoming culturally efficacious educators.* The content and pedagogical knowledge critical in closing the achievement gaps are woven into the culturally relevant practices and magical world of LCM. *Aspirantes* and teachers have opportunities within this space to engage in ongoing learning opportunities and enact transworld pedagogy that will assist them in becoming culturally efficacious educators.

In general, LCM creates opportunities for children and *aspirantes* to engage in transformative and expansive learning. In addition, it is a mutually beneficial partnership that aids in the transformation of a community and changes the way people think by becoming culturally, bilingually, and technologically efficacious. It is vital to sustain such efforts while incorporating the community's cultural heritage as a central tenet to ensure the success of the university, community, and school partnership.

NOTES

1. According to the indigenous vision, only what represents unity or association is of significance because that is the nature of evolution. This has been manifested among the union of families across nations where roots and knowledge are shared across the continent. The enthusiastic cooperative efforts known as *tekio* is a collaborative communal work practice that fortunately we have conserved and in some communities it is longed for with great joy.

REFERENCES

Baum, F., MacDougall, C., and Smith, D. (2006). "Participatory Action Research." *Journal of Epidemiology and Community Health*, 60, 854–857. DOI: 10.1136/jech.2004.028662

Carr, K. and Nevin, P. (2012). "Petroglyphs-Home." Retrieved March 2, 2013 from pa. gov/portal/server.pt/community/petroglyphs/3892

Chevalier, J. M. and Buckles, D. J. (2013). *Participatory Action Research: Theory and Methods for Engaged Inquiry*, Routledge, UK.

Collins, C., Vásquez, O. A., and Bliesner, J. (2011). "Bridging the Gaps: Community-University Partnerships as a New Form of Social Policy." In M. Bowdon and R. Carpenter (eds.), *Higher Education, Emerging Technologies, and Community Partnerships: Concepts, Models, and Practices* (319–328). Hershey, PA: Information Science Reference. DOI:10.4018/978-1-60960-623-7.ch029.

Delgado-Gaitán, C. (2001). *The Power of Community: Mobilizing for Family and Schooling.* Lanham, MD: Rowman and Littlefield.

——— (2012). "Culture, Literacy, and Power in Family-Community-School Relationships." *Theory into Practice*, 51(4), 305–311. DOI: 10.1080/0040505841.2012.72606.

Ek, L.D., Machado-Casas, M., Sánchez, P., and Alanís, I. (2010) "Crossing Cultural Borders: *La Clase Mágica* as a University-School Partnership." *Journal of School Leadership*, 20(6), 820–849.

Flores, B. B., and Claeys, L. (2011). "Academy for Teacher Excellence: Maximizing Synergy among Partners for Promoting College Access for Latino Teacher Candidates." *The Urban Review*, 43(3), 321–338. DOI:10.1007/s11256-010-0153-y.

Flores, B. B., Clark, E. R., Claeys, L., and Villarreal, A. (2007). "Academy for Teacher Excellence: Recruiting, Preparing, and Retaining Latino Teachers though Learning Communities." *Teacher Education Quarterly*, 34(4), 51–69.

Herman, M. (1998). "Open Space World." Retrieved July 17, 2012 from www.openspaceworld.org/cgi/wiki.cgi.

Kemper, R. V. (1982). "The *Compadrazgo* in Urban Mexico." *Anthropological Quarterly*, 55(1), 17–30. Retrieved July 17, 2012 from www.jstor.org/stable/3317372.

Lara, E. (2004) *Mi trascender a través de la cuenta y el juego: Metáfora espiritual matemática.* México City: El Angelito Editor.

Marshall, G. (1998) "A Dictionary of Sociology." Retrieved July 17, 2012 from www.encyclopedia.com/doc/1O88-compadrazgo.html

Making Connections Partnerships~San Antonio, (2012). Retrieved July 17, 2012 from www.mc-sa.org/resident/default.asp

Moll, L., Amanti, C., Neff, D., and González, N. (2005). "Funds of Knowledge for Teaching: Using a Qualitative Approach to Connect Homes and Classrooms." In N. González, L. Moll, and C. Amanti (eds.), *Funds of Knowledge: Theorizing Practices in Households, Communities, and Classrooms*. New Jersey: Lawrence Erlbaum.

Montejano, D. (2010). *Quixote's Soldiers: A Local History of the Chicano Movement, 1966-1981*. Austin: University of Texas Press.

Montemayor, C. (2007). *Diccionario del Náhuatl en el español de México*. México City: Gobierno del Distrito Federal y el Programa Universitario México Nación Multicultural de la UNAM, 237.

Mendoza Ontiveros, M. (2010). "El compadrazgo desde la perspectiva antropológica." *Alteridades. 20*(40), 141–147. Retrieved July 17, 2012 from www.redalyc.org/articulo.oa?id=74720839011

Owen, H. (2008). *Open Space Technology: A User's Guide.* San Francisco, CA: Berrett-Koehler Publishers.

Texas Education Agency. (2011). *2010-11 Texas Academic Excellence Indicator System (AEIS)Report.* Austin, TX: Author retrieved July, 17, 2012 from: ritter.tea.state.tx.us/perfreport/aeis/2011/index.html

Torre, M.E. and Ayala, J. (2009). "Envisioning Participatory Action Research *entremundos.*" *Feminism and Psychology,* 19(3), 387–393. Retrieved May 9, 2012 from http://fap.sagepub.com

U.S. Census Bureau. (2010). *State and County Quickfacts: Bexar County, TX.* Retrieved July 17, 2012 from http://quickfacts.census.gov.

Valdés, G. (1996). *Con respeto: Bridging the Distances Between Culturally Diverse Families and Schools.* New York: Teachers College Press.

Vázquez, O. (2003). *La Clase Mágica: Imagining Optimal Possibilities in a Bilingual Community of Learners.* New Jersey: Lawrence Erlbaum.

Vásquez, O. and Marcello, A. (2009). "Una mirada contextualizada del uso de las prácticas de innovación en comunidades cultural y lingüísticamente diversas: la necesidad de adaptación mutua." *Revista de Investigaciones UNAD,* 8(2), 13–30.

Vélez-Ibáñez, C. G. (1983). *Bonds of Mutual Trust: The Cultural Systems of Rotating Credit Associations among Urban Mexicans and Chicanos.* New Brunswick, NJ: Rutgers University Press.

——— (1988). "Networks of Exchange among Mexicans in the U.S. and Mexico: Local Level Mediating Responses to National and International Transformations." *Urban Anthropology,* 17(1), 27–51.

Yosso, T. J. (2005). "Whose Culture Has Capital? A Critical Race Theory Discussion of Community Cultural Wealth." *Race, Ethnicity, and Education,* 8(2), 69–91.

SIX

Digitizing *El Laberinto*: Integrating Technology and Culture for the Twenty-First Century

Patricia Sánchez, Timothy T. Yuen, Macneil Shonle,
Theresa De Hoyos, Lisa Santillán, and
Adriana S. García

WORKING TOWARD HARMONY

La Clase Mágica (LCM) is an afterschool program that brings together Latina/o school children (*protégés*) and undergraduate students, as *aspirantes*, in an informal learning environment. *El Laberinto* is the magical maze that provided the structure for interactions and activities in LCM. In the original version by Vásquez and her colleagues at the University of California, San Diego, the maze was presented in a paper-based format. *El Laberinto* was sometimes an elaborate box construction that provided participants with supplies to construct a road map, which led to a series of games and activities, mostly commercial computer games. College students served as experienced guides to young elementary children on their magical journey to becoming wizard assistants and maintaining closer communication with *El Maga*[1] (a magical "being" central to LCM (see chapters 2, 3, and 7). At LCM@UTSA, the undergraduate bilingual teacher candidates are the *aspirantes*, who met weekly with the *protégés* during LCM sessions at the elementary school.

Based on Olga Vásquez's work (2003), we at the University of Texas at San Antonio have reinvented LCM for twenty-first century bilingual, bicultural learners by digitizing the learning experience. In this chapter, we describe how an interdisciplinary design team from UTSA consisting of two instructional technologists, two computer programmers, two teacher educators/professors at UTSA, and two local bilingual teachers began the process of reinventing Vásquez's *El Laberinto* for twenty-first century bilingual, bicultural learners. The design team integrated technology and culture by producing an interactive digitized maze for LCM that is reflective of the linguistic and cultural resources of the population being served. This innovative design and implementation of *El Laberinto* for learning and teaching takes elementary children on a new and more magical journey into a digital world that reflects and validates their language and culture.

In this interdisciplinary case study, we begin with an explanation for digitizing *El Laberinto,* and its role in the LCM program at UTSA, followed by a description of both mazes: Vásquez's version and our digitized version of *El Laberinto.* We continue with a discussion of the theoretical frameworks that inform the design of the digital maze and the journey in collaborating and designing this product as a team comprised of subject matter experts (SMEs), instructional technologists (IT), and technology developers. The SMEs included Latina/o educators with ten to fifteen years of experience working with Latina/o bilingual children or who could contribute to integrating the on-the-ground realities the children experience, while the IT and computer programmers were academics with extensive knowledge in instructional technology, multimedia, digital gaming, and programming. Finally, we share some preliminary responses from users who have interacted with the digitized maze, while our closing remarks reflect on our hope for others across the country to develop online tools that are grounded in children's local communities and cultures.

CONCEPTUAL RESONANCE: WHAT DO WE KNOW?

El Laberinto *Goes Digital*

Although Vásquez's original version of *El Laberinto* was used as a tool to integrate technology into their afterschool program in San Diego, California, the maze itself was not implemented in digital format. The maze was created in Microsoft Word by inserting a table and clipart graphics to form a path of rooms on an 8.5" x 11" page. This maze was printed and used by the elementary school children to play and learn as they completed the tasks associated with each room, much like a roadmap that led to a series of games and activities (mostly commercial computer games). It was sometimes presented as a larger wall hanging. The tasks to be completed by children and their college partners were referred to as "task cards" and were also created in Microsoft Word and used in printed format. In order to address the needs of the twenty-first century learners, it was important to reinvent Vásquez's original paper maze by going digital. UTSA's version of *El Laberinto* takes LCM's magical journey to a new level by immersing learners in an interactive digital environment and using multimedia to provide an engaging experience. As a digital environment, *El Laberinto* easily connects to other digital resources, such as websites, online games and simulations, and videos.

Going digital also meant that the design team could create an interactive culturally relevant maze that is reflective of the population being served and validates their language and culture in a digital world. According to Frederick, Donnor, and Hatley (2009), instructional technologies that support culturally relevant pedagogies engage students within a context that is familiar to the learners and allows for students to express their own experiences. Such activities are embedded in a culturally relevant environment as a way to support the learners in achieving instructional objectives. While the original maze incorporated a simple path with twelve rooms and clipart graphics such as stars, crayons, numbers and letters of the alphabet on a white background (see Figure 6.1), the digital version is engaging to our learners because it includes images from their immediate local community and has a bright and colorful banner and background (see Figure 6.2). In the case of *El Laberinto,* the environment included many references to Mexican/Latino cultures and the San Antonio community. The digital maze has a similar layout to the original paper maze, but is flanked by a colorful display of *papel picado* — decorative festive paper decorations that are typically displayed during various Mexican/Latino celebrations — to represent each room. As in the original maze, each of the twelve rooms is associated with task cards, which had a set list of three activities for students to complete. The digital version of *El Laberinto* added more flexibility by allowing students to choose one of eight possible task cards per *cuarto* and having one to three activities per task card. Students must complete at least one task card to advance to the next room and finish the maze.

We intentionally placed different pictures that specifically represent local community or Latino culture in general. These images include: Mayan temples; *El Día de los Muertos* [Day of the Dead] — a local celebration and holiday of deceased loved ones[2], originally from Mexico and gaining popularity across the Southwest; a *panadería* (bakery), common across neighborhoods throughout the mostly Latina/o city; the elementary school itself where LCM is held; a super-scale tile votive candle, depicting *La Vírgen de Guadalupe,* made by a local Latino artist; local grocery stores; a *piñata;* an image of the downtown UTSA campus; images of *la familia,* including a father wearing a plaid work shirt, slightly unbuttoned, that reveals a "Superman" logo — representing his two young children's adoration of him; and finally a soccer ball, symbolizing the culmination of reaching a "goal" or completion of the maze (see Figure 6.2).

These iconic images selected for the digital maze were chosen for their deep symbolic meaning for participants—whether it is a local attachment or a broader Latina/o affinity. As the children navigate along *El Laberinto's* path, they navigate through an alternate world, where the iconography and language reflect and honor who they are. The inclusion of two current bilingual teachers from the local community (doctoral students at UTSA) and UTSA teacher educators ensured that both the digital maze and task cards reflected the culture(s) of the local children and their knowledge by taking photos of the children's school and nearby grocery stores to bring their world into the digital world.

REPOSITIONING METHODOLOGY: BEYOND RELEVANCE TO THE SACRED SCIENCES

Using an interdisciplinary case study approach, we examine the development of our maze. According to Repko, Newell, and Szostak (2012), interdisciplinary case studies examine complex problems using a team approach; as such each of us brought our expertise and experience while

Figure 6.1.   Image of Original El Laberinto by Vásquez (2003), La Clase Mágica: *Imagining Optimal Possibilities in a Bilingual Community of Learners*, Mahwah, NJ: Lawrence Erlbaum.

Figure 6.2.   Image of El Laberinto Digitized. Academy for Teacher Excellence. (2008). University of Texas at San Antonio.

working in harmony to explore and create our culturally relevant maze. Interdisciplinarity by its nature required that we weave a common understanding from our various disciplines, thus we integrated the following theoretical lenses.

Making Funds of Knowledge Accessible and Relevant in an Online Environment

Funds of knowledge is an assets-oriented approach that recognizes and values the homegrown knowledge within households (González, Moll, and Amanti, 2005; Moll, Amanti, Neff, and González, 1992; Vélez-Ibáñez and Greenberg, 1992). It also serves as one of the pillars on which *El Laberinto* is based (Vásquez, 2003). Although funds of knowledge has always been a mechanism of support that facilitates and enriches the learning process of all children—particularly within LCM—in the digital environments we have organized, they become dynamic resources to reflect cultural awareness/affinity for one's family knowledge and background.

In LCM, participants are able to use language, semiotics, gestures, texts, and interact with each other in socially meaningful ways as they navigate through the maze and complete the different tasks. The *protégés* are able to engage in "play" by activating their discursive resources in order to operate within the school setting in ways that affirm their cultural, ethnic, and linguistic identities. They are able to form a "community of practice" (Wenger, 1999) where novices learn through apprenticeship and scaffolding in their interaction with experts, which then allows an affinity space to be fostered where people relate to each other around a common passion, proclivity, or endeavor (Black, 2007). This type of exchange between *aspirantes* and the *protégés* privileges both the adult and the child as co-constructors of knowledge and supports a "joint activity" (Gutiérrez, Baquedano-López, Alvarez, and Chiu, 1999), which affords children the opportunity to create hybrid texts that ingeniously display their bilingual and biliterate skills.

Similarly, LCM contradicts the teacher-centered classroom by providing opportunities for *protégés* to share their interests and inquiries. The following quote by poet and essayist Adrienne Rich (1986) echoes the voices of those who often feel silenced and ignored by the dominant discourse of the school culture:

> When those who have the power to name and to socially construct reality choose not to see you or hear you . . . when someone with the authority of a teacher, say, describes the world and you are not in it, there is a moment of psychic disequilibrium, as if you looked in the mirror and saw nothing. It takes some strength of soul—and not just individual strength, but collective understanding—to resist this void, this non-being, into which you are thrust, and to stand up, demanding to be seen and heard. (p. 99)

This "collective understanding" is enforced at LCM by allowing *protégés* to venture out of the hegemony found within the public school system and encourages them to participate in a more familial community. Children employ their unique linguistic resources, hybrid practices, and "funds" to interpret the social action and construct meaning of the curriculum of LCM. The goal of the LCM curriculum is not only to promote biliteracy and bilingualism among *protégés* and *aspirantes,* but also to "draw from their own as well as each other's linguistic and social cultural resources . . . creating rich zones of development" (Gutiérrez, Baquedano-López, Alvarez, Chiu, 1999, p. 88).

According to Schieffelin and Ochs (1986), "children bring their experiences and expectations to the verbal interactions that take place in formal school settings, and these differing backgrounds contribute to the nature of their participation, the interpretive procedures they employ, and their understanding of these verbal interactions" (p. 170). For example, by providing Latina/o *protégés* with ample opportunities to engage in digital media, they are able to discover new ideas, achieve specific learning objectives and communicative goals. Furthermore, they are able to negotiate tasks and become more digitally fluent and/or competent by developing their bilingual and biliterate skills. Their families' and community's "funds of knowledge" (Moll, Amanti, Neff, and González, 1992; Vélez-Ibáñez and Greenberg, 1992) recognize children's sociocultural and linguistic heritage as well as the myriad of experiences, strategies, and skills that are central to their daily lives. Through this type of collective recognition of the students' "funds," a space is created for them to serve as both knowledge consumers and producers instead of simply passive/receptive learners.

El Laberinto encourages *protégés* to engage in hybrid literacy and linguistic practices/activities (Gutiérrez, Baquedano-López, and Tejeda, 1999; Gutiérrez, Baquedano-López, Alvarez, and Chiu, 1999). Through these practices/activities, the idea of a "Third Space" is supported because it creates authentic interactions that intersect formal and informal spaces and reorganizes what counts as knowledge (Gutiérrez et al., 1999). Furthermore, Gutiérrez et al. (1999) explain that, "these hybrid literacy practices, embedded in a playful and stimulating learning environment, provide a model for understanding how meaningful collaboration can be created and sustained and how difference and diversity can serve as resources for learning" (p. 92). Therefore, LCM is a space that provides Latina/o *protégés* with the tools needed for becoming more socially, linguistically, and cognitively adept biliterate, bicultural digital citizens.

The elementary school *protégés* are also able to negotiate their roles between expert and novice by selecting task cards that vary in difficulty. Likewise, the *protégés* gain knowledge with the help of their *aspirantes* through scaffolding when faced with a complex task. This type of exchange between co-constructors of knowledge allows for a productive space where learners have many opportunities to utilize their larger linguistic, literate, cultural, and social repertoires. According to Gutiérrez and Rogoff (2003), *protégés'* repertoires are supported in LCM by helping them develop "dexterity in moving between approaches appropriate to varying activities and settings" (p. 22). The *protégés* use both their home and school language in their written and pictorial narratives that demonstrate their use of bilingualism as a resource for expressing sentiments and understanding (Vásquez and Duran, 2000), which in turn fosters the formation of a positive sense of self. Throughout their participation in LCM, *protégés* are able to use their unique linguistic, literate, and cultural repertoires to navigate through the playful and collaborative learning environment that embraces their background experiences as resources towards enhancing student learning and performance.

The relationship between the students and their mentors and the sharing of knowledge in LCM set up the mediational contexts and tools for social, emotional, and cognitive development. In this particular setting, *protégés* become competent in "using the concept of funds of knowledge as a heuristic device . . . . [which] allows the possibility of seeing beyond the classroom and glimpsing the circulating discourses and shifting fields of power that shape students' lives" (González, Moll, and Amanti, 2005, p. 44). In this context, learning is more dialogical and fluid in the sense that the child is able to interchange roles while participating in the digital activities. This power exchange occurs through language whereby the *protégés* acquire knowledge of its function, distribution, and interpretation in and across the situations found within the confines of LCM and, ultimately, contributes to the *protégés* feeling empowered by their contribution to learning.

Play and Intrinsic Motivation Theory

Providing culturally relevant learning environments, based on their funds of knowledge, is just one way of getting students to become interested in instructional content (Frederick et al., 2009). Our design of the digital *El Laberinto* was also informed by play and intrinsic motivation theory.

According to one important tenet of play, "the toys and gestures with which children play [are] significant artifacts from their social and cultural settings. . . . In play, children are acquiring the tools and meanings of their culture" (Verenikina, Harris, and Lysaght, 2003, p. 3). Therefore, it makes especially good sense to incorporate into the online play world, the students' funds of knowledge, as previously mentioned. We carefully adhered to this tenet to maximize *protégés'* processes of play—we not only "included culture but also used it as a tool for learning" (Riojas-Cortez, 2001, p. 39). *El Laberinto's* cultural relevance is intimately tied into *protégés'* intrinsic motivation for exploring and piquing their curiosity. Also, the maze-like structure of *El Laberinto* emulates many of the existing board games and puzzles for elementary school *protégés*.

Classical and modern theories of play all point to the ways that play advances *protégés'* emotional, social, and cognitive development. In fact, play is considered the most significant "leading" activity of early childhood years (Vygotsky, 1977; Bodrova and Leong, 1996, as cited in Verenikina, Harris, and Lysaght, 2003). Features of play include opportunities for children to engage in uncertainty, complexity, novelty, problem-solving, role play, imitation, and imagination, to name a few (Christie and Johnsen, 1983). When children are caught up in play, they are motivated to continue their engagement. And when students are intrinsically motivated, they are more likely to learn content (Ryan and Deci, 2000).

Three components intrinsic to a motivating environment are: challenge, curiosity, and fantasy (Malone, 1981; Malone and Lepper, 1987). *Protégés* need to have optimal challenges and goals to be motivated (Harackiewicz and Elliot, 1993; Malone and Lepper, 1987). Optimal challenge is important so that *protégés* can feel a sense of accomplishment and success when they overcome it. If the challenge is too difficult, then the *protégés* can become frustrated and constant frustration may lead to a lower sense of self-efficacy. Those with a lower sense of self-efficacy are more likely to envision failures, have negative attitudes to the content, and not try again (Bandura, 1993).

The design team's goal was to engage and motivate participants the entire time they navigated and worked through the maze, advancing from one *cuarto* to the next. The ultimate motivation feature was their advancement to becoming wizard assistants to *El Maga* at the completion of the maze. Advancing to the next *cuarto* requires a student to complete a task or tasks. The task cards within each *cuarto* provide multiple levels of challenge. When entering a *cuarto*, the *protégé* and *aspirante* select the appropriate level of the task card together (beginner, intermediate, or expert). As indicated by Malone (1980) and Malone and Lepper (1987), giving students the choice of how they accomplish the *cuarto* task card would be intrinsically motivating. Students may select the challenge that they believe is appropriate for their own self-perceived ability. Though a *protégé* is expected to move to the next *cuarto* after completing the task, there is a replayability factor—i.e., they can return to a previous task to complete it, select a higher level, or a lower level, if necessary.

There is also the challenge of completing the task at all levels. For those who have a higher sense of self-efficacy, they are more likely to attempt more challenging problems and try again if they failed (Bandura, 1993). It is up to the *aspirantes* to set and sequence the tasks because after all, they are bilingual education teacher candidates with training in working with *protégés* and their development. They are also serving as a mentor to the *protégés* as they are completing the tasks. Feedback is an essential component of any challenge (Malone and Lepper, 1987). *Aspirantes* facilitate the LCM activity and are the primary sources of feedback given that the task cards refer to some activities outside of LCM (e.g., other websites, online activities, or computer-based tasks) that may not provide adequate feedback. The feedback that *El Laberinto* can provide is the progress at which students are traversing the maze—showing the complete and unvisited *cuarto* which they aspire to reach and explore. Another important motivating factor is that the task cards and the maze's interface are presented in Spanish, providing students with *El Laberinto* in a language they are most comfortable using.

Sparking *protégés'* curiosity was the next principle of intrinsic motivation applied to the design. To take advantage of the digital platform, we tried to evoke a sense sensory curiosity throughout *El Laberinto*. Sensory curiosity uses multimedia stimuli (e.g., graphics, sounds) to draw the learner into the environment (Malone and Lepper, 1987). We first attempted to evoke sensory through using images of San Antonio and Mexican-American culture placed on *El Laberinto* as a way to get the students' attention. We also designed the maze to call attention to those students that have a personal interest in wizards, magic mazes, and similar fantasies. For those *protégés* who do not find any cultural relevance or interest in the wizard fantasy, we relied on extrinsic motivators to spark some situational interest, such as interesting visuals, audios, or textual information, and transition that to a more long-term interest. In today's high tech world, multimedia elements serve as great motivators. We also placed an ongoing interactive animation about *El Maga* being captured by *El Chupacabra*[3]. As students complete parts of the maze, they get to see a new chapter of the animation. Each chapter shows *El Chupacabra* attempting to cause some trouble in the LCM world, while trying to kidnap *El Maga*. The students watch the animation and are presented with a problem that will foil *El Chupacabra*'s mayhem. Placed in the role as an aspiring wizard assistant to *El Maga*, the learner must do a simple activity—such as finding a missing object or pressing a button—to stop *El Chupacabra* and save the day. Though this animation does not necessarily tie in with the instructional objectives of *El Laberinto*, it adds another layer of interactive multimedia to the experience. Most importantly, it supports the fantasy in which LCM *protégés* are trying to become assistant wizards.

Fantasy is one of the guiding principles for an intrinsically motivating environment. There are two types of fantasy that were used in designing *El Laberinto*: intrinsic and extrinsic fantasy (Malone and Lepper, 1987). In intrinsic fantasy, the fantasy is dependent on the skill and the skill furthers the fantasy. That is, the fantasy and the skill depend on each other. In extrinsic fantasy, the skill may further the fantasy, but the fantasy does not depend on the skill. Intrinsic fantasy is preferred since it results in deeper learning. So, it was important for the designers to make *El Laberinto*'s wizard theme an intrinsic fantasy. *El Maga* plays a central role in this fantasy. In order for the fantasy and skill to be related, LCM presents a storyline in which students believe that the path to becoming a wizard assistant to *El Maga* is by going through *El Laberinto*. The tasks in each *cuarto* result in *protégés* gaining new skills and knowledge that is required to become a wizard assistant. As students are completing tasks, they may contact *El Maga* through the interface by sending emails to *El Maga* who, in turn, responds to the students. *El Maga* can also send letters periodically to the students to show that s/he is continuing to observe their progress, providing feedback, and giving words of inspiration. The interaction between *El Maga* and the *protégés* during the maze adds to the fantasy that the students are on their way to becoming wizard assistants.

Another layer of fantasy is superimposing LCM on a more realistic environment: *El Laberinto* is decorated with scenes familiar to the students. The culturally-relevant maze blends different genres, contents, topics, themes, characters and locales so that *protégés* and *aspirantes* can have ample opportunities to display their expertise through linguistic or written forms with the usage of any of the task cards. The blending of "real life" and "fantasy" is a mechanism in which we can get students to become more motivated in completing the maze. By including elements from their everyday lives (e.g., Spanish, local images of San Antonio), there is an effort to make *El Laberinto* relevant to the *protégés*. If they do not respond to the maze's fantasy elements and *El Maga*, they will at least have the community aspects to which they can relate. The *El Chupcabra* animation that students view throughout the *El Laberinto* also solidifies this fantasy by showing the LCM world, which surprisingly shares a skyline just like San Antonio! This was an important step to get *protégés* interested in *El Laberinto*, by providing a familiar yet different environment.

SYNCHRONIZING MULTIPLE WORLDS: FINDINGS AND CHALLENGES

Envisioning New Worlds: A Multidisciplinary Approach in Fusing Culture and Technology

The development of *El Laberinto* was an interdisciplinary, collaborative effort between several on-campus departments in educationa and computer science. Faculty and graduate students from these departments participated in the design and development. Those who were professors in the bilingual teacher education program served as the subject-matter experts, along with the current doctoral students who were full-time bilingual teachers in the local community. A professor and master's student from the instructional technology program served as instructional designers, and a computer science professor and a master's student served as developers. The design team was formed because of a shared interest in education and technology and knowing that students in our city would be using the product we produced was a motivating factor.

The initial conceptualization started in spring 2010, and graduate students were brought onto the project during the summer. Several meetings between all stakeholders were held to discuss the requirements and specifications in terms of content and technology. In a meeting, the SMEs expressed their desire for generic themes that elementary *protégés* would find interesting and their custom-designed task cards would bring the bilingual, bicultural element into play. They also requested that the instructional designers refrain from using stereotypical images that represent the Latino culture. From this meeting, a sufficient amount of information was gained to build a mockup of the application and to begin designing the user interface.

During the process, the development design team had to learn new tools and techniques to provide a useable interface given the technology constraints. Another important aspect of culturally responsive technologies is that they must be open-source (Frederick, et al., 2009). The open-source platform allows for people to access, use, and change software freely (Pfaffman, 2008). Since open-source is free, it does not have the same budgetary and license limitations that most popular commercial software imposes. Open-source software solutions have a broader reach to those who may not have access to similar commercial software. Initially, *El Laberinto* was designed and developed specifically for Google Web Toolkit, an open-source development toolkit for building browser-based applications. Google Web Toolkit was to be used to build *El Laberinto* as an online interactive application that could also be used by others to customize their own *El Laberinto* to meet their local needs by modifying, removing, or adding new features and functionalities. The maze application was built as conceptualized, but during the testing phase of *El Laberinto*, there were problems with transferring the toolkit application to the university's production server and caused a delay in the implementation of the online interactive application. We immediately had to find another solution that would provide us with an interface that could support the SME's specifications. Moodle 1.9 is an open-source virtual learning management system that served as our backup solution.

Since Moodle uses an HTML (Hyper Text Markup Language designed to be read by Internet browsers) editor to build pages, it facilitated the building of the maze and made it accessible on the public school campus. In addition, an instance of Moodle was already in use by the university, making Moodle ideal for hosting LCM and its activities. *El Laberinto* was successfully implemented in the afterschool program as a Moodle course and is only available to our LCM participants with user accounts.

Our team was comprised of members with multiple areas of expertise: subject matter experts, instructional technologists, and technology developers. The subject matter experts created all the content and worked with the instructional technologists in designing the learning environment for *El Laberinto,* as guided by the theories and principles discussed in this chapter. Due to their expertise, the instructional technologists also worked as graphic designers, software developers, and testers. The instructional technologists "translated" the instructional design of *El Laberinto* into a set of requirements, which were then handed to the technology developers who developed the software. This communication process helped our team members to work together as an effective ensemble.

Though they all brought with them their own set of expertise, there was still a substantial learning curve for some of the team members. The graphic designer who created the interface for the maze had to learn new tools and techniques in multimedia applications to create the specific media objects while making the interface culturally relevant. All of these objects had to interface with the backend technology, which required intensive training on programming and using Google Web Toolkit. The content writers—the SMEs—had to be trained to format the task cards to meet the programming requirements that would be needed for the future entering of task cards into the database.

Initially, the development team had planned to create an interactive application that would allow the bilingual teacher candidates or *aspirantes* to choose from a template and build their own themed mazes and develop elaborate rules for when one room on the board could be visited from another. Not only did this plan create complications for the interface's design, the development team found it was not necessary. It was later decided that for the purpose of what was required for the following academic year, only a single maze type would be used, which simplified the rest of the maze development task.

When the instructional designers and application developers presented the SMEs with examples of the five themes *La Playa* (The Beach), *La Escuela* (The School), *El Bosque* (The Wilderness), and an animal zoo-like theme, to offer a choice, and the work in progress; feedback was expected to be minor, cosmetic issues, such as font or color choice. In reality, the five prototype themes that were under development did not receive the expected response and the meeting turned out to be a vital turning point. There was a clear miscommunication in regard to the digital maze; two months of design and development produced products that were visually irrelevant to the project. The five themes did not meet the needs of the SMEs because the themes were too general and were not culturally relevant. It was during this meeting that the instructional designers were provided with the original paper-based maze and expressed their desire to have it represented in digital format. Fortunately, all was not lost. The underlying structure and programming that was used to build the prototypes were similar in layout and still useful. With a visual representation of the maze in hand, the instructional designers were able to proceed with digitizing the maze. The SMEs provided the culturally relevant photo files and graphics as well as suggestions such as incorporating the use of *papel picado,* which simplified the design process for the user interface.

Another challenge during the development phase was the location where *El Laberinto* application was installed. Initially, it was running off of a server housed in the Department of Computer Science, where the developers had access privileges. The plan was to install the application on a server where it could be monitored and maintained by UTSA's College of Education and Human Development (COEHD). Despite mirroring the same settings as the COEHD server onto the computer science server, there were substantial problems with transferring the application to the production server. Thus, at the time of writing this chapter, the full functions of the maze were not available but are being worked on. As previously stated, Moodle was used as a temporary solution to host *El Laberinto*. The animation of *El Chupacabra* was added about a year after the start of this project as another way to motivate students.

Digitizing the Maze's Task Cards

While technology development was underway, the content team was creating the task cards for the maze. Many of the ones developed in San Diego (Vásquez, 2003) were updated to reflect more current content and useable websites. About a third of the new task cards also integrated applications (or apps) for *protégés* that were available on the iPad, iPhone, and iPod Touch, moving away from solely computer-based activities. In addition, the development of the task cards focused on privileging Spanish and incorporating meaningful content. This became a huge challenge because of the difficulty in finding websites in Spanish; however, with continuous and careful deliberations, the SMEs were able to select websites that were educational and fulfilling.

Another challenge was to create exciting and playful task cards that also met educational objectives. According to Gee (2007) "children cannot learn in a deep way if they have no opportunities to practice what they are learning. They cannot learn deeply only by being told about things outside the context of embodied actions" (p. 65). In order for *protégés* to become experts and master the objectives of each task, they must be motivated to engage in plenty of practice and allowed to make mistakes so that they can become critical players and take ownership of their own learning. And because the hope is for future bilingual teacher candidates, as *aspirantes*, to create more task cards each semester they work with their students, the team developed an information card that goes with each task card. This info card includes the following information to help ease the storage and classification of each task card: Title of task card; Website needed, if any; Intended for grade level; Language of digital game to be used; School subject task card covers; and Level of cultural relevance.

Technology Required: Additional Materials

In addition, in LCM the computer is used as a tool to augment thought and to "create opportunities for students to digitally encounter, discover, and articulate their thoughts through digital composing and problem solving" (Labbo, Reinking, and McKenna, 1998, p. 278). Therefore, the myriad of task cards developed include content that is: culturally and linguistically relevant; academically enriching; cognitively challenging, yet with an adequate level of easiness to entice *protégés* to participate; enhanced by interactive simulations; appealing with musical/audio selections; eye-catching with pop-ups when available; accessible on the Internet; "kid friendly" and will keep both *protégés* and *aspirantes* digitally active and engaged. Again, this follows the guiding principles of making a learning environment intrinsically motivating through sparking sensory curiosity and fantasy (Malone and Lepper, 1987). Many of the task cards call for different activities that require frequent written exchanges with *El Maga* through letters and visual representations, which are avenues towards increasing students' literacy development.

Initial Feedback on El Laberinto Mágico

Initial observations on the use of the maze and the task cards proved that both the *protégés* and their families involved in the afterschool program connected with the culturally relevant maze. In fact, the images of the grocery stores, their elementary school, and the *piñata* called the most attention. Parents saw the maze as colorful and kid-oriented. Others suggested additional icons/material, such as a community member who suggested that an image of a local park's lake (and its ducks) be added because many of the families and students were familiar with this place. As the maze reaches full online function, we will gather more data on its use and feedback from all users. However, as the co-creators of *El Laberinto,* we take tremendous pride knowing that our collaborative work proved to be a wonderful initial success. Many members of the team are Latinas and feel a sense of empowerment to have had so much say in the maze's creation—especially to be able to fully incorporate images and concepts central to our own cultural background and life experiences. Indeed, this is what is meant by harmonic balance—synchronization!

RETHINKING RESONANCE: NEW CONCEPTUAL UNDERSTANDINGS

The adaptation process is ongoing and includes making curricular materials relevant to the lives of students—all within a society undergoing rapid transformation to adapt to new and emergent technologies. It is no exaggeration to say that we are all becoming designers now. In this particular project, our team has converted a two-dimensional, real-life paper gameboard maze into a digital, three-dimensional online *laberinto*—a challenge our team learned to face with a great deal of patience. For example, in the beginning of this process, the SMEs were not clear in conveying their goals of cultural relevance and local knowledge to the IT experts; in addition, the delays in having a server that supports the full functions and design of *El Laberinto* had been a major setback in its implementation. However, just as we weaved together our theoretical training from disparate fields to create the final product, we continue to cross-collaborate to troubleshoot and to one day achieve 100 percent function of the maze.

By reinventing and digitizing the original LCM maze to one that is interactive and online—as well as incorporating other media tools like iPads, iPhones, iPod touches, and accompanying apps—our goal to create a twenty-first-century *laberinto* were realized . . . for now. As technology continues to advance at its own rapid pace, *El Laberinto* will need the same flexibility if we truly want to continue to prepare *protégés* who may or may not have the same access to digital literacy as this country's millennial generation. (We have already considered a *laberinto* in Second Life, a virtual environment, or one that is more STEM-based, but our partnering school district does not have compatible hardware nor does it have the infrastructure to support this level of technology. Our hope is for other teacher education programs to seek collaborations with designers and developers on their campuses to work together in harmony to create and produce technological tools that not only reflect the latest in technology, but also the knowledge and cultures of the *protégés* and families being served, generating transworld pedagogy. We also cannot emphasize enough that the key to these projects is not replication nor duplication of one site's product to another, but *adaptation* to the next level of relevance!

NOTES

1. The name *El Maga* circumvents the issue of gender and redefines power in the world of the maze—as the "authority" of the system—because the name *"El Maga"* itself is composed of forms indicating both male *(el)* and female *(maga)*. (See Vásquez, 2003, for more details on the genesis of *El Maga*.)

2. There is a strong cultural exchange between Mexico and the United States, and it is particularly felt in San Antonio—not only because of its proximity to the border but also because this city and region were a part of Mexico long before 1848.

3. *El Chupacabra* literally means "the goat sucker," and is the name of a legendary creature in South Texas and Mexico, known for killing or attacking small animals such as goats. It is famed to be a type of creature that causes inexplicable chaos and damage, leaving evidence behind such as scratched or slashed animals. It is not unlike the legendary Big Foot or Loch Ness Monster.

REFERENCES

Bandura, A. (1993). "Perceived Self-Efficacy in Cognitive Development and Functioning." *Educational Psychologist*, 28(2), 117–148.

Black, R. W. (2007). "Digital Design: English Language Learners and Reader Reviewers in Online Fiction." In M. Knobel and C. Lankshear (eds.), *A New Literacy Sampler*, 115–136. New York: Peter Lang.

Bodrova, E. and Leong, D. J. (1996). *The Vygotskian Approach to Early Childhood*. Columbus, OH: Merill, Prentice Hall.

Christie, J. F., and Johnsen, E. P. (1983). "The Role of Play in Social-Intellectual Development." *Review of Educational Research*, 53(1), 93–115.

Frederick, R., Donnor, J. K., and Hatley, L. (2009). "Culturally Responsive Applications of Computer Technologies in Education." *Educational Technology and Society,* November-December.

Gee, J. P. (2007). *What Video Games Have to Teach Us About Learning and Literacy.* 2nd ed. New York: Palgrave Macmillan.

González, N., Moll, L. C., and Amanti, C. (2005). (eds.), *Funds of Knowledge: Theorizing Practices in Households, Communities and Classrooms.* Mahwah, NJ: Lawrence Erlbaum.

Gutiérrez, K. D., Baquedano-López, P., and Tejeda, C. (1999). " Rethinking Diversity: Hybridity and Hybrid Language Practices in the Third Space." *Mind, Culture, and Activity,* 6(4), 286–303.

Gutiérrez, K. D., Baquedano-López, P., Alvarez, H., and Chiu, M. M. (1999). "Building a Culture of Collaboration through Hybrid Language Practices." *Theory Into Practice,* 38(2), 87–93.

Gutierrez, K. D., and Rogoff, B. (2003). " Cultural Ways of Learning: Individual Traits or Repertoires of Practice." *Educational Researcher,* 32, 19–25.

Harackiewicz, J. M., and Elliot, A. J. (1993). "Achievement Goals and Intrinsic Motivation." *Journal of Personality and Social Psychology,* 65, 904–915.

Labbo, L., Reinking, D., and McKenna, M. (1998). "Technology and Literacy Education in the Next Century: Exploring the Connection between Work and Schooling." *Peabody Journal of Education,* 73(3–4), 273–289.

Malone, T. W. (1980). "What Makes Things Fun to Learn? Heuristics for Designing Instructional Computer Games." Paper presented at the Proceedings of the Third ACM SIGSMALL Symposium and the First SIGPC Symposium on Small Systems.

——— (1981). "Toward a Theory of Intrinsically Motivating Instruction." *Cognitive Science,* 4, 333–369.

Malone, T. W., and Lepper, M. R. (1987). "Making Learning Fun: A Taxonomy of Intrinsic Motivations for Learning." In R. E. Snow and M. J. Farr (eds.), *Aptitude, Learning, and Instruction,* (Vol. 3, pp. 223–253). Hillsdale, NJ: Lawrence Erlbaum.

Moll, L., Amanti, C., Neff, D., González, N. (1992). "Funds of Knowledge for Teaching: Using a Qualitative Approach to Connect Homes and Classrooms." *Theory Into Practice,* 31(2), 132–141.

Pfaffman, J. (2008). "Transforming High School Classrooms with Free/Open Source Software: It's Time for an Open Source Software Revolution." *The High School Journal,* 91(3), 25–31.

Repko, A. F., Newell, W. H., Szostak, R., (2012) *Case Studies in Interdisciplinary Research.* Thousand Oaks, CA: SAGE.

Rich, A.C. (1986). *Blood, Bread, and Poetry: Selected Prose, 1979-1985.* New York: W. W. Norton.

Riojas-Cortez, M. (2001). "Preschoolers' Funds of Knowledge Displayed through Sociodramatic Play Episodes in a Bilingual Classroom." *Early Childhood Education Journal,* 29(1), 35–40.

Ryan, R. M., and Deci, E. L. (2000). "Intrinsic and Extrinsic Motivations: Classic Definitions and New Directions." *Contemporary Educational Psychology,* 25(1), 54–67.

Schieffelin, B.B., and Ochs, E. (1986). "Language Socialization." *Annual Review of Anthropology,* 15, 163–191.

Vásquez, O. A. (2003). *La Clase Mágica: Imagining Optimal Possibilities in a Bilingual Community of Learners.* Mahwah, NJ: Lawrence Erlbaum.

Vásquez, O. A., and Duran, R. (2000). "La Clase Mágica and Club Proteo: Multiple Literacies in New Community Institutions." In M.A. Gallego and S. Hollingsworth (eds.), *What Counts as Literacy: Challenging the School Standard.* New York: Teachers College Press.

Vélez-Ibáñez, C., and Greenberg, J. (1992). "Formation and Transformation of Funds of Knowledge among U.S. Mexican Households." *Anthropology and Education Quarterly,* 23(4), 313–335.

Verenikina, I., Harris, P., and Lysaght, P. (2003). "Child's Play: Computer Games, Theories of Play, and Children's Development." Australian Computer Society: IFIP Working Group 3.5 Paper Series.

Vygotsky, L. (1977). "Play and Its Role in the Mental Development of the Child." In J.S. Bruner, A. Jolly, and K. Sylva (eds.), *Play: Its Role in Development and Evolution.* New York: Basic Books.

Wenger, E. (1999). *Communities of Practice: Learning, Meaning, and Identity.* Cambridge, UK: Cambridge University Press.

III

Enacting Transworld Pedagogy

"Live here on earth, blossom! As you move and shake, flowers fall. My flowers are eternal, my songs are forever: I raise them: I, a singer. I scatter them, I spill them, the flowers become gold: they are carried inside the golden place. Ohuaya ohuyaya."

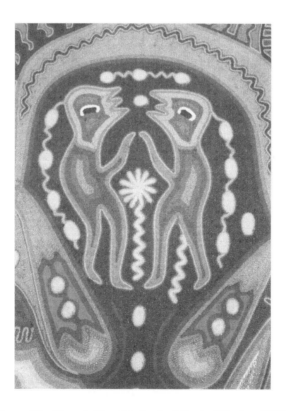

The Flower Song of the Hungry Coyote, Ancient Poet of Mexico (1402–1472). (2) The Flower Tree. *Ancient American Poets.* **Translated and compiled by John Curl from** *Cantares Mexicanos* **#20 (16v–17r) (2005). University of Arizona: Bilingual Review Press. (Original publication date 1560–1592)**

SEVEN

Preparing *Aspirantes*: Synchronizing Culture and Digital Media

Iliana Alanís

WORKING TOWARD HARMONY

Technology has changed the way schools across the country operate in their daily functioning. Skype and emails often take the place of school and classroom visits; PowerPoint presentations have become pedagogical tools, while SMART boards and YouTube videos now replace hands-on activities. These technological changes have become critical for the academic and professional success of students. It is also critical for bilingual education teacher candidates (*aspirantes*) who will enter a work force that assumes they already have the strong technology skills to use digital media as a pedagogical tool for learning. As Elizabeth, an *aspirante* from *La Clase Mágica* conveys: *Me encanto el uso de la tecnología y el poder convivir de esta manera con nuestros estudiantes!* [I loved the use of technology and the ability to engage in this way with our students!]

Additionally, we face demographic shifts that predict the Latino student population will surpass all other groups in schools by 2040 (Murdock, 2003). *Aspirantes* must be digitally literate if they are to meet the needs of their young bilingual learners, particularly those without access to technology. The presence of digital literate teachers in twenty-first century classrooms, however, is dependent on their technology skill development in teacher preparation programs.

This chapter draws from the larger corpus of data related to the impact of *La Clase Mágica,* funded by the Academy for Teacher Excellence at the University of Texas at San Antonio (LCM@UTSA) (Ek, Machado-

Casas, Sánchez, and Alanís, 2010). *La Clase Mágica* is an after school tech-nology-based project designed to promote the academic achievement of bilingual Latino/a elementary-aged students (see Vásquez, 2003 for a de-tailed description of *La Clase Mágica*). Children's bilingual and biliterate skills are developed through the use of technology in meaningful learn-ing activities (see chapters 8 and 9) led by *aspirantes*. The goals of this research will lend additional insight into the direction that teacher prep-aration programs must take to better serve *aspirantes* and an increasingly culturally and linguistically diverse school-age population. In the sec-tions that follow, I provide a brief review of the literature on the integra-tion of technology in teacher preparation programs and the need for bilingual education teachers to integrate technology in instructional classrooms with young Latino learners.

CONCEPTUAL RESONANCE: WHAT DO WE KNOW?

Technology and Teacher Preparation

There is little doubt that the integration of technology with pedagogy has had a significant influence on how we view and interact with stu-dents in K-12 settings and in teacher preparation programs. Use of com-puters in the classroom has changed the teacher's role from knowledge provider to facilitator, as students explore and guide their own learning experiences (Lee, 2006). However, Russell, Bebell, O'Dwyer, and O'Connor (2003) noted that, although new teachers exhibited higher tech-nology skills than veteran teachers, they did not display higher levels of technology use in the classroom, especially in the category of student use. Their research indicates two reasons for this phenomenon: (1) new teach-ers focus on learning about how to use technology rather than on how to integrate technology in the content areas and (2) the extremely challeng-ing aspect of their first few years of teaching (p. 308). Thus, new teachers typically spend most of their energy in developing lessons and in class-room management, leaving little time for technology integration.

Schrum (1999) argued that three aspects of experience are crucial for teacher candidates to integrate technology in their teaching. Teacher can-didates must:

1. be exposed to various types of technological tools in skill-based courses
2. learn how these technology tools can be integrated in subject areas
3. be placed in a technology-rich field environment where they can receive on-going guidance as they implement technology-sup-ported lessons (p. 85).

Hence, teacher candidates' development of technology skills needs to be complemented by pedagogical knowledge and extensive practice of how to integrate technology skills to augment student learning (Chen, 2010; Vásquez, 2008ab); transworld pedagogy creates this possibility (see chapter 2). Additionally, necessary support from administration and cooperating teachers have been shown as key factors influencing teacher candidates' intention and use of technology resources (Bullock, 2004; Dexter and Riedel, 2003). For teacher candidates, one-on-one technology support was considered a necessary part of many projects aimed at improving their capacity to use technology in their teaching (Mims, Polly, Shepherd, and Inan, 2006).

Chen (2010) revealed that self-efficacy had a stronger influence on technology integration than the perceived value technology incorporation. This confirms a previous research finding that, although most teachers see the value and benefits of technology in education, many do not use technology in their teaching (Russell, Bebell, O'Dwyer, and O'Connor 2003). Essentially, teacher candidates' perceptions of the benefits of instructional technology and their perceived efficacy of teaching with technology act as mediators that shape how teacher candidates' training is enacted in their decisions on technology use (Chen, 2010).

Dexter and Riedel (2003) argued that teacher education programs should set high expectations for the use of technology during student teaching. Additionally, Russell, Bebell, O'Dwyer, and O'Connor (2003) suggested that preparing teachers, both preservice and inservice, to use technology should focus on specific instructional uses of technology rather than on familiarizing them with technology in general. They add that teaching to use technology should focus on designing and implementing technology-supported projects where students use technology in their own learning. Benmayor (2008) identified digital storytelling, for example, as a social pedagogy, approaching learning as a collaborative process. The process of story development is one of refinement through the telling and re-telling of ideas; digital storytelling is self-reflexive and becomes a recursive process (Benmayor, 2008). Introducing multiple media into this process allows learners to express their understanding visually as well as verbally. Technology-mediated learning becomes transformative praxis "to achieve new ways of enhancing the intellectual capacity of learners" (Vásquez, 2008b, p. 183); through transworld pedagogy, bilingual learners' cultural and linguistic capacities are also optimized (see chapter 2)

Technology and Latino Learners

Technology has become an instructional tool often used to create a certain "form" of culture—the culture of the future (Ek, Machado-Casas, Alanís, and Sánchez, 2010; Vásquez, 2008b). Technology is cultural in that people who are digitally literate have particular values, beliefs, norms, and identities (Knobel and Lankshear, 2007). Technology itself is culture specific—based on the English language and Western norms. It is critical; therefore, to pay close attention to the role technology has as a cultural practice in our society and in our schools.

Latinos comprise 14 percent of the U.S. adult population and over half of this rapidly increasing group (65 percent) goes online. Non-English-speaking Latinos, however, remain a group with alarmingly low rates of Internet access and use (Fox and Livingston, 2007). Fairlie (2007), reports that only 13.1 percent of "Spanish only" Mexican or Mexican American families in the United States had home Internet access, as compared with a home Internet access rate of 40.1 percent among English-speaking Mexican or Mexican American families. Much of this gap held true even when controlling for education, family income, immigrant status, and other factors (Fairlie, 2007).

As a result, public classrooms may be the only source of advanced technology for many low-income Spanish-speaking Latinos/as. Moreover, in schools where students of color are the majority, only 64 percent of classrooms were connected to the Internet, and computers were used mostly for rote skills (Gorski, 2003). Thus, technology use in schools often heightens educational inequity (Warschauer and Matuchniak, 2010). A comparative study of school technology use in high- and low-socioeconomic status (SES) communities revealed the low-SES neighborhood schools tended to have less stable teaching staff, administrative staff, and technology support staff, which made planning for technology use more problematic. The high-SES schools invested more in professional development and hiring full-time technical support staff that promoted digital networks (Warschauer, Knobel, and Stone, 2004). Many teachers found it a complex undertaking to actually integrate computers in their teaching. Several factors contributed to this complexity, the pressure of high-stakes testing, differential home computer access, and the challenge of teaching English language learners were all thrown into sharp relief in the low-SES schools (Warschauer et al., 2004). Additionally, working with Latino/a immigrant families in northern California, Sánchez and Salazar (2012) found even when school-aged children acquire computational skills at school, they may not know how to set up a computer at home. In addition, their public school classrooms did not offer this explicit skill in their weekly computer lab sessions exacerbating the differential technology access.

Addressing the Disparity

The LCM@UTSA is an after-school technology project that brings together young bilingual learners and *aspirantes*. LCM@UTSA is designed to promote the academic achievement of bilingual Latino/a children, ages four to ten, and the areas of bilingualism, biliteracy, and technology. Using meaningful learning activities through the medium of technology, *aspirantes* engage with young Latino/a learners and their families. LCM@UTSA has created opportunities for children to develop their technological skills along with their family (Ek et al., 2010; see chapter 12). While the children collaborate with *aspirantes*, family members work with a UTSA faculty member who teaches them how to use the iPhone, netbooks, and iPods used in the program (see chapter 12). Yet, for those who do not have access to technology, it has become a mark of segregation and marginalization (Sánchez and Salazar, 2012). As a consequence, technology creates and perpetuates social inequalities. It is therefore crucial for teachers to feel comfortable with the use of technology as they work with young Latino learners.

REPOSITIONING METHODOLOGY: BEYOND RELEVANCE TO THE SACRED SCIENCES

The methodological approach used in this study was that of a qualitative survey (Knobel and Lankshear, 1999). This approach involves comprehensively examining a context and includes field-based observations, interviews, questionnaires, and artifact collection. Qualitative survey designs maximize data collection within a minimum amount of time and thus allow qualitative data to be efficiently gathered and analyzed (Marsland, Wilson, Abeyasekera, and Kleth, 1999). The approach enabled a team of four researchers to gather data from the after-school technology project over a 1.5 year period.

Participants

Because the study sought to focus on the relationship between technology and academic preparation, *aspirantes* from the UTSA's Department of Bicultural Bilingual Studies were chosen as target participants. A total of twenty bilingual teacher candidates, as *apirantes*, participated in the study. The majority were first-generation college students in their early twenties and in the third year of their teacher preparation program. All were of Mexican origin with varying levels of Spanish/English bilingualism and technology experience.

The twenty *aspirantes* were asked to take two undergraduate courses simultaneously to create an LCM cohort. One course emphasized Latino/cultural experiences with children's literature and focused on the use of literature as a pedagogical tool. The other, focused on the relationship between children's play and cognitive, social, and affective development. Both of these courses were taught primarily in Spanish by two of the faculty in LCM@UTSA study. *Aspirantes* took university classes one day of the week and spent an additional three hours a week at the elementary school's computer room—the LCM classroom. The UTSA Academy for Teacher Excellence provided *aspirantes* with netbooks, iPhones, and iPods to use with elementary school students (see chapters 6–9).

Aspirantes and their professors attended the LCM program every Tuesday afternoon for three hours for a 10 to 14-week period over three semesters. Each *aspirante* was assigned to a young student in grades K-5 in an effort to develop rapport and *confianza*. This pairing was organized to create an opportunity for children to negotiate meaning with a more experienced peer through digital media such as, computer games, digital stories, and other educational software (Vygotsky, 1978; also see chapters 8 and 9).

DATA COLLECTION

Data collection occurred over the three semester period at the school site. The following sources of data were collected:

Field notes

Aspirantes documented their experiences in the afterschool LCM technology program through weekly field notes, using an ethnography template. Through this activity, they were asked to become researchers and observers of the development of biliteracy and digital literacy development in multi-situational spaces. Their detailed accounts of interactions with the *protégés* revealed teacher candidates' ideas related to the project and their reactions to weekly assignments.

In-class Discussion

Following participation in the LCM after school technology and literacy program, the teacher candidates engaged in weekly in-class discussions. These discussions, led by UTSA faculty, focused on *aspirantes'* experiences, struggles, and lessons learned at LCM. They lasted from thirty to forty-five minutes and were audio or video recorded in order to document the program's development. The recordings were then professionally transcribed for data analysis.

Artifacts

Drawing on Darder's (1991, 1995) notion of bicultural voice, digitally-based assignments were used to interpret the observations, reflections, and experiences of the aspirantes in the program. Auto-narratives were based on the premise that, as human beings, we come to understand and give meaning to our lives through story (Andrews, Squire, and Tambokou, 2008). Grounded in interpretive hermeneutics and phenomenology, it is a form of qualitative research that involves the gathering of narratives—focusing on the meanings that people ascribe to their experiences, seeking to provide "insight that (befits) the complexity of human lives" (Josselson, 2006, p. 4). *Aspirantes* developed auto-narratives around their experiences related to their journey as a bilingual education teacher candidate.

Data Analysis

All of the data, including the auto-narratives field notes, and in-class discussion transcriptions, were coded and analyzed to identify salient themes, patterns, and relationships (Emerson, Fretz, and Shaw, 1995). These codes helped identify emerging themes and patterns. To ensure interrater reliability, the researchers independently analyzed the same set of transcripts, field notes, and artifacts, meeting approximately every other week for three months over the 1.5 year term to compare and make decisions in identifying and coding the data for themes. Three major themes emerged from the data: (1) the role that digital media plays as a learning tool for *aspirantes*; (2) *aspirantes'* expectations and perceptions about young Latino learners; and (3) the need for a new bilingual/multilingual technology toolkit for bilingual *aspirantes*.

SYNCHRONIZING MULTIPLE WORLDS: FINDINGS AND CHALLENGES

Data reveals that *aspirantes* and their *protégés* were creative and skillful in their use of the virtual/electronic resources and tools available to them (i.e., iPhone, netbook, digital camera). Importantly, the collaborative use of media with the children helped candidates realize that literacy development relies on social interaction and the opportunity to play with a more knowledgeable other (Riojas-Cortez and Alanís, 2011). *Aspirantes* also discovered the immediacy of learning when using the computer in a dialogic learning environment as they developed strong relationships with their a*miguitas/os (protégés)*. This experience creates a harmonic balance that promotes learners to thrive.

Promoting Aspirantes' *Capacity with Digital Media*

The LCM@UTSA project provided multisituational spaces where aspirantes and their amiguitos/as used technology as a medium for communication and learning. This provided practical applications for *aspirantes* to see meaningful and purposeful uses of technology as a pedagogical tool—transworld pedagogy they will use with ease in their future classroom. Three activities were significant for this understanding of how social interaction plays a significant role in facilitating the acquisition of language and content in context. *Aspirantes* used digital media with children as they reflected on their own biliteracy journeys to create collaborative digital auto-narratives entitled *Cómo aprendí a leer y escribir en mi primer y segundo idioma* (How I learned to read and write in my first and second language). Elementary school protégés enrolled in the LCM afterschool technology program became co-authors and co-editors on the assignment, which included a three to five page paper and a virtual narrative. Maribel, an *aspirante,* best captures the connection she felt with her *protégé* Lucia.

> *La autonarrativa me ha dado la oportunidad de usar la tecnología para conocer a Lucia más. Ella trajo fotos de su casa y su familia y yo de la mía. Esto nos ha ayudado a hablar acerca de donde vinimos y de que va primero y porque en la narrativa. Hemos hablado mucho de cómo va a ser la autonarrativa y ahora siento que ella me conoce más y yo a ella. Este proyecto me encanto.* [The self-narrative has given me the opportunity to use technology to know Lucia more. She brought pictures of her house and family and I of mine. This has helped us to talk about where we came from and that comes first and because in the narrative. We have talked a lot about how the self-narrative will be and now I feel that she knows me more and I know her more as well. I loved this project.]

These kinds of personal experiences have provided the *aspirantes* with a way to connect with their *amiguita/os* in a more authentic way. In this case, the creative, purposeful, and personal use of technology has given *aspirantes* and their *protégés* deeper and more meaningful ways of getting to know each other and build trust; an important context for authentic teaching and learning. This is what Agustina, another *aspirante,* had to say about the experience of creating a digital auto-narrative.

> What I liked best was creating my auto-narrative with Nico in Spanish. I loved the way we added phrases that you can only understand in Spanish. I loved it and Nico did too. For me it was so good to practice my Spanish and to have to learn technology words in Spanish. It was so much fun and also good because he does not speak English good. So he was able to feel really good because we were doing it in Spanish. I also learned about how we all learn to write and some differences that mostly depend on how they learned it at home.

As stated above, the creation of the digital narratives provided Agustina and her *amiguito* with a unique opportunity to engage in technology-based activities in the child's native language, giving the child the opportunity to be the expert, and allowing him to feel comfortable and connected to the *aspirante*. It also gives the *protégé* and the *aspirante* a culturally and linguistically diverse activity that incorporates the child's culture, background, language, past experiences, and new technological knowledge—a means to bridge the child's funds of knowledge in the acquisition of technological knowledge and skills. Furthermore, it provides a way to learn how bilingual children maintain their home language as they develop biliteracy. Paola, another *aspirante*, had this to say about her experience with this activity:

> As a future teacher doing the auto-narratives gives me an idea of all the cool things I can do when I become a teacher. It really made me see that I can use activities like this one [the creation of the auto-narrative] to connect and get to know my students but also to make it interesting and not scary. I think that before *tenía miedo* (I was afraid) but now I know that I will do this again when I have my own class.

Auto-narratives provide both the *aspirante* and the children with a way to connect in appropriate, authentic, culturally and linguistically diverse ways, while at the same time using new technological tools as mediators of learning.

iPhone Applications

Learning and media theorists, such as Gee (2003, 2004) and Jenkins (2009), make a compelling case that youth's engagement with new media provides vital learning experiences. Our study reveals how the integration of the iPhone and its various applications provided *aspirantes* the opportunity to use it as a pedagogical tool to negotiate meaning with their young bilingual learners through digital mediated collaboration. As children progressed through the maze (see chapter 6), questions arose as did opportunities to problem-solve or co-construct new knowledge in various content areas including technology. One example is Vivian's response to her *amiguita*, Ana's enjoyment with literature, "Ana seemed to enjoy the story reading and I found an app that might help her a little more next week when I see her again." Vivian realized that iPhone applications could be used to develop children's literacy and enjoyment of text. Without direction, Vivian took it upon herself to find additional activities for her *amiguita*. That initiative is exactly what we want to see in teachers!

Teacher candidates were also asked to create iPhone task cards based on their students' academic needs. Task cards were created to facilitate the use of iPhone applications or Internet games. They provided directions in Spanish for children to follow. Because *aspirantes* were enrolled in a course focusing on play theory and its significance for young children's learning, Jessica found an application that was playful using music as a tool for learning. Jessica explains how her *amiguita* responded to her task card:

> I opened up the task card and she was like "Miss, you made this?!" I chose an iPhone application that incorporated the different grammar components. It introduced each component at the beginning with a

catchy tune and song. Kayla was able to go through the application and enjoyed singing and dancing along with the different tunes.

Creating task cards using iPhone applications provided *aspirantes* with an opportunity to use digital media to advance children's academic knowledge in a fun, relaxing space.

Playing with iPhone applications also provide scaffolding opportunities for the children's learning. Liliana discovers in watching an interaction between two *amiguitos:*

> I noticed that Mario works better when he works with Alex. Because Alex knows more about how to use the iPhone and how to play the applications, Mario likes to play with him and at the same time learns from him. I think that they are good partners when it comes to the Zone of Proximal Development theory developed by Vygotsky. I think it is good that they help each other because it helps them build their self-esteem and often it may make them feel more confident to learn from each other.

Alex's ability to teach Mario how to use the iPhone provided a much needed boost for Alex who often struggled with academic work. At the same time, it revealed to Liliana the power of collaborative learning.

Both *aspirantes* and young bilingual learners were in the process of acquiring digital literacies, content knowledge, and technology-based pedagogical knowledge. "I was able to learn some new skills in regards to technology; believe it or not my students actually showed me some new skills that I was unaware of." This was further revealed in Vivian's comment:

> Overall, this semester I have accomplished new knowledge that will prepare me as a future bilingual education teacher. I have learned that children learn better when working with a partner, as Vygotsky states. . . . because through Letty's and my help we have learned many new things. Throughout the *La Clase Mágica*, Letty's learning and development increased. At the beginning, her typing and communication skills were really low, but as the weeks passed, these increased.

This idea was exhibited in another *aspirante's* statement, "I found that they were teaching me how to use the iPhone." Another stated, "Additionally, my thought about the computer games, play, and science projects are that all of them were very educational. The maze was a really good example and it was culturally relevant to all the students." The collaboration was beneficial for both young bilingual learners and the *aspirantes* who worked with them.

Internet Games

Aspirantes need varied and ample opportunities for hands-on experience with technology, where both teacher candidates and young bilingual learners can create digital spaces of autonomy and creativity in becoming technological risk-takers in their learning process. Playing computer games and exploring the Internet are just some of the ways in which technology can stimulate the imagination as revealed by Nelda's comment, "I love how we stimulate the children's mind with computer games and how we stir their imagination."

The use of Internet games provided *aspirantes* with an opportunity to experience the power of learning through play on children's level of confidence with subject matter. Melinda explains:

> *Hoy vi que Marissa en realidad ahora está intentando sumar y restar, al principio en cual quier juego de matemáticas se negaba a hacerlo. Esta vez ella estaba tratando de contestar todas las respuestas su intento fue muy intenso y verdadero y me dio orgullo.* [Today I saw that Marissa is now actually trying to add and subtract, at first in whatever game of mathematics she could do. this time she is trying to answer all the questions. Her attempt was very intense and real and gave me pride.]

Marissa's change in attitude toward mathematics not only impacted her as a learner, but also the *aspirante*, who feels a sense of pride and accomplishment with her *amiguita*.

Aspirantes also discovered how the computer could be used to further learning through easy and quick configurations of comprehensible and enhanced input.

> I found the activity *"Un juego del espacio nivel 1,"* [A game from level 1] very interesting because the students were learning about the space and at the same time playing educational games. I also liked that when the students were reading about the solar system or the sun, difficult words would appear on light blue and if they did not know the word they could click on the word and the definition would appear on a different website showing you several vocabulary words.

The ability to click on words that may be beyond a child's level of comprehension allows them to learn at a much quicker pace than stopping to look it up in a dictionary or continue reading without a true understanding of the information.

Access to technology, a supportive school culture, and adequate time for teacher candidates to explore educational uses of technology are essential for successful integration into lessons (Chen and Ferneding, 2003; Franklin, 2007). The ability to create auto-narratives provided the *aspirantes* with an educational opportunity to see digital media as a tool for learning in multi-situational occasions carried out in joint communication activities between experts and novices, using technology as a mediating tool.

In the LCM@UTSA after school technology project laboratory, *aspirantes* bring their technological expertise to share with the young learners and at the end find that they also learn from their protégés. Both, the

teacher candidates and the elementary school students, are being social-
ized to digital culture and their role as learners while developing their
language and literacy skills (Ek et al., 2010). This approach provided the
researchers and participants alike with opportunities to test technology's
potential to create innovative learning environments and to study its
effect on language, literacy, and cultural development of young bilingual
learners. Thus, it allowed us to develop educational expertise and resources to fulfill the needs of both learners—the *aspirantes* and their *protégés*. *Aspirantes'* reactions indicate an overall positive experience and an
understanding that we hope will increase their capacity to utilize technology for playful learning in the elementary classrooms they will one day
organize and manage. Although the technology is crucial to attracting
and maintaining the child's active participation, the collaboration between the *aspirantes* and the *protégé* is the major factor behind their engagement and motivation. These relationships help build the self-efficacy
of our aspirantes as they develop their identities as educators.

RETHINKING RESONANCE: NEW CONCEPTUAL UNDERSTANDINGS

Recommendations for Bilingual Education Teacher Preparation

This work illuminates the importance of preparing bilingual education teacher candidates to meet the demands of the twenty-first century
classroom in terms of transworld pedagogy (see chapter 2) with cultural
and linguistic/global relevance. It also reveals a deeper understanding of
aspirantes' needs when teaching young bilingual learners through digital
media with specific innovative instructional uses of technology. We have
found that multi-dimensional technology use will only be effective if
teacher education providers distinguish various types of technology uses
and articulate each use. These experiences, however, require access to the
latest technology such as mobile devices and an understanding of how
these innovative tools can mediate the development of language and
literacy for young bilingual children.

One recommendation for teacher education is to develop a design-
based approach to preparing teachers; an approach where efforts would
focus on implementing technology-supported projects into the curriculum. In this approach, teacher candidates would utilize technology in
their education while they are engaged with young children through
collaborative learning. *Aspirantes* can benefit from seeing how technology
can be specifically integrated seamlessly into the curriculum, rather than
an addition to existing lessons. It would also include the strategic placement of *aspirantes* in the field. Placements would need to be in locales
where technology is seen as a viable pedagogical tool. In addition, there

is a need for teacher preparation programs to have reciprocal exchanges where both parties benefit from the placement of *aspirantes* and the collaboration between local education agencies and institutes of higher education.

After school technology programs such as *La Clase Mágica* at UTSA provide an avenue for teacher preparation programs to attend to achieving the optimal potential of their teacher candidates while preparing them for a world that privileges critical and reflective skills related to sociocultural learning processes and digital literacies. Bilingual bicultural teachers have social and cultural capital that, if nurtured, can create culturally responsive zones of proximal development for their own bicultural students (Monzo and Rueda, 2001) through the medium of transworld pedagogy that incorporates technological tools.

Chapelle (2005) indicates, "Teachers need to know how learning can best be accomplished through technology and apply that knowledge to their teaching" (p. 3). Additional dimensions of research must consider the evolving views of teacher candidates as they gain additional expertise over time. Specifically, research needs to help us understand:

- What are some of the challenges that *aspirantes* in preparation programs face in integrating technology into their coursework?
- How can programs like LCM increase *aspirantes'* self-efficacy in transworld pedagogy?
- How do programs such as LCM impact teachers' integration of technology over time?

REFERENCES

Andrews, M., Squire, C., and Tambokou, M. (eds.) (2008). *Doing Narrative Research.* London: Sage.

Benmayor, R. (2008). "Digital Storytelling as a Signature Pedagogy for the New Humanities." *Arts and Humanities in Higher Education*, 7(2), 188–204.

Bullock, D. (2004). "Moving from Theory to Practice: An Examination of the Factors that Preservice Teachers Encounter as They Attempt to Gain Experience Teaching with Technology During Field Placement Experiences." *Journal of Technology and Teacher Education*, 12(2), 211–237.

Chapelle, C. (2005). "Hints about CALL Use from Research." *PacCALL Journal*, 1(1), 1–8.

Chen, R.-J., and Ferneding, K. (2003). "Technology as a Heuristic: How Pre-Service Teachers Learn to Think about Mathematics Instruction Using Technology." In C. Crawford, N. Davis, J. Price, and R. Webber (eds.), *Proceedings of the 14th Annual Meeting of the Society for Information Technology and Teacher Education (3441–3444).* Norfolk, VA: Association for the Advancement of Computing in Education.

Chen, R. J. (2010). "Investigating Models for Preservice Teachers' Use of Technology to Support Student-Centered Learning." *Computers and Education* 55, 32–42.

Darder, A. (1991). *Culture and Power in the Classroom: A Critical Foundation for Bicultural Education.* New York: Bergin and Garvey.

———— (1995). "Bicultural Identity and the Development of Voice." In J. Frederickson (ed.), *Reclaiming our Voices: Bilingual Education, Critical Pedagogy, and Praxis* (35–52). Covina, CA: California Association for Bilingual Education.

Dexter, S., and Riedel, E. (2003). "Why Improving Preservice Teacher Educational Technology Preparation Must Go Beyond College's Walls." *Journal of Teacher Education,* 54(4), 334–346.

Ek, L.; Machado-Casas, M.; Alanís, I.; and Sánchez, P. (2010). "Crossing Cultural Borders: *La Clase Mágica* as a University-School Partnership." *Journal of School Leadership* 20(6) 820–849.

Emerson, R., Fretz, R., and Shaw, L. (1995). *Writing Ethnographic Fieldnotes.* Chicago: University of Chicago Press.

Fairlie, R. W. (2007). "Explaining Differences in Access to Home Computers and the Internet: A Comparison of Latino Groups to Other Ethnic and Racial Groups." *Electronic Commerce Research* 7(3–4), 265–291.

Fox, S. (2007). "Pew Internet and American Life Project." Gretchen Livingston, Pew Hispanic Center.

Franklin, C. (2007). "Factors that Influence Elementary Teachers' Use of Computers." *Journal of Technology and Teacher Education,* 15(2), 267–293.

Gee, J. P. (2003). *What Video Games Have to Teach Us about Learning and Literacy.* New York: Palgrave Macmillan.

———— (2004). *Situated Language and Learning: A Critique of Traditional Schooling.* New York: Routledge.

Gorski, P. (2003). "Privilege and Repression in the Digital Era: Rethinking the Sociopolitics of the Digital Divide." *Race, Gender, and Class* 10 (4), 145–176.

Jenkins, H. (2009). "Confronting the Challenges of Participatory Culture: Media Education for the 21st Century." Cambridge: MIT Press. Retrieved July 1, 2009, from http://mitpress.mit.edu/books/chapters/Confronting_the_Challenges.pdf.

Josselson, R. (2006). "Narrative Research and the Challenge of Accumulating Knowledge." *Narrative Inquiry,* 16(1), 3–10.

Knobel, M., and Lankshear, C. (1999). *Ways of Knowing: Researching Literacy.* Newton, Australia: Primary English Teachers' Association.

Knobel, M. and Lankshear, C. (2007). *A New Literacies Sampler.* New York: Peter Lang.

Lee, R. (2006). "Effective Learning Outcomes of ESL Elementary and Secondary School Students Utilizing Educational Technology Infused with Constructivist Pedagogy." *International Journal of Instructional Media,* 33, 87–93.

Marsland, N., Wilson, I., Abeyasekera, S., and Kleth, U. (1999). *A Methodological Framework for Combining Quantitative and Qualitative Survey Methods.* Reading, UK: Social and Economic Development Department, Natural Resources Institute and the Statistical Services Centre, University of Reading.

Mims, C., Polly, D., Shepherd, C., and Inan, F. (2006). "Examining PT3 Projects Designed to Improve Preservice Education." *TechTrends,* 50(3), 16–24.

Monzo, L. D., and Rueda, R. S. (2001). "Professional Roles, Caring, and Scaffolds: Latino Teachers' and Paraeducators' Interactions with Latino Students." *American Journal of Education,* 109(4), 438–471.

Murdock, S. (2003). *The New Texas Challenge: Population Change and the Future of Texas.* College Station, TX: Texas A&M University Press.

Riojas-Cortez, M. and Alanís, I. (2011). "El aprendizaje por medio del juego: Teaching in Bilingual Early Childhood Settings." In B. B. Flores, R. Hernandez Sheets, and E. Riojas Clark (eds.), (103–114). *Teacher Preparation for Bilingual Student Populations: Educar para transformar.* New York, NY: Routledge.

Russell, M., Bebell, D., O'Dwyer, L., and O'Connor, K. (2003). "Examing Teacher Technology Use: Implications for Preservice and Inservice Teacher Preparation." *Journal of Teacher Education,* 54(4), 297–310.

Sánchez, P. and Salazar, M. (2012). "Transnational Computer Use in Urban Latino Immigrant Communities: Implications for Schooling." *Urban Education.* 47(1), 90–116.

Schrum, L. (1999). "Technology Professional Development for Teachers." *Educational Technology Research and Development,* 47(4), 83–90.

Vásquez, O. A. (2003). *La Clase Mágica: Imagining Optimal Possibilities in a Bilingual Community of Learners.* Mahwah, NJ: Lawrence Erlbaum.

——— (2008a). "Reflection: Rules of Engagement for Achieving Educational Futures." In L.L. Parker (ed.), *Technology-Mediated Learning Environments for Young English Learners: Connections In and Out of School.* New York: Taylor and Francis Group.

——— (2008b). "Technology Out of School: What Schools Can Learn from Community-Based Technology." In L. Smolin, K. Lawless and N. C. Burbules (eds.), *The 106 Yearbook of the National Society for the Study of Education: Information and Communication Technologies: Considerations of Current Practice for Teachers and Teacher Educators.* Vol. 106, 182–206.

Vygotsky, L. S. (1978). *Mind in Society.* Cambridge, MA: Harvard University Press.

Warschauer, M., Knobel, M., and Stone, L. (2004). "Technology and Equity in Schooling: Deconstructing the Digital Divide." *Educational Policy,* 18(4), 562–588.

Warschauer, M. and Matuchniak, T. (2010). "New Technology and Digital Worlds: Analyzing Evidence of Equity in Access, Use, and Outcomes." *Review of Research in Education,* 34(1), 179–225.

EIGHT

Aspirantes' Consejos on *El Maga* and the Role of Technology

María Guadalupe Arreguín-Anderson and Kimberley D. Kennedy

WORKING TOWARD HARMONY

"Por mi raza hablará el espíritu" (The spirit shall speak for my race), wrote Mexican philosopher and educator José Vasconcelos when proposing the motto for the Universidad Nacional Autónoma de México. Within this phrase, Vasconcelos encapsulated both spirituality and the spoken word as forces that fuel change, not only at a personal level, but in the wider context. We argue that the spoken word becomes socially transformative when it emerges within dialogic spaces in which students dare to dream, imagine, and visualize reality different from what it is. This transworld pedagogy of possibility is congruent with the liberatory principles that act as a guiding force in *La Clase Mágica* (LCM), where just like Vasconcelos suggested, *nuestra raza*, our people, can be empowered to "construct a culture of new trends with the most spiritual and freest of essence" (Universidad Nacional Autónoma de México, 2012).

In this chapter, we seek to illustrate how, when invited to dialogue, LCM *aspirantes*—bilingual teacher education candidates—eagerly embrace an ideological discourse of possibility and transformation. Shifting the research lens to *aspirantes* is important, not only because they bring fresh eyes into the process, but also because they are affectively invested in LCM. Using qualitative methodologies, we explored the experiences of five *aspirantes* who participated in UTSA's inaugural semester of LCM during the fall of 2009. Drawing primarily from a series of reflective *pláticas* (discussions or chats) with the *aspirantes,* our findings centered on themes and corresponding *consejos* (advice) specific to *El Maga* (the wizard) and the role of technology as an educational tool.

Delgado-Gaitan (1994) described *consejo* as a notion that extends the meaning of advice, which in English is defined merely as an opinion. *Consejos,* Delgado-Gaitan states, imply "a cultural domain of communication sparked with emotional empathy and compassion, as well as familial expectation and inspiration" (p. 300). In the Latino culture, *consejos* are permeated by "caring" behaviors and relationships that seek to empower and transform. The use of this word emerged from the *aspirantes* themselves as they sought to contribute to the betterment of a project in which they had participated.

CONCEPTUAL RESONANCE: WHAT DO WE KNOW?

We situate *consejos* as the natural outcome of dialogic conversations in which *aspirantes* link reflection and action. Within a dialogic conversation, Rodriguez, Zozakiewics, and Yerrick (2005) suggest, "the goal is not just to understand what is being said, but the reasons (emotional tone, ideological and conceptual positions) the speaker may have chosen to say what he or she says in that particular context" (p. 355). In LCM, dialogue is crucial for making the transformation process both democratic and contextually situated.

Dialogue is democratic and, therefore, an open-ended process. We use the following definition for dialogue in relation to LCM: "the capacity and inclination of human beings to reflect together on the meaning of their experience and their knowledge" (Shor, 1992, p. 86). To be democratic, a dialogue must become a meeting ground where horizontal relationships are created. That is, LCM participants talk mutually with no preset agenda allowing ideas to be generated over the course of the conversation. In essence, this open-ended process allows participants to problematize their experiences within LCM as they explore and learn.

Dialogue is a contextually situated approach to education. In giving *consejos, aspirantes* shaped their discourse to match the cultural make up of the predominantly Latino community that hosts LCM as an afterschool program. Each one of the *aspirantes' consejos* and words "tastes of the context and contexts in which it has lived its socially charged life" (Bakhtin, 1981, p. 293). Therefore, when *aspirantes* dialogued, they identified *El Maga* and the role of technology as generative themes; that is, themes generated within the context of their experience in LCM that inspired them to foresee possibilities for change.

El Maga (e.g., Wizard, Golem), the first generative theme mentioned by *aspirantes,* exists at each site to coordinate and mediate participants (Gallego, 2001). In Vygotskian terms, *El Maga* (the all-knowing wizard) is a "cultural artifact in action" who corresponds through electronic messaging with elementary students in both English and Spanish to discuss a variety of topics ranging from their academic progress and learning to personal interests and happenings (Vásquez, 2003). In LCM, *El Maga* represents an electronic entity who regularly communicates with children and tracks their progress in the *Laberinto Mágico*. The *Laberinto*, or magical maze, presents a series of self-selected activities formatted as task cards that include beginner, intermediate, and advanced levels of difficulty. *El Maga*, whose identity remains anonymous, must regularly exert a position of power to monitor and provide input as protégés complete their task cards using technology.

Technology, the second generative theme discussed by *aspirantes*, served as in other contexts, as "a distributed system of meaning making" (Sharples, Milrad, Sanchez, and Vavuola, 2009, p. 4) that has gradually evolved. The role and the description of technological tools utilized within this program have changed dramatically since the inception of LCM in 1989. Unlike the earliest LCM sites that were equipped with cutting-edge technologies, which are now considered bulky desktop computers static in nature, today's technology-based literacy tools have been adjusted in response to changing contexts. As a result, LCM has embraced mobile technologies (e.g., iPhones, netbooks, iPads) that are congruent with the nature of today's learner.

REPOSITIONING METHODOLOGY: BEYOND RELEVANCE TO THE SACRED SCIENCES

In her analysis of *La Clase Mágica*'s ability to achieve sustainable change, Nocon (2004) emphasized that participants "have a voice and opportunities to make visible needs, concerns, and potential solutions to the shared problems of productive integration of the reform" (p. 729). In order for LCM to be a sustainable program that effectively blurs the mystical and the scientific together, we need to seek out and examine the experiences of past and present participants. Therefore, this two-phase qualitative study utilized purposeful homogeneous sampling of *aspirantes* who participated in the inaugural semester of LCM at our university. Table 8.1 provides a snapshot of the major methodological components for each phase of the study.

Of the five participants, four were native Spanish speakers of Mexican descent and one native English speaker who stated, "My dad's side is white; my mom's side is Hispanic, Mexican." As university undergraduates enrolled in a Hispanic-Serving Institution (HSI), many of the *aspirantes* juggled the demands of their course loads, their part-time jobs, and, in many cases, their roles as parents.

Table 8.1. Synthesis of Methodology

Data Collection	Participants	Criteria for Purposeful Sampling	Data Sources
Phase 1: Fall 2010	Osiel Matthew Martha Joann Karen	Fall 2009: Participated in LCM Fall 2010: Enrolled in one or both of the researchers' courses (that were not engaged in LCM)	• Focus-group interviews • Email correspondence • On-line chats • Member-checking feedback
Phase 2: Spring 2011	Osiel Matthew Martha	Aforementioned criteria plus: Spring 2011: Enrolled in courses that required LCM fieldwork	• Researcher field notes from monthly LCM observations • Focus-group interview • Member-checking feedback

The five *aspirantes* from Phase I of the study met all three criteria to be included in the purposeful sampling pool. First, the *aspirantes* were accepted formally prior to fall of 2009 into the teaching preparation program seeking Bilingual Education certification. Secondly, *aspirantes* participated in the inaugural semester of LCM as part of required fieldwork for their university coursework in the fall of 2009. As part of the field experience requirements, the inaugural group of LCM *aspirantes* spent an average of two hours per week at Las Palmas Elementary School in fall 2009. Lastly, *aspirantes* were enrolled in one or both of the researchers' university courses in the fall of 2010: Reading Comprehension and Approaches to Teaching Science. During that semester, our *aspirantes* did not participate in LCM as part of their fieldwork. Data sources from Phase I included focus-group interviews, email correspondence, on-line chats, and member-checking feedback.

Three of the Phase I *aspirantes* participated in Phase II during the spring of 2011 as part of their required fieldwork for their courses. Data sources from Phase II included: researcher debriefings from monthly LCM observations, focus-group interviews, and feedback from member-checking regarding Phase I data analysis. For the purpose of this study, we maintained ongoing informal conversations regarding *aspirantes'* previous experience as *participants* in *La Clase Mágica*.

As major stakeholders from the UTSA's inaugural semester of LCM, the *aspirantes* played a key role in a system of collaboration in which the university and the community combined efforts in their quest for change. They have a unique perspective on the design and implementation of LCM as they are the eyes and the ears of the project. They witnessed firsthand and documented the complex process of transformation in the context of an after-school project at Las Palmas, an urban elementary school located in a primarily Mexican American community.

Initially, a handful of themes emerged from initial conversations: suggestions on the use of technology within the project; opinions on the role of *El Maga* as overseer of the protégés' progress; children's attitudes towards writing, the importance of structure and organization; and the importance of infusing interactions with elements of choice. After initial analysis and member checking (i.e., verifying our preliminary analysis with *aspirantes*), we collapsed our themes and conducted follow-up focus group interviews in which we sought answers to the following questions: (a) What would it take to transform *El Maga* and the technological components of LCM into more effective artifacts of *La Clase Mágica*? and (b) What would you suggest in order to improve the experience of all LCM participants? Through the data collection and analysis, an interesting and unexpected purpose transpired in that the *aspirantes'* voices (and subsequent findings/themes) took the shape of *consejos*, or advice, specifically regarding *El Maga* and the role of technology.

Trustworthiness was achieved through triangulation of various data sources, member checking with *aspirantes* during both phases of the study, examining positionality of researchers, and peer-debriefing with the LCM research group. The first author/researcher is a Mexican-born Latina and the second author/researcher is a White native English speaker. Both have been bilingual (Spanish/English) educators since the early 1990s.

SYNCHRONIZING MULTIPLE WORLDS: FINDINGS AND CHALLENGES

El Maga

In essence, our conversations with *aspirantes* served as dialogic spaces in which they sought to synchronize a real world in which they actively participated and an imagined virtual LCM world. As key "participants in the production of tomorrow" (Freire, 2007), *aspirantes* identified *El Maga* as an essential component in LCM and one whose interactions must be permeated by consistency and depth. In doing so, they also identified themselves as potential facilitators of the interaction process by assuming the role of *El Maga*. *Aspirantes* also suggested that protégés' written communication with *El Maga* be adapted to the child's literacy levels while making use of available technologies.

Consistency and Depth

In LCM, *aspirantes* are to assume the role of a guide who travels through the maze with the elementary student often prompting them to initiate or extend communication with *El Maga*. To *aspirantes*, elaboration was important, not only because it conveyed a message of relevancy of *El Maga* as a figure, but because of the sense of motivation that *El Maga* can potentially build as Karen, an *aspirante*, conveyed:

> The UTSA students as well as [Las Palmas] students understood *El Maga*'s concept in relation to the class. It just didn't work because since *El Maga* is a very busy person many times it just wrote a general email to all the students so they caught on to it not being *El Maga*. Other times *El Maga* would completely forget to answer back to some students. The students originally wanted to talk to *El Maga* and ask questions to it but *El Maga* was very vague.

As a result of an irregular flow of vague emails, the *aspirantes* argued for more personalized correspondence with *El Maga*. Osiel, another *aspirante*, commented that this also had an emotional impact on the protégés, "The idea was that *Maga* was supposed to know about everything and that it could ask about anything, but also *El Maga* sometimes didn't answer and then kids were kind of disappointed." From this perspective, it is important to preserve *El Maga* as a magical figure who motivates children to engage in literacy and language practices in a nonhierarchical structure (i.e., non teacher- or administrator led) at Las Palmas. We think motivated children are more likely to willingly engage in dialogical exchanges, ultimately leading to the development of literacy and language skills.

Engaging in "Wizarding" Tasks

"Wizarding," Vazquez (1993, p. 206) asserted, occasionally occurs within LCM projects. In this type of assignment, undergraduates take over live-chats and answering letters. The collaborative wizarding can have an additional benefit of forming an intimate professional community where all members take vested interest in the elementary students' progress much like grade level planning and pre-referral procedures that take place in public schools. Interestingly, this was the *aspirantes'* first *consejo:* allowing *aspirantes* to act as chief "wizard" assistants on a regular basis. *Aspirantes* saw a diminishing and neglecting of the prominence of *El Maga* as a central figure in LCM and proposed that each one of them be assigned to correspond with the child on behalf of *El Maga*. In their focus group interview, they also suggested that teams of three university students be established within the project so that these teams can monitor each other's progress occasionally substituting for *El Maga* when someone could not fulfill the role.

Written Communication to El Maga

During our chat room session, *aspirantes* suggested that communication with *El Maga* mirror the ownership and levels of choice available to students as they initiated their journey through the Maze or *Laberinto Mágico*. This power of decision making reinforces elementary students' emerging identity as independent self-motivated thinkers and learners. Aside from being able to select "which direction to take, what game and level to play, and what culture and language to use" (Vasquez, 2003, p. 108), *aspirantes* envisioned empowerment opportunities for children to select the type of technology to use in their written communication with *El Maga* as they reported their progress, posed questions, and provided answers.

Children displayed varied levels of literacy development that affected the length of the responses produced. Therefore, kindergartners took considerably longer to type and send messages than fifth grade students. Writing to *El Maga* turned out to be a time consuming endeavor and both, *aspirantes* and protégés faced major challenges in completing this cognitively demanding activity. Difficulties emerged when children attempted to rush through this assignment or plainly refused to do it, as stated by another *aspirante*, Matt:

> For me, it was the world's biggest process to be able to sit there . . . and maybe for a student like him, he had a really hard time typing, so he would want to make it as brief as possible. There was never any interest, no matter how enthusiastic I tried to read what the *maga* was saying. I think my student was a special case. He was very in-tuned into what he wanted to be in-tuned to and that is that.

To alleviate the difficulties in writing to *El Maga*, the *aspirantes' consejo* consisted in providing alternatives to typing. *Aspirantes* also suggested a deeper exploration into using cell phones built-in technologies to increase the spectrum of choices available to students in communication with *El Maga*. Freedom of choice, seldom a topic of curricular conversation in public schools, is a type of instructional strategy generally reserved for children in gifted and talented programs. In their regular routines, elementary students generally do not have a voice on topics, methodology, products or the technologies they will utilize in creating those products. However, the *aspirantes* followed LCM's responsive approach to local context, and perceived the potential of technology as a situated system of meaning making.

Traditionally, computer-mediated learning has been favored as a practice that allows varying degrees of freedom of choice (Maker, 1996). In today's learning environments, computers have shrunk in size, but have expanded in the processing capabilities and the types of technologies now contained within pocket-size devices. In this sense, communication with *El Maga* entails a decision-making process that *aspirantes* suggest should begin with a thoughtful selection of the type of technology to use. The iPhones and netbooks provided *aspirantes* with a variety of applications to engage in and complete projects. Therefore, *aspirantes* proposed that iPhone technologies such as video recorder, voice-memo application, podcasting applications, and texting capabilities be used to facilitate communication with *El Maga*. For example, they suggested a video clip/audio file could be recorded, saved in a video sharing website, and accessed remotely by *El Maga*.

The Role of Mobile Technology: A Tool for Inquiry

In LCM, children bridged the divide between academic and social environments and embraced their position as mobile learners. Mobile learning is defined as a "process (both personal and public) of coming to know through exploration and conversation across multiple contexts amongst people and interactive technologies" (Sharples et al., 2009, p. 5). Using these technologies, elementary students reached beyond the confines of their homes assuming their role as social agents, and contributing to transworld "pedagogical validation of household knowledge" (González, Moll, and Amanti, 2005, p. 40). Therefore, *aspirantes* recommended the use of technology as a tool for inquiry and knowledge construction. This *consejo* was based on their observations that, in LCM, *aspirantes* and their *protégé* moved in and out of technologies as they learned and in doing so, they seamlessly entered and left virtual and physical spaces through devices that include netbooks and iPhones. This continuous connectedness, they suggested, should be shaped by a well-defined guiding question and tied to a project as expressed by Osiel:

> I think . . . use the technology that you have. Use the instruments that you have . . . to either tell a story, to take pictures, make something with the instruments that you have with the kid. That is what I think was supposed to happen and it didn't go that way. Maybe have them take the phone and make a story using the phone only. Take your netbook and make a story. Write something. Add pictures.

Aspirantes visualized themselves using technology to conduct self-selected or guided inquiries with LCM children. In their view and subsequent *consejo*, the implementation of a project approach must begin with a needs assessment and a plan that clearly defines a basic set of technologies to be used along with applications or software needed as stated by Osiel: "Students might not understand how to use technology (e.g., computer, iPhone). They might not have experience with it due to their young age," and lack of expertise may place both *aspirantes* and elementary students on similar levels of authority and power. During our focus group session, Osiel questioned the amount of time consumed in trying to figure out technical details embedded within the wide variety of technologies infused within daily experiences in this after-school project: "When you want to use technology . . . have the software . . . during the class it is not the time to be experimenting . . . if you are going to use the iPhone make sure that you don't have to go and get something at that moment."

In sum, *aspirantes* argued for a system of meaning making that did not interfere with protégés' inquiries and explorations. They proposed a systematic use of technology in which the overall goal for student empowerment is to expand the learning context to include social and cultural spaces not obstructed by embedded technicalities. *Aspirantes* suggested a gradual exposure to the myriad of technologies built-into or accessible for use in netbooks and cell phones. In their view, a harmonic balanced approach and more efficient use of time are vital in achieving the goals of the project.

Witnessing Transformation

During the spring 2011 semester, the inaugural *aspirantes* enrolled in a course that required participation LCM. Once again, three of the original five *aspirantes* who participated in this study returned to the LCM site to assume their role as guides. This allowed us to revisit with *aspirantes* and extend their perspectives regarding their LCM experience. Key transformations had taken place since their last visit to Las Palmas Elementary. As a result, they had more *consejos* to prepare LCM for the new cohort of *aspirantes*.

The opportunity to revisit LCM allowed *aspirantes* to witness transcendence of LCM activities. For example, they commented on how *El Maga* was more focused on tailoring its electronic correspondence with the children in LCM, because a graduate assistant was assigned to fulfill this role providing individualized and consistent messages. Although *aspirantes* themselves were not wizarding, *aspirantes* applauded *El Maga's* efforts to maintain good communication. This consistency resulted in students being more motivated to correspond with *El Maga* in comparison to the inaugural semester when children avoided this activity. Osiel stated, "*Esta es una de las ventajas más grandes que he visto. Si dedicas un maestro solamente a LCM hace mucho la diferencia.*" [This is one of the advantages I have noticed. If you dedicate a teacher exclusively to LCM, there will be a great difference.]

Perhaps one of the most crucial transformations noticed by returning *aspirantes* was the newfound sense of independence displayed by participating children. Martha made an observation regarding her original protégé from four semesters prior: "*Cuando a mí me tocó, no sabía el teclado ni nada. Ahora él contesta a El Maga . . . Ya sabe deletrear. Me sorprendió su avance.*" [When he was assigned to me, he did not know how to use the keyboard or anything . . . Now he answers to *El Maga* . . . He now knows how to spell. I am amazed at his progress.] Additionally, families have commented to the *aspirantes* that their children's mastery of technological tools, literacy skills, and confidence have increased as a result of participating in LCM.

Continuous Reflection: Más Consejos

After this second experience with LCM, our Phase II participants proposed several new *consejos*. They once again recommend an inquiry-based approach as a central aspect of the LCM experience. Specifically, they favored the infusion of open-ended activities into the design of task cards. This would imply opening spaces for self-selected topics leading to child-envisioned projects. This type of exploration, our participants concluded, may include regular conversations (*aspirante*-protégé) regarding emergent topics of interest proposed on an as-needed basis.

A second *consejo* related to a child-centered focus. For example, this may occasionally entail assisting with homework, discovering technology tools, etc. They commented that sometimes children may be distracted with a predetermined agenda that does not allow for them focus on their priorities. For example, children occasionally were specially burdened with a lot of homework, so Osiel mentioned that he would have like to have the opportunity to assist protégés with their homework as needed.

As part of their *consejos*, the *aspirantes* supported a play-based environment. Both physical and academic play were perceived as key ingredients of this after-school project. In their previous experience, they recalled, children had an opportunity to engage in physical activities involving traditional games. This semester, they stated, participating children had missed this component and would have liked to see it become part of the schedule. Additionally, they also perceived play as a dynamic construct ideally infused into technology-based activities.

RETHINKING RESONANCE: NEW CONCEPTUAL UNDERSTANDINGS

Dialogue, we propose, is the continuous search for harmony. In joining a dialogic space, *aspirantes* framed *consejos* that sought to bring harmonic balance between "what is" and "what ought to be," with the intent of moving towards synchronization. *Consejos* from *aspirantes'* centered on *El Maga* and the role of technology in LCM. As a prominent figure in this after school program, *El Maga* embodies spiritual and mystical qualities whose daily interactions are potentially empowering and transformative. Its role in engaging protégés both affectively and cognitively is too important to ignore.

The prominence of *El Maga* is paralleled by the role of technology within LCM. As a multidimensional component that facilitates interdisciplinary connections while children explore and engage in conversation, technology deserves special attention. Its use, as *aspirantes* suggested, must give protégés opportunities to not only access knowledge but to actively produce it and disseminate it. In the case of the *aspirantes*, this experience affords the opportunity to fully understand the tenets and the application of learning and empowerment within a virtual space. Thereby, LCM becomes the liberating space for employing a transworld pedagogy of possibility and transformation.

REFERENCES

Bakhtin, M. M. (1981). *The Dialogic Imagination: Four Essays by M. M. Bakhtin*. M. Holquist (ed.), C. Emerson (trans.). Austin, TX: University of Texas Press.

Delgado-Gaitan, C. (1994). "'Consejos': The Power of Cultural Narratives." *Anthropology and Education Quarterly*, 25(3), 298–316.

Freire, P. (2007). *Daring to Dream: Toward a Pedaogy of the Unfinished*. Boulder, CO: Paradigm Publishers.

Gallego, M. A. (2001). "Is Experience the Best Teacher?: The Potential of Coupling Classroom and Community-Based Field Experiences." *Journal of Teacher Education*, 52(4), 312–325.

Gonzalez, N., Moll, L. C., and Amanti, C. (2005). *Funds of Knowledge*. Mahwah, NJ: Lawrence Erlbaum.

Maker, C. J., and Nielson, A. B. (1996). *Curriculum Development and Teaching Strategies for Gifted Learners*. Austin, TX: Pro-Ed.

Nocon, H. D. (2004). Sustainability as Process: Community Education and Expansive Collaborative Activity. *Educational Policy*, 18(5), 710–732.

Rodriguez, A. J., Zozakiewics, C., and Yerrick, R. (2005). "Using Prompted Praxis to Improve Teacher Professional Development in Culturally Diverse Schools." *School Science and Mathematics*, 105(7), 352–362.

Sharples, M., Milrad, M., Sanchez, I., and Vavuola, G. (2009). "Mobile Learning: Small Devices, Big Issues." In N. Balacheff, S. Ludvigsen and T. D. Jong (eds.), *Technology Enhanced Learning: Principles and Products* (233–249). Heidelberg: Springer.

Shor, I. (1992). *Empowering Education: Critical Teaching for Social Change*. Chicago: The University of Chicago Press.

Universidad Nacional Autónoma de México. (2012). "UNAM Identity." Retrieved January 21, 2012, from http://www.unam.mx/acercaunam/en/identidad/lema.html

Vásquez, O. A. (1993). "A Look at Language as a Resource: Lessons from *La Clase Mágica*." *The Yearbook of the National Society for the Study of Education*, 92(2), 199–224.

——— (2003). *La Clase Mágica: Imagining Optimal Possibilities in a Bilingual Community of Learners*. Mahwah, NJ: Lawrance Erlbaum.

NINE

Latino Children: Constructing Identities, Voices, Linguistic, and Cultural Understandings

Lucila D. Ek, Adriana S. García, and Armando Garza

WORKING TOWARD HARMONY

The application of technology in the classroom has become increasingly important as researchers and educators seek innovative ways to teach and engage learners that meet the new social realities. The use of technology in out-of-school programs has raised great interest in recent educational research (Masters and Nykvist, 2006). Of particular concern is the digital divide where Latino/a working-class students have limited access to technology (Ek, Machado-Casas, Sánchez, and Alanís, 2010). This chapter highlights *La Clase Mágica* at the University of Texas at San Antonio (LCM@UTSA) as an after-school program that provides children (protégés), teacher candidates (*aspirantes*), and researchers with opportunities to tap into technology's potential to create innovative learning environments that focus on language, literacy, and cultural development.

Miller (2003) asserts that afterschool enrichment activities have been shown to have long-term social and academic benefits for participants. After-school programs have the advantage of providing children an informal learning setting. In contrast to school, where teachers design activities to engage children in learning goals, after-school settings afford children opportunities for learning that addresses their unique, desired goals (Masters and Nykvist, 2006). Afterschool programs have been shown to bring positive outcomes, especially to a culturally diverse student population (Dyson, 2003; Vasquez, 2003).

Informed by sociocultural theories of learning and development (Vygostky, 1978) and an "anthropolitical linguistics" (Zentella, 1997, 2005) that focuses on the political aspects of language and literacy learning for marginalized groups, this chapter examines the ways that Latino/a bilingual children in grades PreK–5 engage in language and literacy practices with undergraduate bilingual Latina/o teacher candidates (*aspirantes*) during LCM. LCM provides children with a space to make sense of and develop their identities, voices, linguistic, and cultural understandings. In joint activity with the undergraduate teacher candidates, children construct and display themselves in positive ways that counter stereotypical and deficit views of bilingual Latino/a children and their families.

The corpus of data includes the children's digital autonarratives, their letters to *El Maga* [the Wizard], and bilingual teacher candidate fieldnotes. A significant presence, *El Maga* oversees the playful world of *La Clase Mágica*. *El Maga's* practice of communicating in Spanish and English via email provides ample opportunities to scaffold children's bilingualism and biliteracy. At LCM, each child writes a paragraph-long letter to *El Maga* every week then gets a personalized response from *El Maga*. From 2009 to 2011, the children wrote over 800 letters to *El Maga*.

CONCEPTUAL RESONANCE: WHAT DO WE KNOW?

Focusing on the importance of social context, LCM strives to create conditions for optimal learning. LCM draws on Vygotsky's (1978) premise that a child's mental, linguistic, and social development is supported by more competent others through social interactions. Sociocultural views of learning and development are socially mediated as well as socially motivated; children learn through interacting with a more knowledgeable person where they engage in a developmental zone of proximal development (ZPD). This sociocultural view of learning reconceptualizes the nature and purpose of cooperation and collaboration. The more knowledgeable other is able to scaffold the child's development of complex skills and concepts (Tharp and Gallimore, 1988). In addition, children are also able to be both novices and experts as these positions shift throughout joint activity.

The informal learning experiences and skills culturally and linguistically diverse children bring to school can be critical sources of prior knowledge that children can use to understand new concepts (Monzó and Rueda, 2003). The goal, then, is to create rich zones of development in which all participants learn by collaborating in activities in which they share sociocultural, linguistic, and cognitive resources. Cole, Olt, and Woodbridge (1994) believe that in these activities, students' participation is based on authentic competence that is not based on school criteria such as age, language background, education, or specific abilities.

An additional framework that informs our research is an anthropolitical linguistics, which argues that language and language learning are not neutral, but intertwined with politics, particularly for traditionally marginalized working-class non-dominant communities (Zentella 1997, 2002, 2005). One of the principal aims of an anthropolitical perspective is to illuminate the existence of multiple routes to literacy and education and demonstrate that Latino families of all types may contribute to this goal in manners that are different from those prescribed by the school. For example, LCM provides a space where both children and their parents, mothers in particular, develop digital literacies (see chapter 12).

Developing Students' Voices

Education cannot stand apart from its constituent communities (Vásquez, 2008). Embedded in their families, schools, and communities, bilingual/bicultural children construct complex selves, voices, and identities (Quíocho and Ríos, 2000; Tellez, 1999; Weisman, 2001). Voices imply having power over some kind of presentation of reality and meaning, and the ability to construct one's experience as it is presented to others (Blake, 1997; Gilligan, 1982). Consequently, students need to have the opportunities to express their own voice, including the rich local knowledge they possess. As such, schools must use knowledge that stems from relevant cultural systems such as family, community, and multiple institutional contexts that may provide socializing systems for literacy development. Students' voices must be heard and understood.

Technology as a Literacy Tool

Many countries now regard mastering the basic skills and concepts of information and communication technologies (ICTs) as part of the core of education, alongside reading and writing (Fairlie, 2004). Yet, the rapid diffusion of information and communication technology has also widened the gap in communication-based competency between Hispanic and non-Hispanic youth (Warschauer, Knobel, and Stone, 2004; Fairlie, 2007). Three factors have been found to significantly contribute to Latino youth's underachievement in this area: (1) lack of equal access to ICT technologies (Sánchez and Salazar, 2012); (2) low access to high quality ICT technologies available in Latino homes and schools (Warschauer, and Matuchniak, 2010); and, (3) poor use of ICT technology in the classroom as a result of inferior instruction (Fairlie, 2004; Hess and Leal, 2001; Tripp and Herr-Stephenson, 2009). Yet, ICTs play an important role in the lives of youth today, including Latino/a youth (Lam and Rosario-Ramos, 2009).

Vásquez (2008) argues that the use of technology can be seen as a tool to develop literacy skills. Learners are not only seen as processors of information, they are also actors who engage in activities that are significant to them, that give them voice, and that can transform the meaning of learning experiences. The computer as a language tool is seen as a medium for both collective sharing and for transmission of new forms of consciousness across generations and circumstances that may express voice and stories full of vivid knowledge. In addition, through technology, children can express identity within sociocultural contexts (Vásquez, 2008). Specifically, a technology literacy after-school program may provide literacy events that might serve as socializing practices in which children can appropriate sociocultural knowledge about their own culture (Gutiérrez, Baquedano-López, Álvarez, and Ming, 1999).

REPOSITIONING METHODOLOGY: BEYOND RELEVANCE TO THE SACRED SCIENCES

We draw from an ongoing qualitative research study on the Latino/a bilingual children and the bilingual teacher candidates who participate in LCM@UTSA. Our guiding question was: How do Latino/a bilingual children develop their bilingualism and their biliteracy at an after-school technology program? We analyzed data from the first two years (2009–2011) of the study. We found that through interaction with the teacher candidates and *El Maga,* children produced oral, written, and visual texts in Spanish and English.

Two courses targeting undergraduate bilingual teacher candidates produced the LCM@UTSA cohort over the span of three semesters. One course focused on play and creativity and the relationship between children's play and cognitive, social, and affective development. The other course focused on children's literature with a special emphasis on Latino/a and Mexican American cultural experiences. Both of these courses were taught primarily in Spanish with some English. The undergraduate students, all Spanish-English bilinguals of Latino/a origin, took both classes once a week and then spent another day at Las Palmas Elementary School in the after school LCM program. The fourth semester, the bilingual teacher candidates who participated in LCM were enrolled in a bilingual language arts course.

The UTSA undergraduate teacher candidates were trained to engage their younger partners in robust, theoretically informed interactions that support active engagement in learning and development. Through the Academy for Teacher Excellence (see chapter 5), teacher candidates, or *aspirantes*, were provided with netbooks and iPhones/iPods to use with the elementary school students. The *aspirantes* and the children (protégés) used computer-based educational games and collaborative activities specifically selected to emphasize technology as a tool for the development of language, literacy, and problem-solving skills. Each semester, the teacher candidates attended Las Palmas Elementary every Tuesday afternoon for three hours over a ten to fourteen week period. Each UTSA teacher candidate was paired with a young elementary student in grades PreK–5 for the duration of the semester. Adult-child (*aspirante*-protégé) pairs were organized to create an opportunity structure in which each learner collaborated with a more experienced peer (Vygotsky, 1978). Every activity was mediated by instructional task-cards, *aspirante*-protégé interactions, and computer games which were structured to develop the learners' interests and emergent skills. Learners were afforded a space to use their linguistic, sociocultural, and academic repertoires as intellectual tools (Gutiérrez et al., 2002). That is, they could use their multiple linguistic codes and dialects.

Two activities that leveraged children's linguistic repertoires were the digital autonarratives and the letter writing to *El Maga*. For the first activity, the elementary students collaborated as co-authors and co-editors with the *aspirantes* to create collaborative digital autonarratives entitled *Cómo aprendí a leer y escribir en mi primer y segundo idioma* (How I learned to read and write in my first and second language). The assignment included a three to five page paper and a virtual narrative, and required the creative use of every virtual/electronic resource and tool available to them (i.e., iPhone, laptop, camera, etc.). For the second activity, each child participant received email messages every week from *El Maga,* a gender-neutral cyber entity. *El Maga* remained anonymous throughout the semester and interacted with children on both a personal and an academic level. Each semester, the majority of the children wrote about ten letters to *El Maga* and, in turn, *El Maga* replied to each letter. Through these writings, the children became increasingly engaged with *El Maga,* allowing for deeper, more critical exchanges highlighting the children's biliteracy practices and how they narrate their own life stories. *El Maga* is bilingual in Spanish and English and she/he writes to the children in both languages or can code-switch.

In 2009–2010, *Maga* used code-switching in his/her responses to the children as compared to the following year. In 2010–2011, because one of the goals of LCM was to increase the use and value of Spanish, *El Maga* wrote to the children primarily in Spanish. For example, in fall 2010, *El Maga* wrote only one letter in English to see how the children would respond. In addition, when some of the children who are English-dominant wrote in English, *El Maga* responded in Spanish and suggested that these children ask the *aspirantes* to help them decipher the letter. However, if children used specific words in English such as "cupcakes," "Thanksgiving," "spring break," then *El Maga* would also use these terms.

To analyze the autonarratives and letters, we employed an iterative process of qualitative data collection and analysis in which researchers went back and forth between data looking for authenticity and entertaining alternative conclusions (Miles and Huberman, 1984). We read through transcripts of email correspondences with *El Maga, aspirante* fieldnotes, and viewed the digital autonarratives several times. We coded these data for themes and patterns that provided insight into children's development of voice, and their linguistic and cultural understandings. Three major themes emerged from the data: (1) the assertion of bilingualism in children's postings; (2) the use of local and cultural knowledge to make sense of LCM practices; and (3) the construction of self and family in positive ways. Pseudonyms are used to maintain children's anonymity.

SYNCHRONIZING MULTIPLE WORLDS: FINDINGS AND CHALLENGES

Code-switching represents the acquisition and use of two or more languages particularly among Latino/a immigrants (Zentella, 1997). Myers-Scotton (2007) states that "[b]y using two codes in two different turns, the speaker encodes two identities" (p. 116). Hence, bilinguals may purposefully code-switch on the basis of the roles they play and who they exchange dialogue with. For example, *El Maga* writes to the children primarily in Spanish, but sometimes uses English. The use of language in both the children's and *Maga's* letters is found in the following email exchange between *El Maga* and second grader Ramon. The exchange also shows how language use is negotiated by the children.

> *El Maga: Hola, quería saber porque no me pones tu nombre* [Hi, I wanted to know why don't you put your name] . . . How are you? I hope you are well. How did you like the activity of last week. . . .
>
> Ramon: *Hola soy [Ramon]* . . . *porque me escribistes en ingles? Yo prefiero que me escribas en espanol. Espero tu respuesta sea en espanol. A mi me gusta el ingles, pero no me gusta leer el ingles pero aun asi trate de leer lo que me escribiste.* [Hi I am Ramon. . . why did you write to me in English? I prefer that you write to me in Spanish. I hope that your response is in Spanish. I like English, but I don't like to read English even so I tried to read what you wrote to me.]

As the exchange demonstrates, *El Maga* begins the letter to Ramon in Spanish and continues in English. In his response, Ramon voices his language preference as he questions why *El Maga* wrote to him in English. Constructing himself as biliterate/bilingual, he explains that he likes English but he does not like to read in English. Ramon's writing contains grammatical errors, but his response also shows his high level of literacy in Spanish as he uses various verb tenses including the present subjunctive "escribas" (*you write*) and "sea" (*is*), the preterite "escribistes" (*you wrote*, non-standard), "escribiste" (*you wrote*, standard), and the adverbial phrase "*aún así*" (even so).

Another example of children's use of English, Spanish and codeswitching of their two languages is seen when second grader Ricardo writes to *El Maga* about the end of the semester celebration:

> Ricardo: *En el festival yo quiero juegos como las escondidas, un* Moonwalk ballon hot potato *y* tag. *Tambien comida como* pizza, hot dogs, *nachos*, cotton candy *y* ice cream. [At the festival I want games like hide and seek, a Moonwalk balloon, hot potato, and tag. Also food like pizza, hot dogs, nachos, cotton candy, and ice cream.]

In this example, Ricardo codeswitches to communicate his likes and dislikes to *Maga*. His linking of a particular language with certain items reflects his bicultural experiences. For example, he uses the Spanish *las escondidas* rather than the English "hide-and-seek" but other games are described in English such as "Moonwalk," "hot potato," and "tag." In the second sentence, he starts off in Spanish also, but lists foods in English including pizza, hot dogs, cotton candy, and ice cream. In the last line, his use of "*y*" rather than "and" indicates that he is writing and possibly thinking primarily in Spanish but he associates certain games and foods with English rather than Spanish.

Local Cultural Knowledge as a Resource for Biliteracy

The data show that in addition to their bilingualism, children draw on their local cultural knowledge as a resource to make sense of their experiences during LCM. Local knowledge includes what the children know about their state, Texas, as well as cultural identities such as that of "Tejano." Children's constructions of the mysterious *El Maga* provide a lens into how they use their local cultural knowledge. The following exchange between *El Maga* and first grader Adan provides an example of such kinds of sense making.

> El Maga: *¿Dime como te imaginas que soy yo el Maga? ¿Donde crees que vivo? ¿Cuando piensas en mi como me piensas? ¿Si me pudieras dibujar como me vería? ¡Espero que me contestes! El Maga.* (Tell me how do you imagine that I am? Where do you think I live? When you think of me, how do you think of me? If you could draw me how would I look? I expect your reply! El Maga)

> Adan: *Creo que eres un hombre que vivies en una casa en Tejas. dibujar cafe y con ropa azul. te espero tu mensaje. adios. Adan.* [I think you are a man that lives in a house in Texas. [I] draw you brown with blue clothing. I await your message. Bye. Adan.]

Adan draws upon his cultural awareness and knowledge to depict *El Maga* as *un hombre* [a man] that lives in "Tejas", spelled with a "j." Adan's spelling signals a Tejano identity and culture that is connected to Mexican-American/Chicano history and experiences in Texas. "Tejano" refers to Texans of Mexican ancestry, who resided in Texas before it was even a state (Ballí, 2012). Interestingly, Adan also writes the word "Texas," indicating his understandings that the state can be spelled with either a "j" or an "x." These orthographic choices may signal Adan's biculturality as Mexican American. Moreover, in Adan's imaginings, *El Maga* wears a cowboy hat and drives a truck—which is local cultural knowledge. The red truck in the drawing evokes the trucks that are common in Texas. Adan writes that he drew *El Maga* in brown which may signal his assumption *of El Maga* as being brown-skinned and Latino or Tejano like him.

Children's Construction of Themselves and their Families

Biliteracy practices during LCM afford the elementary school children opportunities to depict themselves and their families in multiple and positive ways. For example, as stated previously, the protégés with the help of the *aspirantes,* created digital autonarratives where they used pictures and videos to depict who they are. Children incorporated photos of themselves and their families. First-grader Craig, for example, chose to highlight his athletic side as he incorporated pictures that showed him

Figure 9.1.   Drawing of *El Maga*

playing basketball, swimming, jumping on the trampoline, and climbing the monkey bars. Creatively, Craig chose to modify some pictures by using computer software. In the captions of his autonarrative, he wrote, "I like my photos [to] look cool and different. . . . I don't like having my pictures taken. . . . That's why I have made my photos look strange." The autonarrative format gave Craig the flexibility to choose how his images were displayed. He was able to depict his individuality and uniqueness through his use of color and photo editing. In another set of pictures, Craig is shown playing tea with his younger cousin Amanda. The caption under the photo reads "I really hated to play pretend here, but I was made to." Craig displays his collaborative side by taking on the role of a playmate to younger children and even participates in games he does not necessarily want to play.

Like Craig, second-grader Ricardo chose photos that highlighted his roles in his family. One picture shows him reading to his mother and younger brother at the library. The mother and brother appear to be listening attentively. Thus, Ricardo is socializing his little brother to shared reading and constructs himself as an able reader for his family. Highlighting Latino/a family reading practices such as Ricardo does in these pictures disrupts deficit perspectives of Latino/a families as not having literacy.

The children's families were central to their narrations of themselves. In a letter to *El Maga*, third-grader Abigail, emphasized the connection between her name and her family. She wrote:

> *Si es importante el tener un apellido porque es para saber en que familia estas y quien eres. Como yo tengo 2 apellidos pero solo es 1 familia. Me gusta tener 2 apellidos porque puedo escribir largo*

> (Yes it is important to have a last name because you know what family you are in and who you are. Like me, I have 2 last names but it is only 1 family. I like to have two last names because I can write it [my name] long).

Abigail expresses her enjoyment of writing as she explains that an additional perk of having two last names is that she can write more. In Mexico, and many parts of Latin America, both the mother and father's last names are used so children have two last names— all Mexican children have the right to have the paternal names of their parents as stated by the *Código Civil Federal* (Cámara de Diputados, H. Congreso de la Unión, 2012). Abigail is aware of how these names are linked to identity, *quien eres* (who you are), and to familial belonging. She is also aware of how two families merge to become only one as she explains that her two names represent *"solo"* [only] one family. Other children also constructed their families in positive ways such as *Mi familia es amable y divertida* (My family is nice and fun) and *Mi familia siempre está unida* (My family is always united).

When talking about or writing about their families, many of the children included their extended family both in the United States and in Mexico. Jose, for example, included a picture of his uncle's birthday celebration and a picture of traveling to Mexico. In his autonarrative, he wrote:

> *A mi familia y a mi nos gusta celebrar cumpleanos. Mi familia celebrando el cumpelanos de mi tio. . . . Cantando las mananitas y partiendo el pastel. . . . Viajando a Mexico con mis hermanos y papas.*

> (My family and I like to celebrate birthdays. My family celebrating my uncle's birthday. . . . Singing "las mananitas" [a traditional birthday song] and cutting the cake. . . . Traveling to Mexico with my brothers and parents.)

Through his photos, Jose gives insight into his daily familial practices. He explains that for his uncle's birthday, the family sings "*Las Mañanitas*," a traditional Mexican birthday song. In addition, Jose's picture highlights his transnational experiences. Research has shown that for Latino/a bilingual students sustained transnational contact with communities in their or their parents' home countries provides linguistic and cultural resources for language, literacy, and culture maintenance and development (Ek, 2009; Sánchez, 2007). Hence, as captured in photos, children provide glimpses of various cultural practices and artifacts that are meaningful to them.

Children's pictures also provided a lens into religious influences in their and their family's lives. For example, second-grader Laura took a picture of her grandmother standing near a statue of *La Virgen de Guadalupe*. According to Petty (2000), "*La Virgen de Guadalupe* is the religious icon around which Mexican Catholicism centers . . . [and] the embodiment of feminine purity as well as the virtues of nurturing and self-sacrifices. Thus she is venerated in Mexican culture as the proper symbol for womanhood" (pp. 120–121). In Laura's picture, her grandmother stands with her head held high and her hands on her waist depicting a strong confident woman with her *Virgencita* nearby.

As these examples demonstrate, children can and will assert their voices and understandings if given the space and opportunity to engage in activities that foster their language and literacy development. Analysis of Latino/a children's writings, drawings, pictures, and talk, give educators and researchers a deeper understanding of how these children construct themselves in ways that complicate monolingual, monocultural identities. Latino/a children's constructions of their families disrupt the nuclear norm prevalent in U.S. discourse. Children's texts reveal their extended, multi-generational families both in the United States and in Latin American countries.

RETHINKING RESONANCE: NEW CONCEPTUAL UNDERSTANDINGS

LCM creates rich contexts for learning for Latino/a children and families—particularly in a time when English-only and anti-immigrant sentiments dominate educational policy and practice. Children's engagement in these hybrid literacy practices (Gutiérrez, Baquedano-López, Alvarez and Chiu, 1999), embedded in a playful and stimulating bilingual learning environment, creates harmonic balance, while providing spaces in which learners can develop their voices, cultural understandings, and identities in positive ways. The Latino/a children's writings and digital autonarratives illuminated their language use and choices, their local cultural knowledge, and their positive constructions of themselves and their families. Importantly, children depicted engagement in meaningful language, literacy, religious, and transnational practices. Also important to our research are computer-based resources that are key to both attracting Latino/a children's active participation and giving children access to quality learning materials and resources that they would otherwise not have at home or at school (Ek, Machado-Casas, Sánchez and Alanís, 2010). This kind of transworld pedagogy could be incorporated into the classroom in lieu of traditional classroom practices and scripts that often limit children's learning opportunities. More after school programs like *La Clase Mágica* are needed to highlight and build on working-class Latino/a bilingual children's bilingualism and biliteracy.

REFERENCES

Ballí, C. (2012, April). "The True Meaning of the Tejano Monument." *Texas Monthly— Daily Post.* Retrieved from www.tmdailypost.com/article/culture/true-meaning-tejano-monument

Blake, B. (1997). *She Say, He Say: Urban Girls Write Their Lives.* Albany, NY: State University of New York Press.

Código Civil Federal (2012). *Cámara de diputados,* Retrieved from www.diputados.gob.mx/LeyesBiblio/pdf/2.pdf.

Cole, M., Olt, A., and Woodbridge, S. (1994, April). "Documenting Children's Problem Solving Behaviors Using Fieldnotes of Participant Observers." Paper presented at the annual meeting of the American Educational Research Association, New Orleans, LA.

Dyson, A. H. (2003). *The Brothers and Sisters Learn to Write: Popular Literacies in Childhood and School Cultures.* New York: Teachers College Press.

Ek, L.D. (2009). "'Allá en Guatemala': Transnationalism, Language, and Identity of a Pentecostal Guatemalan-American Young Woman." *High School Journal,* 92(4), 67-81.

Ek, L. D., Machado-Casas, M., Sánchez, P., and Alanís, I. (2010). "Collaborating Across the Divides: *La Clase Mágica* as a University-Community-School Partnership." *Journal of School Leadership*, 20(6), 822–850.

Fairlie, R. W. (2004). "Race and the Digital Divide." *Contributions to Economic Analysis and Policy*, 3(1), 1–38.

——— (2007). "Explaining Differences in Access to Home Computers and the Internet: A Comparison of Latino Groups to Other Ethnic and Racial Groups." *Electronic Commerce Research*, 7(3–4), 265–291.

Hess, F. and Leal, D. (2001). "Quality, Race, and the Urban Education Marketplace." *Urban Affairs Review*, 37(2), 249–266.

Gilligan, C. (1982). *In a Different Voice*. Cambridge, MA: Harvard University Press.

Gutiérrez, K. D., Baquedano-López, P., Álvarez, H. H., and Chiu, M. M. (1999). "Building a Culture of Collaboration through Hybrid Language Practices." *Theory into Practice*, 38(2), 87–93.

Gutiérrez, K. D., Asato, J., Pacheco, M., Moll, L. C., Olson, K., Horng, E., Ruiz, R., García, E., and McCarty, T.L. (2002). "Sounding American: The Consequences of New Reforms on English Language Learners." *Reading Research Quarterly*, 37(2), 328–343.

Lam, W. E. and Rosario-Ramos, E. (2009). "Multilingual Literacies in Transnational Digitally Mediated Contexts: An Exploratory Study of Immigrant Teens in the United States." *Language and Education*, 23(2), 171–190.

Masters, J. and Nykvist, S. (2006). "Supporting Play with Digital Media: Informal Learning in the Fifth Dimension." *Current Developments in Technology-Assisted Education*. Retrieved October 4, 2012 from uclinks.org/reference/research/masters.pdf.

Miles, M. B. and Huberman, A. M. (1984). *Qualitative Data Analysis, 16*. Newbury Park, CA: Sage.

Miller, B. M. (2003). *Critical Hours: After School Programs and Educational Success*. Quincy, MA: Nellie Mae Education Foundation.

Monzó, L. D. and Rueda, R. (2003). "Shaping Education through Diverse Funds of Knowledge: A Look at One Latina Paraeducator's Lived Experiences, Beliefs, and Teaching Practice." *Anthropolgy and Education Quarterly*, 34(1), 72–95.

Myers-Scotton, C. (2007). "Code-Switching as Indexical of Social Negotiations." In L. Wei (ed.), *The Bilingualism Reader* (97–122). New York: Routledge.

Quíocho, A. and Ríos, F. (2000). "The Power of their Presence: Minority Group Teachers and Schooling." *Review of Educational Research*, 70(4), 485–528.

Petty, L. (2000). "The 'Dual'-ing Images of La Malinche and La Virgen de Guadalupe in Cisneros's *The House on Mango Street*." *Melus*, 25(2), 119-132.

Sánchez, P. (2007). Cultural Authenticity and Transnational Latina Youth: Constructing a Metanarrative Across Borders. *Linguistics and Education*, 18(3–4), 258–282.

Sánchez, P. and Salazar, M. (2012). "Transnational Computer Use in Urban Latino Immigrant Communities: Implications for Schooling." *Urban Education*, 47(1), 90–116.

Tharp, R. G. and Gilmore, R. (1988). *Rousing Minds to Life: Teaching, Learning, and Schooling in Social Context*. New York: Cambridge University Press.

Tellez, K. (1999). "Mexican-American Preservice Teachers and the Intransigency of the Elementary School Curriculum." *Teaching and Teacher Education*, 15, 555–570.

Tripp, L. M. and Herr-Stephenson, R. (2009). "Making Access Meaningful: Latino Young People Using Digital Media at Home and at School." *Journal of Computer-Mediated Communication*, 14(4), 1190–1207.

Vásquez, O. (2003). *La Clase Mágica: Imagining Optimal Possibilities in a Bilingual Community of Learners*. Mahwah, NJ: Erlbaum.

——— (2008)."Reflection: Rules of Engagement for Achieving Educational Futures." In L. L. Parker (ed.), *Technology-Mediated Learning Environments for Young English Learners: Connections In and Out of School* (99–110). New York: Erlbaum.

Vygotsky, L. S. (1978). *Mind in Society: The Development of Higher Psychological Processes*. Cambridge, MA: Harvard University Press.

Warschauer, M., Knobel, M., and Stone, L. (2004). "Technology and Equity in School-ing: Deconstructing the Digital Divide." *Educational Policy*, 18(4), 562–588.

Warschauer, M. and Matuchniak, T. (2010). "New Technology and Digital Worlds: Analyzing Evidence of Equity in Access, Use, and Outcomes." *Review of Research in Education*, 34(1), 179–225

Weisman, E. M. (2001). "Bicultural Identity and Language Attitudes: Perspectives of Four Latina Teachers." *Urban Education*, 36, 203–225.

Zentella, A. C. (1997). *Growing Up Bilingual: Puerto Rican Children in New York*. Malden, MA: Blackwell Publishers.

——— (2002). "Latino Languages and Identities." In M. Páez and M. Suárez-Orozco (eds.), *Latinos: Remaking America* (321–338). Berkeley, CA: University of California Press.

——— (2005). *Building on Strength: Language and Literacy in Latino Families and Commu-nities*. New York: Teachers College Press.

TEN

Digital Literacies and Latino Literature Supporting Children's Inquiries

Carmen M. Martínez-Roldán

WORKING TOWARD HARMONY

I say feed me.
She serves red prickly pear on a spiked cactus.
I say tease me.
She sprinkles raindrops in my face on a sunny day.
The desert is my mother.
El desierto es mi madre.
The desert is my strong mother.
(Verses from the poem "The Desert is My Mother," by Pat Mora, 2000)

In this poem, Latina author Mora captures a view of the earth that reflects what many Chicanos and indigenous people have learned from their ancestors, "the belief that all creation is sacred and that we are to live in harmony with nature" (see chapters 1 and 2). In the organization of the after-school program, the Longhorn Amigos Clase Mágica in Austin, Texas[1], I purposefully sought to harmonize various types of cultural tools and artifacts, such as Latino literature that reflected perspectives, stories, and traditions from non-dominant communities, as well as technology. The goal of this integration was twofold: (a) to provide a culturally relevant learning experience to the primary grade children participating in the program; and (b) to respond to the 2010 Recommendations for the Reauthorization of the ESEA report that "English language learners must be provided with an equal opportunity to acquire the same content and high-level skills that school reform movements advocate for all students" (p. 2), which in the twenty-first century includes, among other things, access to the discourse of science and technology and the development of multiliteracies.

The use of digital tools in the classroom represents a challenge for some teachers who do not see themselves as "digital natives" (Prensky, 2001) and who are teaching children who may well be quite technologically literate. An additional challenge may come from the perceived dichotomy some adults express between the use of print-based materials and some digital materials, and their concern regarding the potential negative impact of video and computer games on student learning (Gee, 2007). In fact, it is not uncommon to see that when digital technologies are embraced by teachers, these technologies are often incorporated in ways that keep conventional print-based literacy at the center of the curriculum (Reinking and Carter, 2007). Therefore, a third goal of the program was to provide the bilingual education teacher candidates (*aspirantes*) with experiences mediating the use of these tools to support children's learning.

In this chapter, I illustrate through a case study how digital resources, specifically the program Animoto that enables the creation of video clips and Latino literature, were integrated into the after-school program to support the children's introduction to some components of the discourse of science, specifically, the development of an inquiry perspective.

CONCEPTUAL RESONANCE: WHAT DO WE KNOW?

It was important for this study to examine this mediation from a situated perspective toward learning, a perspective concerned with how individuals become members of a learning community—in this case, a bilingual community that values inquiry and multiliteracies. I was especially interested in understanding how children learn through participation and how they appropriate and transform the discourse, identities, and tools (Vygotsky, 1978) available to them through the mediation of the technologies/games and children's literature (Gee, 2007; Lave and Wenger, 1991; Rogoff, 2003).

Gee (2007) proposes that any specific way of reading and thinking is, in fact, a way of being in the world, a way of being a certain "kind of person," and a way of taking on a certain sort of identity. For instance, learning within the Science Technology Engineering and Mathematics (STEM) disciplines should be, following Gee (2007), a matter of the learning of new semiotic domains rather than the learning of content. This approach involves becoming familiar with "an area or set of activities where people think, act, and value in certain ways . . . a set of practices that recruits one or more modalities to communicate distinctive types of meanings" (pp. 18–19), which includes the codes or representations used by a particular group to make meaning. In my study of the children's (protégés) participation in the after-school program, I have investigated the types of representations and meanings available for protégés through both cultural tools: children's literature and online games.

Latino Literature

Multicultural children's literature has the potential to broaden students' perspectives by introducing them to the lives, languages, social practices, and ways of thinking of groups different from their own, thereby helping these children to enhance their knowledge about the social world and develop an appreciation of diverse cultures. Of interest in this study is the role of Latino children's literature—"literature written by Latino and Latina authors, whether they write in English or in Spanish and regardless of the topic they address" (Ada, 2003, p. 36)[2]—as a cultural tool that mediates student learning and identity. Many Latino authors experience the very texts they are creating as spaces for the interpretation of their collective and personal experiences and identities. For instance, Yarbro-Bejarano (1996) notes that the Latina/Chicana writer finds that the self she seeks to define and love is not merely an individual self, but a collective one; thus, her literary work becomes a mediational tool for the negotiation and development of identities, especially for Latino teachers and students (Fránquiz, Martínez-Roldán, and Mercado, 2010; Medina, 2006).

Literature can also support some of the skills and dispositions that characterize scientists, specifically, that literature written as informational text. It is important that *aspirantes* familiarize themselves with the quality body of Latino literature available for children so that they can incorporate it into the classroom to mediate learning.[3]

Computer Games and Digital Learning

Play, school, and work have been identified within the cultural-historical perspective as three main leading activities that mediate individual development. "In play," Vygotsky (1966/1933) maintains, "a child is always above his average age, above his daily behavior; in play it is as though he were a head taller than himself" (p. 25). Play within online games and digital sites results in supporting experimentation, playing with ideas, testing boundaries, trying out possibilities, and engaging in other forms of open-ended activity that may involve failure rather than fun (Gee, 2007). As Gee (2007) argues, because the stakes of the experimental activity tend to be low—there is no external punishment for failure—an unsuccessful playful effort can benefit the learner's knowledge by helping to inform the next attempt and by developing the concept of the activity.

Digital spaces also afford youths the opportunity to remix the worlds that they inherit into new configurations that suit their needs as they shape their identities in the worlds that they find online (Knobel and Lankshear, 2008; Martínez-Roldán and Smagorinsky, 2011). Digital programs that encourage the production of digital text, such as Animoto, are especially suitable for children as they remix their worlds.

REPOSITIONING METHODOLOGY: BEYOND RELEVANCE TO THE SACRED SCIENCES

Drawn from a larger study employing Erickson's (1986) interpretive methods, this case study brings the participants' voices and experiences to the center and recognizes Latino students and Latino authors as holders and creators of knowledge (Delgado-Bernal, 2002). Participant observation, field notes, audio recordings, and video recordings of protégés' interactions with undergraduates about books and computers were the means of data collection for the study. For the case study presented in this chapter, audio recordings from eight sessions between September and November 2010 provided the data for the focused analysis.

Two times per week for one year, thirty-one *aspirantes* enrolled in my bilingual reading class, which met for an hour at the end of the school day with sixteen second-grade bilingual students, mainly Latinos, who attended a neighborhood bilingual school. Half of the *aspirantes* worked with the children on Wednesdays, and the other half of the candidates worked with the same students on Thursdays. The sessions formally opened with the *aspirantes* reading a children's book to or with the protégés. The reading time was centered on Latino literature, and online games were at the center of the computer time.

This chapter focuses on the program Animoto as the digital tool that mediated the case study, César's learning, while the informational text *Magic Windows/Ventanas Mágicas*, written and illustrated by Chicana artist and writer Carmen Lomas Garza (1999), was the literature used to mediate the child's reading and learning. The author uses her experiences to paint and describe the Southwest landscape, her family, her ancestors, and their traditions integrating the use of the technique known as *papel picado* (cut-paper art).

The research also used a qualitative case study design (Dyson and Genishi, 2005) that focused on individual dyads of *aspirantes*-protégés and their meaning-making processes. Diana and Celia were the two *aspirantes,* who worked with César, a third-grade bilingual learner during the Fall 2010 semester. In Martínez-Roldán and Smagorinsky (2011), we presented César's learning during the first semester of the program (spring of 2009) when he was working with Antonia. In that discussion, we focused on how the line between expert and learner became blurred for many of the children and teacher candidates participating in the program, thus raising questions about the nature of the mediation in the zone of proximal development for both children and interns. In this chapter, I extend that case study by focusing on the second semester, when César was working with Diana, to show how the boundaries between the two artifacts that are the focus of this analysis, literature and computer learning, were also blurred.

César liked mystery and scary stories as well as informational texts. Consequently, Diana selected Latino literature within these different genres. César also liked math and the program Cool Math was one of his favorite online games. Table 10.1 provides a list of texts and games used during Diana's sessions with César.

Transcripts of interactions between Diana, the *aspirante*, and César, protégé, were examined and categorized according to the different roles and sub-activities in which César and Diana engaged during both parts of each session, the thirty-minute reading time and the thirty-minute digital learning time. In the next section, I present the last day of interactions to illustrate the range of roles that the protégés and *aspirantes* assumed during the after-school program and the types of learning afforded by the two cultural artifacts highlighted in this chapter. Specifically, I compared the two parts of a session across sixteen categories, which included characteristics of interactions and roles.

SYNCHRONIZING MULTIPLE WORLDS: FINDINGS AND CHALLENGES

Reading Time

During the reading time, some *aspirantes*, such as Diana, observed that when the books they had chosen appeared too long, it helped facilitate the discussion of the book and the entire reading event, in general, if the *aspirante* and the protégé distributed the role of reading. For example, *Magic Windows/Ventanas Mágicas* (1999), is organized in short scenes that can be discussed individually, so Diana and César each chose and read different scenes from the book and discussed those sections, commenting on and elaborating upon the information provided, as the following excerpt illustrates (the text from the book appears within quotation marks). The *aspirante,* Diana introduced the bilingual book and asked César to choose the language for the reading and he chose English and began to read.

Table 10.1. Schedule, Texts, Websites, and Games Used with César during Fall 2010.

Fecha	Children's Literature	Website and Games
9/22/10	*The Lottery/La lotería* by René Colato Laynez	Free Choice
9/29/10	*Prietita and the Ghost Woman/Prietita y la Llorona* by Gloria Anzaldua	www.pbskids.org/fetch Germinator
10/6/10	*El cucuy* by Joe Hayes	www.animoto.com
10/13/10	*Chato y su cena* by Gary Soto	www.pbskids.org/cyberchase Logical Zoo
10/20/10	*Ghost Fever* by Joe Hayes	www.scholastic.com/magicschoolbus/ games Space Chase Student preferred to play Fetch: Make it or Luge it & Germinator (most of the time) Coolmath (5 minutes)
11/3/10	*A Spoon for Every Bite* by Joe Hayes	www.pbskids.org/superwhy Superwhy (5 minutes) Coolmath: Civiballs, Construction Fall, and Rotate and Roll (most of the time)
11/10/10	*La mariposa* by Francisco Jiménez	www.scholastic.com/ magicschoolbus/games: Build a Bug Animoto (10 minutes) Coolmath: Civiballs (most of the time)
11/17/10	*Magic Windows* by Carmen Lomas Garza	www.animoto.com (most of the time) Coolmath.

César: "I've always loved to watch the work that people do with their hands. This is a close-up of my grandfather's hands. . . . In this piece, the cactus spines are the connectors."

Diana: "Have you seen nopalitos? Tunas?" [The child gives a nonverbal response indicating that he has not seen them.] *Sometimes the cacti have those fruits that come, that grow out of them and you can eat them.*

[Diana reads and comments on the section about the altar and explains that the *papel picado* was used to represent the Day of the Dead.]

César: [César chooses to read the section, "Horned Toads"]: "This piece is in honor of the camaleones. We used to call them horned toads."

Diana: "*Horned*" [pronouncing it slowly].

César: "*Horned*" [keeps reading.] "Actually, they're not toads. . . . They have spikes all over their bodies to protect themselves . . . their habitat has been destroyed by humans, and so today they are an endangered species."

Diana: "Hmm. Have you ever seen one?"

César: "In the picture."

Diana: "In the pictures?" [Laughs.] "But not up close, right?"

César: "No."

Diana: "They usually live in the desert."

César: "Can we make a video out of it?"

Diana: "Okay! We can look those up. Yeah, that's a good idea."

César: "Don't they have like a lot of spines?"

Diana: "Uhum . . . yes, like these."

César: "Like the barbed wire?"

Diana: "Kind of."

César: "I got caught by one of those one time."

Diana: "You did? By one of these? Was it in your backyard?"

[Talk about barbed wire.]

Diana: "And we use fences to protect our houses, right? That's how they [chameleons] use their spines, they use them for—"

César: "No, they are like . . . [inaudible]"

Diana: "Oh! Okay!"

[They alternate reading the sections, both contributing comments and information about the pictures. César asks questions and makes connections to personal experiences, and Diana poses follow-up questions.]

César: "An eagle eating a snake . . . isn't that [the] symbol for Mexico['s] flag?"

Diana: "Yes, it is."

César: "Yeah, it's green, white, and red."

[They continue talking about his learning of the Mexican flag, reading, and discussing the text. César shares information he knows about the pythons.] (Excerpts from session on 11/17/2010.)

This excerpt is typical of their interactions during the first part of the *Longhorn Amigos Clase Mágica* (LCM) after-school program sessions, and it shows the distribution of roles during reading time. Salient aspects of these roles include Diana, as the *aspirante*, choosing Latino literature after taking into account César's interests in informational books (during the semester, sometimes César chose between two texts brought in by Diana). César also chose the language of the reading event (the language was, at times, negotiated to include exposure to both Spanish and English). This day, César also negotiated the task for the computer time. He knew that Diana always had a plan for the use of computer time, so on this day, he took the lead during reading time to shape the activity for the second part of the session, linking both activities by creating a video of one of the animals he was reading about in the book. Both Diana and César contributed information during the reading (e.g., Diana about *nopalitos* and *chameleons'* use of spines and César about the Mexican flag and pythons). Each asked questions. Diana, as an *aspirante*, assessed César's knowledge and understanding to adjust the amount of information she was giving and also to follow up on the protégé's connections to personal experiences, asking him to extend his descriptions of those experiences. César asked questions seeking information to confirm his hypotheses and knowledge. For example, *"Don't they have like a lot of spines?"*

Computer Time

After thirty minutes of reading and discussing the book, the class moved to the computer room where the following interactions occurred. The session began with Diana confirming the task that César had negotiated for this computer time.

Diana: "Do you want to get onto Animoto?"

[César tries to find the site but cannot.]

Diana: "Why don't we look it up on Google since that didn't work?"

César: "I can look up things . . . aha!"[Inaudible; found the site.]

César faces his first problem when he cannot access the Animoto site, and Diana proposes another way to search for it, that is, using Google. The *aspirante* documented, based on her own experience, how important this type of teaching/learning was for her protégé so that he, too, could become familiar with this popular research tool:

> As a college student, I use Google all the time, not only for images but also for other topics. It is important that César starts using this tool now so that he knows where to turn to in case he is seeking information for his personal use or for a class project. Google is a good starting point for answering questions (Final Paper, Dec. 2010).

Another instance to support César's digital skills occurred when, once he found the Animoto site and saw his two previous videos, he wanted to create a third video. Diana, however, demonstrated another way to access and obtain relevant information.

César: "Yeah, it's the video. I want three. Okay, we have to go right here, right?"

Diana: "Yes. But let's open another tab. Do you remember how to open a tab?"

César: "Yeah, 'command plus'"[Laughs] [Tries, but his way did not work.]

Diana: "The way I do it is I go to 'file' and then open a tab." [Inaudible.]

César: "Ah!"

Diana: "And there it is!"

César: "Look at all the snakes!"

Diana: "Yeah, look at all the snakes! Look at that!"

César: "I wonder what is this one? It looks like it is biting or something, like a wire or something."

Diana: "Oh, look how big! Do you open your mouth that big?"

César: "Uh-uh" [in the negative].

Diana: [Laughs]

César: "It looks like an anaconda! I thought they didn't have teeth. Look at all those teeth!" [Continues to comment on the pictures.]

During the whole session there were many surprises and expressions of exclamation, thus revealing their engagement and aesthetic experiences. They also searched for information, commented on the pictures, and speculated about them. César posed questions, adopting an inquiry perspective (Lindfors, 1999; Martínez-Roldán, 2005): "*I wonder what is this one?*" Their interactions were also characterized by some mutual teasing.

> César: "This is 'creeping' me out." [laughs] "I think it's a coral snake. . . . Oh, it looks like this is an anaconda!"
>
> Diana: [Reading information from the screen:] "Hmm . . . it doesn't say what they are."
>
> César: "I think it is an anaconda. Anacondas are that big!" [César reads aloud from the screen.]

In this segment, it is clear that, at times, the aspirante challenged César's interpretations. She also read the text accompanying the pictures, which César also started to read. For Diana, reading the text (captions) that accompanied the images was an important part of reading informational text as "practice" for research, as she reflected in her final paper.

As it happened in the beginning of the session, when César proudly announced, "*I can look up things*" (in Google), there were other exchanges during the making of the video in which César showed his sense of efficacy, as evidenced in this next excerpt:

> César: "I haven't blinked the whole time.">
>
> Diana: "You haven't blinked? . . ."[César shows Diana some images of snakes.] "Don't show! I don't need to see that." [Laughs.]
>
> César: "Wow! This one is a little one!"
>
> Diana: "Yes, it's like a skinny one. That's such a good picture."
>
> César: "Uhh, it is." [Inaudible.]

César comments on his sense of efficacy because he has been able to stay focused for so long looking for pictures [or perhaps because he can stand strong/scary images]. At any rate, he has a positive image of himself and an image of success. His self-efficacy reflections contrast with previous negative statements about himself as a reader and about school. César had previously expressed that reading and school were boring. He had previously described himself, stating "*I am not very good at that*" when Diana asked about the sequence of events in a story in an earlier session where she was conducting a mini lesson as part of an assignment for the teacher candidates. However, during the creation of the video, an activity full of challenges, he proudly stated, on two occasions, "*I can look up things*" and "*I haven't blinked the whole time.*"

The *aspirante* and César continued to comment on the photos. César then tried to capture photos for his video but was having difficulties. He then talked to himself, or to the computer, "*Come on, I can't even have them stand up.*" He managed to select the pictures and continued working until he was satisfied. "*I think I'm done,*" he said. He then moved on to upload the pictures from the desktop to the program, Animoto.

> César: "Would you grab one of those if they give you a million dollars?"
>
> Diana: "No, would you?"
>
> César: "No! Look at its heart!"
>
> Diana: "Oh, that's a snake eating a mouse. This color part is the mouse [not the heart]."
>
> César: [Makes a sound as if he is throwing up.]
>
> Diana: [Reads from the screen information about snakes and extends it] ". . . so they can't really see, but they can trap . . ." [inaudible] "You know how they find their prey? They use their sense of smell."

César continued to upload photos, which was taking a great deal of time and was becoming impatient. "I don't want to wait 30 seconds!" (He actually waited longer than that.) Therefore, the *aspirante* took over the last part of the uploading process. They then proceeded to add the music and the background to the video. Diana searched for the music and César listened to it, rejecting the first choice she presented and asking her to change it. He finally chose the hip-hop song "Quiet Dog" by artist Mos Def. With the selection of the song, Diana and the protégé, César integrated the scientific process of learning about animals and looking for popular culture until they were both satisfied with the final product.

> Diana: "Look! I am watching your video. It's done!">
>
> Diana: "I like it! Those were good pictures! Did you like the song?"
>
> César: "Aha, yeah!"
>
> Diana: "That was good, that was really good!" (Excerpts from session on 11/17/2010.)

Some of these excerpts are examples of how the line between expert and learner could be blurred at times because both the *aspirante* and the protégé shared some of the roles and were coordinating their moves to contribute to the main goals of the activities. The goals established by the *aspirante* were to read for understanding and support digital literacy learning and research skills and the goal established by the child was to create a third video.

Emergent Learning of the Discourse of Science and Technology Outcomes

The LCM afterschool program provided a context in which texts written by Latino authors, which presented personal perspectives and experiences, made it possible to engage protégés in starting learning of technology and tools employed by scientists.

Problem Solving

The main activity in the creation of the video involved problem solving. The process presented the learner with several technological challenges or problems that needed to be solved. In this case, the protégé had difficulties finding the site, Animoto; opening a new tab; capturing images; and uploading pictures, especially with respect to the time required to upload the images.

When faced with these challenges, the protégé used different strategies. For example, he tried to solve the problems and made a few attempts. When those efforts failed, he asked for assistance. He also talked to himself (or to the computer) when he could not capture and transfer images. Nevertheless, in spite of these challenges and some failed attempts, César maintained a strong sense of self-efficacy and a positive view of himself as a user of digital tools. The *aspirante* also used different strategies when supporting César. For example, she proposed alternative/solutions, demonstrated how she would solve the problem, acknowledged when she did not know how to do something, and attempted to solve the problem with him. She also offered various levels of support, from finding music and images for him to use for his video to assisting with and taking over the most challenging parts, always giving him choices, such as asking him what types of music he liked. The protégé, as previously mentioned, sometimes accepted and at other times rejected those solutions.

An Inquiry Perspective

Developing an inquiry perspective was a primary objective of both activities—during the reading of the informational text and during the production of the video. Both the *aspirante* and the protégé engaged in inquiry through two types of inquiry language acts that Lindfors (1999) called information seeking and wonderings. Information seeking inquiry acts include facts, clarifications, justifications, explanations, and confirmations that support the speaker in understanding or making sense of something. Wondering inquiry acts are those in which the speaker invites speculations, conjectures, entertains ideas, considers possible words, and engages another in playing with possibilities, reflecting, considering, and exploring.

Making Choices

During the creation of the video, making choices was one of the defining characteristics of the main activity although, as illustrated, it was a salient characteristic of the reading time. The protégé showed urgency as he negotiated the activity and attempted to complete it during the computer time. The protégé took the lead, established goals (to make a third video), initiated the next step in the process, asked for support, listened and considered alternatives presented by the *aspirante* (e.g., music for the video), rejected alternatives, and selected from different alternatives what he wanted for the video. He also established the end of process to his satisfaction and evaluated the final product.

The *aspirante* also made choices and varied her roles from following his lead, supporting his goal, reminding him of the next step, inviting him to take the next step, and asking him about his knowledge as she assessed the protégé's learning and adjusted the information she wanted to share. She also deliberated about the next step, assisted the protégé as he completed the next steps, and took over when the task was too difficult. The latter occurred at the end of the learning experience when, searching for alternatives for background images and music to complete the last details of the video, the protégé made certain final decisions. She also evaluated the final product, giving it a score of "very good."

Attention to Accuracy

Although kept to a minimum, during the reading event, the teacher candidate corrected the pronunciation of some words, such as "horns" and *Tenochtitlán*, even though the focus of the reading event was clearly on meaning rather than on accuracy of pronunciation (given that there were many difficult words). The protégé also interrupted the *aspirante* and corrected her or offered alternative explanations about the animals in the pictures. During the creation of the video, the *aspirante* sometimes clarified, challenged, or further probed the protégé's interpretations or information. These corrections and interpretations were integrated harmoniously within the flow of the main activities.

RETHINKING RESONANCE: NEW CONCEPTUAL UNDERSTANDINGS

Integrating digital literacies and literature into a curriculum should not be an issue of "either/or" for both types of texts provide unique and important experiences that can better prepare children to participate in twenty-first-century learning and literacies (see also Dewey, 1938, p. 90 and Short, 1999, who discuss the need to overcome the "either-or" mentality). This case study offers an example of how the protégé's transactions with literature informed the digital text that he created that day by challenging the dichotomy some may see between digital texts and print-base texts. Both types of texts have the potential to provide children with an aesthetic experience, an experience that helps children to enjoy and engage in reading and learning, and an inquiry stance that equips them with some of the tools used by scientists, as learners need both experiences.

César's engagement during the two activities that made up the session raises questions about the nature of the readings and reading activities that we provide in schools that lead a curious and smart child, such as César, to develop a negative view of himself as a reader (and of reading and school, in general) and a positive view of himself as creator of multimodal challenging texts/videos on the computer.

In fact, the trends to standardize education prevent teachers of Latino students from incorporating meaningful pedagogical practices, such as transworld pedagogy, that support learning of twenty-first-century digital literacies and deep learning because the curricula that most bilingual children receive focus heavily on providing only conventional basic literacy skills in English. Moll (2010) describes such mandates as a regime of standardization that fails to mobilize the social, cultural, and linguistic processes of diverse communities as the most important resources for positive educational change.

The Longhorn Amigos Clase Mágica research project joins the body of work showing that Latino children (from working class families) are not passive or disinterested learners, but rather, they are active meaning makers who are engaged in interpretive work as readers and users of technology and who, with the proper support, can engage in inquiry and become producers of their own multimodal texts. The three short videos that César created in the after-school program could be considered the "buds" or "flowers" of development that Vygotsky (1978) referred to, rather than the "fruits" of development (p. 86) in terms of digital literacy learning and in the learning of science discourse. These types of learning practices allow the learner to begin to act, with some degree of effectiveness, before becoming completely competent (Gee, 2007), which helps the learner to develop an identity as a technology literate individual. Building curriculum taking into account learners' interests remain a key element to sustain learners' engagements with school work. There is a clear implication for teacher preparation programs to prepare teacher candidates to enact transworld pedagogy that facilitates hybrid learning contexts where children learn through literature, digital literacies, and multiple languages.

NOTES

1. The after-school program mirrored and adapted *La Clase Mágica* program developed by Vásquez (2003).
2. The children also read culturally relevant literature from the Southwest, such as Joe Hayes's stories.
3. For a list of recommended texts, see books recognized in the Américas Book Awards for Children and Young Adult Literature (www4.uwm.edu/clacs/aa/index.cfm); the Tomás Rivera Mexican American Children's Book award (riverabookaward.org), and the Pura Belpré award (www.ala.org/alsc/awardsgrants/bookmedia/belpremedal).

REFERENCES

Ada, A. F. (2003). *A Magical Encounter: Latino Children's Literature in the Classroom* (second ed.). Boston, MA: Pearson Education.
Delgado-Bernal, D. (2002). "Critical Race Theory, Latino Critical Theory, and Critical Raced-Gendered Epistemologies: Recognizing Students of Color as Holders and Creators of Knowledge." *Qualitative Inquiry*, 8(1), 105–126.
Dewey, J. (1938). *Experience and Education*. New York: Collier Books.
Dyson, A. H., and Genishi, C. (2005). *On the Case: Approaches to Language and Literacy Research*. New York: Teachers College Press.
Erickson, F. (1986). "Qualitative Methods in Research on Teaching." In M. C. Wittrock (ed.), *Handbook of Research on Teaching* (third ed.) (119–161). New York: Macmillan.
Fránquiz, M., Martínez-Roldán, C. I., and Mercado, C. (2010). "Teaching Latina/o Children's Literature in Multicultural Contexts: Theoretical and Pedagogical Possibilities." In S. Wolf, K. Coats, P. Enciso, and C. Jenkins (eds.), *Handbook of Research on Children's and Young Adult Literature* (108–120). New York and London: Taylor and Francis and Routledge.
Garza, C. (1999). *Magic Windows/Ventanas mágicas*. San Francisco, CA: Children's Book Press.
Gee, J. P. (2007). *What Video Games Have to Teach Us About Learning and Literacy*. New York: Palgrave MacMillan.
Knobel, M., and Lankshear, C. (2008). "Remix: The Art and Craft of Endless Hybridization." *Journal of Adolescent and Adult Literacy*, 52(1), 22–33.
Lave, J., and Wenger, E. (1991). *Situated Learning: Legitimate Peripheral Participation*. Cambridge, UK: Cambridge University Press.
Lindfors, J. W. (1999). *Children's Inquiry: Using Language to Make Sense of the World*. New York: Teachers College Press.
Martínez-Roldán, C. M. (2005). "The Inquiry Acts of Bilingual Children in Literature Discussions." *Language Arts*, 83(1), 22–32.
Martínez-Roldán, C. M., and Smagorinsky, P. (2011). "Computer-Mediated Learning and Young Latino/a Students' Developing Expertise." In P. R. Portes and S. Salas (eds.), *Vygotsky in Twenty-First Century Society: Advances in Cultural Historical Theory and Praxis with Non-Dominant Communities* (162–179). New York: Peter Lang.

Medina, C. (2006). "Interpreting Latino/a Children's Literature as Critical Fictions." *ALAN Review*, 33(2), 71–77.

Moll, L. C. (2010). "Mobilizing Culture, Language, and Educational Practices: Fulfilling the Promises of *Mendez* and *Brown*." *Educational Researcher*, 39(6), 451–460.

Mora, P. (2000). *My Own True Name: New and Selected Poems for Young Adults*. Houston, TX: Piñata Books/Arte Público Press.

Prensky, M. (2001). "Digital Natives, Digital Immigrants." *On the Horizon (NCB University Press), 9*(5). Retrieved September 19, 2012 from www.marcprensky.com/writing/prensky%20%20digital%20natives,%20digital%20immigrants%20-%20part1.pdf.

Reinking, D., and Carter, A. (2007). "Accomodating Digital Literacies within Conceptions of Literacy Instruction for a New Century." In B. J. Guzzetti (ed.), *Literacy for the New Millennium* (Vol. 2, 139-155). Westport, CT: Praeger.

Rogoff, B. (2003). *The Cultural Nature of Human Development*. New York, NY: Oxford University Press.

Short, K. G. (1999). "The Search for 'Balance' in a Literature-Rich Curriculum." *Theory Into Practice*, 38(3), 130–137.

Vásquez, O. (2003). La Clase Mágica: *Imagining Optimal Possibilities in a Bilingual Community of Learners*. Mahwah, NJ: Lawrence Erlbaum.

Vygotsky, L. S. (1966/1933). *Play and its Role in the Mental Development of the Child* (C. Mulholland, trans.). *Voprosy psikhologii, 6*. Retrieved August 11, 2010, from www.all-about-psychology.com/support-files/play-and-its-role-in-the-mental-development-of-the-child.pdf

——— (1978). *Mind in Society: The Development of Higher Psychological Processes*. (M. Cole, V. John-Steiner, S. Scribner, and E. Souberman, eds. and trans.) Cambridge, MA: Harvard University Press.

Yarbro-Berjano, Y. (1996). "Chicana Literature from a Chicana Feminist Perspective." In M. Herrera-Sobek, and H. Viramontes (eds.), *Chicana Creativity and Criticism: New Frontiers in American Literature* (second ed.), (213–219). Albuquerque, NM: University of New Mexico Press.

ELEVEN

Chanzas: The Probability of Changing the Ecology of Mathematical Activity

Craig Willey, Carlos A. LópezLeiva, Zayoni Torres, and Lena Licón Khisty

WORKING TOWARD HARMONY

Latinas/os[1] continue to be this country's educational problem children in mathematics. Their pattern of underachievement in this content area is tenacious, and is among the lowest of all the major racial and ethnic groups in our society (Perie, Grigg, and Dion, 2005; Robelen, 2011). Moreover, Latinas/os' performance is weakest in mathematical problem solving (NCES, 2004), the area that involves the most language use (for example, word problems) and understanding of meanings as opposed to memorization of procedures.

As we examine Latinas/os' status in mathematics, it is worth considering if and how Spanish relates to mathematics learning. A significant proportion of Latinas/os are bilingual/bicultural students in that they either speak, to some extent, both Spanish and English, live in homes and communities where two languages are used substantially, and/or have caretakers who use one or both languages to communicate. In other words, we can safely assume that students have experiences, knowledge, and histories that are bilingual even if they are not proficient in Spanish. Socially, culturally, and politically, Spanish is a critical factor to understanding Latinas/os' learning and education. However, for too long, we have failed to worry about Spanish in mathematics education, effectively discounting the role it plays in the learning process of Latina/o youth.

Over the years, research has pointed to aspects of classroom dialogue that support or hinder Latinas/os' learning of mathematics and has noted that effective teachers of mathematics with Latinas/os use and develop Spanish in instruction (e.g., Khisty, 1995, 2001, 2004a; Khisty and Viego, 1999). In addition, other work has documented how students use Spanish and English together to make sense of complex mathematical ideas (Moschkovich, 2002, 2007). Nevertheless, there remains a dearth of knowledge in terms of how the utilization of Spanish facilitates Latinas/os' mathematics learning, or how the marginalization of Spanish influences students' interactions with mathematics. While mathematical concepts certainly can be represented in symbolic form, we must still think critically about how the meaning of those symbols is developed via language.

In spite of research that points to the importance of bilingualism in Latinas/os' learning mathematics, English is still designated, either explicitly or de facto, as the language medium for learning mathematics. In essence, by this act, the cognitive and cultural connections between students and the language of their home, community, and histories are ignored or dismissed by teachers, researchers, teacher educators, and/or mathematics curriculum developers (Pitvorec, Willey, and Khisty, 2011). The result is a disconnect with the knowledge and background students bring to mathematics, which can eventually lead to their alienation, or lack of harmony with the subject. In this chapter, we describe an after-school project, *Los Rayos*,[2] that was specifically designed to reinforce and enhance Latinas/os' connection to mathematics through a bilingual/bicultural approach to doing mathematics (Khisty, 2004b).

For many years before *Los Rayos*, the work around *La Clase Mágica* (e.g., Vásquez, 1994, 2003, see chapter 2) appeared to offer tremendous potential for exploring and addressing issues related to Latinos/as' performance in mathematics. Thus, it was this which we drew upon *La Clase Mágica*—with its principles rooted in cultural historical activity theory, play, and biliteracy—for exploring rearrangements in the ecology of Latinas/os' engagement in mathematical activity. In addition, *Los Rayos* drew on an effective model of bilingual integrated mathematics, science, and literacy, *Finding Out/Descubrimiento (FO/D)* (De Avila, Duncan and Navarrete, 1987). Together, *La Clase Magica* and *FO/D* provided us with a conceptual model for examining a bilingual/bicultural approach to mathematics with Latinas/os. This model is discussed in a later section.

Lastly, we wish to note that in our project, we used *Los Rayos* (i.e., lighting bolts) to depict the energetic, magical, transformative, and spontaneous yet complex occurrence of Latina/o students learning mathematics bilingually. In addition, we use the term *chanzas* deliberately to capture the complex role of language in mathematics. We use it to mean "opportunity" for Latinas/os to gain experience in advanced mathematical content such as probability. *Los Rayos* specifically was non-remedial, choosing instead to use dialogues to support the application of mathe-matical content that was just beyond what students could do at the given moment, and which they might not get in their regular classrooms. More importantly, *chanzas* represents the "opportunity" for students to utilize Spanish—and all the experiential and cultural knowledge associated with it—to learn mathematics. Finally, *chanzas* means our "opportunity" to demonstrate the positive possibilities inherent in utilizing a bilingual/bicultural ecology of learning mathematics with Latinas/os. *Chanzas* (i.e., opportunities), then captures Latinas/os learning mathematics through the *mestizaje* of linguistic, cultural, and mathematical practices that syn-chronize the dual nature of both Latino culture and knowledge and the application of the sacred sciences (see chapters 1 and 2).

In the sections that follow, we begin by briefly presenting the intellec-tual foundation of *Los Rayos,* along with a description of *Los Rayos.* We then discuss three patterns of language use that emerged as students engaged in mathematics to demonstrate the affordances offered by native language use as a learning resource for participants' transformation. Through this, we also highlight the complex ways we interact with lan-guage (i.e., Spanish and English) while doing mathematics. We close our discussion with some concluding thoughts and implications regarding the importance of synchronizing a subject like mathematics with the world of Latina/o students and as bilingual "doers" of mathematics.

CONCEPTUAL RESONANCE: WHAT DO WE KNOW?

In this section, we provide a general background of *Los Rayos,* including some of its key features. Importantly, this project was developed with considerations for the political and educational situation of Latinas/os in the United States. While public discourse has historically located the source of underachievement within the Chicana/o family or community (Tejeda, Martinez, and Leonardo, 2000), *Los Rayos'* model moves away from a deficit perspective and specifically confronts prevalent assump-tions about bilingual students in mathematics, the role of bilingualism in this content area, and approaches to learning the content in general, while simultaneously offering visions of more and better *chanzas.* Like other domains, mathematical concept development does not occur with-out plentiful and meaningful opportunities to engage in dynamic prob-lem-solving situations. More often than not, these experiences are charac-terized by dialogic interactions. If Spanish is a student's strongest learn-ing resource, then Spanish ought to be utilized and built upon not only to access important mathematical ideas, but also to develop a mathematical biliteracy, one that is operable in multiple language environments.

Unfortunately, mathematics education among Latinas/os is over-whelmingly characterized by an over-emphasis on low-level content, basic procedures, and remediation; curriculum and instruction primarily in English; and individual and silent work norms (Gándara and Contreras, 2009; Lipman, 2004). Flores (2007) demonstrates unequally distributed opportunities to learn mathematics amongst students. Specifically, he notes that African American, Latino, and low-income students are less likely to have access to experienced and qualified teachers, more likely to face low expectations, and less likely to receive equitable funding per student. He suggests "reframing the problem in terms of opportunity gaps focus[ing] attention on examining the lack of access to the very resources that contribute to the success of more privileged students" (p. 40).

Our intention was to challenge this reality and to give Latinas/os opportunities, or *chanzas*, to do more advanced mathematics than they typically received in school, provide them with experiences where biliteracy—particularly related to mathematics—was valued, and socialize them toward a more dialogic and problem solving orientation to mathematics. However, it should be noted that our objective was not to "teach" mathematics. Instead, our focus was to have students experience, do, and communicate mathematics bilingually.

For four years, *Los Rayos* met for one and a half hours, twice a week, at a hosting public school. The dual-language (Spanish and English) school, located in a large urban area, has a population of 98 percent Latino, 91 percent low income students, 9 percent special education students, and 62 percent English Language Learners (Office of Research, Evaluation, and Accountability, 2008). The students were either U.S.-born or immigrants, and mostly come from a Mexican background. *Los Rayos* served approximately fourteen to twenty Latina/o students each semester. The program began when the students were in third grade and lasted through their sixth grade year. Most students continued participation after the first year of *Los Rayos*, even though the school offers a variety of after-school activities such as tutoring, guitar lessons, and martial arts. In essence, we have known most of these Latina/o students (with a majority female) for four academic years.

The Intellectual Foundation of Los Rayos

Like *La Clase Mágica*, our work drew from sociocultural and activity theory (e.g., Engeström, 1999; Vygotsky, 1978). A major assumption of this perspective is that human development is fundamentally social in nature, rooted in concrete communicative activity and/or participation in local practices. Additionally, development stems from increased familiarity with cultural-historical mediating tools and artifacts, especially language (Vygotsky, 1978). Here language emphasizes dialogue as a key element in development (Bahktin, 1981; Wells, 2002). This perspective shifts us from the view that learning is an individual, internal phenomenon to a view that learning is rooted in social interaction. As Holt (2008) explains:

> concepts such as identity exist and persist because of encounters with, and orientations to, the language, manners, and material arrangements of the social world. . . . We control who we are and create a new identity . . . through the external control of mediating artifacts. . . . Our experience of the world is shaped by our existing competence in using objects, itself influenced by the experience of our peers and the accumulated wisdom of previous generations. (p. 55)

The model below (Figure 11.1) provides an overview of how we conceptualized this particular activity system:

Los Rayos' main objective was the activation and development of participating students' resources through a system of mathematical activity in which students' own resources were challenged and supported. At the same time, the development of these resources took place through a series of highly cognitive demanding tasks to be elaborated on and solved through a dialogical learning process in a community of participants who share similar resources (cultural, linguistic, and mathematical), but at different academic and developmental levels.

In designing *Los Rayos*, our goal was to use this activity system as a means to better understand how best to support linguistically diverse

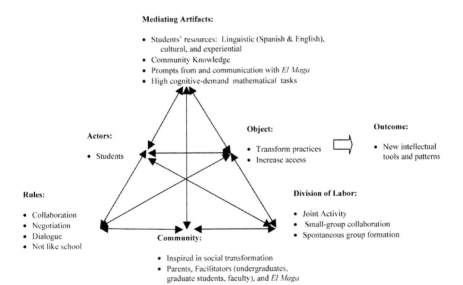

Figure 11.1. Activity System of Los Rayos (adapted from Engeström, 1999). Engeström, Y. (1999). "Activity Theory and Individual and Social Transformation." In Y. Engeström, R. Miettinen, R-L. Punanmäki, (eds.), *Perspectives on Activity Theory* (pp. 19–38). New York: Copyright © 1999 Cambridge University Press.

learners in mathematics (Khisty, 2004b). As such, it was composed of multiple layers of complementary, interacting elements that included the participation of an intergenerational-organized community of adults (teacher candidates [*aspirantes*], research fellows, and mothers of participating children) and protégés around mathematical activities, norms, and expectations that set direction for the after-school club. Overarching all of this and based on the work of *FO/D*, the environment emphasized the value of Spanish and biliteracy, or the use of two languages for communication, including writing—in this case, mathematically. Following *La Clase Mágica* and the Fifth Dimension (Cole, 2006) after-school projects, one of the basic principles comprises the intersection of learning and play. For example, mathematics was presented in whimsical or humorous short stories and/or games defusing the pressures or anxieties typically found in mathematics classrooms.

Design Features of Los Rayos

As mentioned above, one of the objectives of *Los Rayos* was to put protégés in a situation where they had to construct new meanings around what it means to do mathematics; in essence, they were actively co-constructing new sociomathematical norms. Per our leadership, protégés were encouraged and supported to be self-directed, creative, interactive, and self-responsible in everything they do. They were expected to make decisions of various kinds, such as what particular sets of problems they would like to work on (e.g., probability, patterns, etc.). They chose whether to work in groups that included other students, university representatives, and/or, in some cases, parents. They also had the option to work one-on-one with a favorite peer; however, they were discouraged from choosing to work alone. Protégés could even change the direction of activities, as when they asked to use some of the after-school time to draw and connect these drawings to mathematics. In voluntarily responding to an invitation to participate in *Los Rayos*, the students implicitly self-identified themselves as "someone interested in mathematics."

A second objective of our after-school project was to give protégés experiences in mathematics that they would not normally get in classrooms for many reasons. Our assumption was that all protégés are able to do much more in mathematics than is often expected and that with various mediational tools, especially dialogue with more experienced others (Vygotsky, 1978), they can accomplish a good deal, including traditional skill development. Through the different tasks, they not only engaged in operating numbers and concepts expected for their grade-level, but they also explored concepts often included at later grades. Latinas/os are often willing and capable of achieving at high academic levels, though schools often view them at risk and in need of remedial interventions (Vásquez, 2005). In general, the after-school activities focused on problem-solving and non-remedial mathematics, as presented in the examples below. Many of the mathematics problems were adapted from reform-oriented, upper-level, or high school curricula, such as the Interactive Mathematics Program (Fendel, Resek, Alper, and Fraser, 2000). The problems were written in both Spanish and English and in a style more appropriate for younger learners. Protégés solved open-ended problems in probability and algebraic thinking (patterns), and activities that emphasized rational numbers (e.g., creating recipes using proportional reasoning) or explored mathematics in everyday life situations, such as their community and home. Protégés also created digital stories to "re-tell" their problem-solving process, as well as put forth related, self-devised mathematical problem situations for the audience to solve.

Third, we prioritized the inclusion of a bilingual role model and bilingual mathematical communication. As in other Fifth Dimension-inspired projects, students communicated electronically with a whimsical mathematics wizard, *El Maga*, who lives in cyberspace (Cole, 2006; Vásquez 2003, see chapter 6). At the end of each after-school session, protégés wrote to *El Maga* about their mathematical experiences for that day, asked questions they had about mathematics or *El Maga*, and/or posed their own problems. *El Maga*, in a friendly and informal way, responded to protégés, encouraging them to capitalize on their cultural, linguistic, and personal resources to engage in new problem solving situations and concepts. *El Maga*, on the one hand, represented the magical, imaginative side of protégés' engagement and thinking; on the other hand, *El Maga* represented the continuous source of challenges and wisdom, encouraging all participants to work collaboratively and solve the challenging tasks.

In our context, *El Maga* served three primary functions: the wizard was a role model for a mathematical expert who always communicated in Spanish, but who could also use a hybrid combination of Spanish and English similar to what protégés may use; the wizard prompts protégés to explain their mathematical thinking and to explore their own ideas, and thus, encourages and models mathematical communication and norms; and, lastly, by the nature of electronic communication, the wizard fosters mathematical writing including the use of drawings. This electronic writing is a key mediational tool and is part of creating a natural purpose and context for communicating mathematically. Protégés exchanged messages with *El Maga* sharing their ideas, solutions, feelings, conceptualizations, accomplishments, and limitations while engaging with the tasks. Communication between *El Maga* and the protégés engaged them in writing mathematically through the necessity to re-articulate their arguments and mathematical concepts that they worked on at Los Rayos. This important process in teaching and learning mathematics is frequently neglected in the classroom (Chval and Khisty, 2009). Facilitators also developed meta-awareness of the protégés' mathematical thinking and abilities through virtually taking the place of or becoming *El Maga* via cyber-learning exchange (*El Maga*-student), and at the same time, maintained the wittiness, the charm, the wisdom, the emphasis on mathematics, and especially the care characteristic of *El Maga*. This activity system provides a multilayered, multidimensional teaching-learning process that affects all its participants at their own developmental level in mathematics.

Fourth and perhaps most important, the Spanish language is strategically used to reinforce the social and cognitive value of language and to dispel its association with deficit perspectives, especially academic ones such as mathematics. All materials are in both Spanish and English, which radically distinguishes *Los Rayos* from most mathematics classrooms across the country. Another critical aspect of the project is that Latina/o youth interact with "role models" (e.g., Latina/o undergraduate students[3], faculty, and graduate students) who proudly use two languages not only for social communication, but for engaging in mathematics, too. Since most of the other after-school "personnel" speak Spanish, Spanish was utilized even when students themselves may speak in English. However, both languages were used as linguistic tools for meaning-making.

Lastly, the afterschool club involved multiple participant groups: grade-school students, Latina/o undergraduate students (many of whom were *aspirantes*), graduate student researchers, post-doctoral researchers, university faculty, and frequently, parents of the children. Everyone acted as a facilitator for assisting protégés with comprehending the tasks to be accomplished and doing the mathematics. However, emphasis was placed on encouraging protégés to be active problem solvers and minimizing "telling" protégés how to do the mathematics. Graduate students and faculty actively participated in the activities with the protégés and built relationships with the participants and, therefore, were not detached observers. These adults continued the modeling of bilingual mathematicians. Parents, too, became critical to the success of the afterschool club for their ability to speak Spanish and make connections to protégés' experiences outside of school (Morales, Vomvoridi, and Khisty, 2010).

REPOSITIONING METHODOLOGY: BEYOND RELEVANCE TO THE SACRED SCIENCES

The issues and concepts related to the use of Spanish in mathematics that we present are based on extensive ethnographic work carried out during four years of conducting the after-school program (Khisty, 2004). Qualitative data (i.e., videotapes of participation, individual and focus group interviews, fieldnotes, and student work) were gathered as part of our work to investigate and document the language and cultural resources Latinas/os bring to doing mathematics. What we discuss hereafter is a result of collaborative reflection upon the patterns or themes that surfaced as we conducted numerous analyses on various aspects of this work and from our own participant observations.

In addition to gathering observation field notes, the various working groups of student participants were videotaped during each after-school session, or twice per week, for approximately eighteen weeks of each school year. Each session yielded approximately five sets of video data, one set per working group, along with electronic writings of each student. Additionally, protégés were periodically and informally interviewed both individually and in focus groups. All names used are pseudonyms.

We, the authors of this chapter, were all participant observers, so we witnessed first-hand the dynamics we describe below. The video data were analyzed using an iterative process drawn from methods of grounded theory (Glaser and Strauss, 1967), whereby patterns or themes emerged from initial holistic viewing of the data, and then analytic categories and themes were refined by revisiting the data. No fewer than six people collaborated to identify relevant themes (including those presented in this chapter), survey the extensive data set for additional instances, and collectively analyzed and interpreted the situation to assure accuracy and validity.

SYNCHRONIZING MULTIPLE WORLDS: FINDINGS AND CHALLENGES

Protégés' Use of Spanish for Conceptual Understanding in Mathematical Activity

One of the protégés' favorite activities was the Counters Game, a probability activity from a high school curriculum that we modified for fourth grade students (see Razfar, Willey, Radosavljevic, and Khisty, 2008). Players tried to predict which sums of two dice would "come up" most frequently by placing counters on the possible sums of 2-12. Players took turns rolling the dice, summing the two numbers, and removing counters until one person had removed all of his or her counters to win the game. After a few rounds, players began to realize that the sums in the middle of the range were rolled more frequently, mirroring a normal distribution.

In our observations of protégés playing this game, we found them switching between English and Spanish regularly and in purposeful ways (Razfar et al., 2008). During the Counters Game, there were over 500 instances of Spanish use, 270 instances of English use, and nearly 100 instances of code-switching or hybrid practices. Given the dynamic participation structure, code-switching occurred systematically for the purposes of assistance, making tasks more comprehensible, asking questions, making jokes, including others, and even sometimes excluding central or peripheral participants. Students often indexed their awareness of speakers and non-speakers of a particular code by switching to accommodate the speaker and to maximize understanding. The amount of Spanish use was substantially more than English (approximately 2:1), and this ratio increased over time as participants became more comfortable with each other and with the game.

One explanation of this phenomenon relates to the tensions that exist within a bilingual language environment where protégés interact, they make language choices (Razfar, Khisty, and Chval, 2011). It is not as though protégés only operate in the language in which they are most proficient, nor that their proficiency in either language remains the same. Furthermore, as will be discussed below, it is not as though both languages hold the same status. Each unique, sociomathematical interaction comes with certain dynamics and conditions, and each corresponding language choice is made purposefully. Naturally, these interactions are filled with a variety of different tensions. It may very well be that protégés are becoming accustomed to maneuvering within and through these tensions as they become masterful participants in a different kind of mathematical community (see Khisty and Willey, 2013), moving towards an acceptance of new norms and practices—one being the regular use of Spanish in mathematical activities.

Another explanation could be the elimination of specific anxieties. For example, as the protégés got to know each other better and became more familiar with the game, they appeared to shed any insecurities related to language and engage more in the social and meaning-making process. Student conversations, while engaging in the mathematical task, were many times more likely to be in Spanish, which also suggests that protégés used Spanish as they became more "expert" in doing the task. These observations reinforce the idea that Spanish (and a hybrid of Spanish and English) is an integral part of Chicana/o protégés' engagement in mathematics and counter the long-standing notion that mathematics ought to be taught exclusively in English amongst bilingual learners given its symbolic form.

Spanish as a Resource for Advanced Mathematical Work

Within the mathematics community, problem solving is considered a critical goal in advanced mathematical thinking (Van de Walle, Karp, and Bay-Williams, 2010). In yet another probability activity, we observed that protégés tended to use Spanish as a means of engaging in mathematical problem solving, particularly as they worked with each other to create meaning; they also used Spanish for their written explanations of their problem solutions. For example, in a problem that asked how many different kinds of pizza can be made of two toppings given a certain number of toppings, two students, Katia and Marisol, use Spanish to make sense of the problem as evidenced in the following dialogue ("MR" represents Marisol, and "KA" represents Katia; both students are working with an *aspirante* as facilitator "F"):

MR: (Reads the problem) My favorite toppings are mushrooms and onions, I don't know how you call them, olives. What are yours? Write and tell me your favorite toppings.

F: *Ahorita están escribiendo tus ingredientes favoritos.* [Right now you are writing down your favorite ingredients.]

MR: Okay this is mine. (Reads what she has written thus far, see Figure 1) *Mi favorito es queso y piña y lo que más me gusta es comer la pizza . . .* mmmm. [My favorite is cheese and pineapple and what I like most is eating the pizza . . . .mmmm.]

MR: *Yo leo en inglés.* [I will read in English.]

KA: *¿Cuál es la pregunta?* [What is the question?]

F: *Dice cuántas pizzas diferentes con dos ingredientes va tener que preparar? ¿Qué vamos a hacer para encontrar la respuesta?* [It asks how many different pizzas with two ingredients do you need to prepare? What are we going to do to find the answer?]

KA: *Yo puse hongos, aceitunas, y cebollas, y pepperonis.* [I put mushrooms, olives, and onions, and pepperonis.]

F: *¿Entonces los combinaste?* [So you combined them?]

KA: (KA nods agreeing). *Y éste es el que le gusta.* [And this is what he likes.]

As we can observe in this dialogue, all the participants move between Spanish and English as they please. They choose to read in English even though the mathematics task is presented in both languages. However, most of their discussion is carried out in Spanish. They make sure they understand the question—which is a critical step in problem solving—by going back and reading in Spanish. Nevertheless, the protégés make an error and use more ingredients than the problem indicates. The discussion continues among the three participants to clarify the exact conditions of the problem. This is the type of dialogue that is hoped for from a mathematical perspective in that having the right answer is not the most important item. Instead, the process of making sure one understands the conditions of the problem, developing a plan to solve it, and thinking it through are more important. These protégés are clearly engaged in problem solving—and doing it in Spanish, rather than English most of the time.

In Figure 11.2, we note how Katia writes her solution in Spanish and provides a picture representation of the problem. In mathematics learning, constructing representations of a mathematical idea is a key element

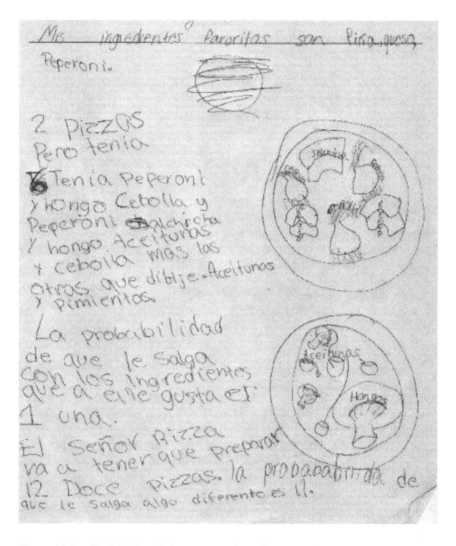

Figure 11.2.   Katia's pictorial representation of a probability activity.

in problem solving. Katia, throughout this episode, used Spanish to create meaning, and used Spanish vocabulary to label the ingredients on the pictures of the pizzas. She also used Spanish to show her thought process and to write a solution to the mathematical problem. From this example, we notice how Spanish was a necessary tool to help Katia make meaning of, to think through, and to solve the mathematical problem.

Challenges: Language Bias (Despite Efforts to "Privilege" Spanish)

Even though the context of this study is a predominantly bilingual community (i.e., dual language school and Spanish-speaking neighborhood), there is still a considerable amount of language bias apparent in the interactions amongst *Los Rayos* participants. Specifically, we found evidence of protégés being marginalized because they were Spanish dominant and certain protégés were reluctant to speak in Spanish. Each year of the after school program, approximately fifteen to eighteen Chicana/os participated. Of these protégés, only three were monolingual English speakers, five were Spanish-dominant, and the rest were bilingual and biliterate. LópezLeiva and Khisty (2009) reported one phenomenon that recurred more than once each year of the three years of the after school program. It always involved one monolingual English protégé (the student was not always the same) "demanding" that the mathematics activities be read in English and that all discussion be done in English likewise. The group members, including the bilingual adult facilitator, would acquiesce to this demand and all interactions after this would be in English. This occurred even though at least one of the protégés in the group only spoke Spanish. The result was that this protégé stopped participating with the group as they engaged in mathematics.

In this example, English was subtly deemed the privileged medium for knowledge and participation and became the means for exclusion. Furthermore, in this instance, we have an example of microaggression, where an English-speaking child, along with the implicit approval of an adult, essentially pushed another student out of the mathematics and signaled to the others a warning of what can happen to them if they speak Spanish. Many things are troubling about this; however, two things are worth noting. First, Chicana/o protégés as young as third grade have already adopted the social "manners" and definitions of which language is for dominance and knowledge—even in a school and an after-school project that strive to develop bilingualism and biliteracy, and even in a community where parents speak Spanish. Second, the bilingual adult (and others who were part of a version of the same event) did not take any action to stop the exclusion of the Spanish-dominant child nor to bring the child back into the group. This is highly significant in that nearly all of the bilingual adult facilitators in the after-school program were Chicana/o pre-service teachers, or persons we hope would be sensitive to exclusionary actions. Moreover, none of the bilingual pre-service teachers raised questions during debriefing about what strategies might be used to meet the needs of both the English-dominant protégé and the Spanish-dominant protégé. The lack of concern for how to deal with such a situation suggested an acceptance that this was simply the way things were—and most likely, the way things would be in their own future classrooms.

Many of the protégés in the after-school program would respond to adult Spanish-speakers in English indicating that they preferred to speak in English even if it was more difficult for them to express complicated ideas in that language. Several would speak only English causing some of the after-school workers to think the protégés did not speak Spanish. Often it was when a parent was present that a student would reveal that she/he could speak Spanish. From these actions and non-verbal signals, it appeared that protégés were embarrassed to speak Spanish publicly, except when their parents were present. Also, even though all materials were in the two languages, protégés often chose the ones in English and ignored what was in Spanish. Here, it should be pointed out that the protégés, most of the *aspirantes*, and even many of the participating researchers had difficulty with mathematics materials or problems written in Spanish. The *aspirantes*—and the researchers—especially noted that they had had little experience in K–12 schooling or at the university doing mathematics in Spanish, and thus, were not as proficient in this form of Spanish compared to conversational Spanish. In essence, even in a bilingual school, mathematics materials and instruction were still in English, and those of us who consider the need for bilingual mathematics instruction could not adequately use this knowledge, because our lack of experience with mathematics in Spanish made it difficult to use Spanish.

Protégés' reluctance to speak Spanish and the difficulty in using Spanish in mathematics points to a general social definition that Spanish is not to be used in schools, especially in the area of mathematics teaching and learning. This message is given through the lack of Spanish materials in mathematics (in some cases, materials exist but are not used) and the lack of mathematics being taught in Spanish. Recently, we encountered a national organization's listserv message where the sender proudly described a new school where all subjects would be taught in both Spanish and English—except for mathematics, which would be taught in English. Our experience in the after-school along with many instances of encountering attitudes such as the one expressed above, suggests an ideology that excludes Spanish from being a viable mediating tool for learning, and results in de facto discrimination against Chicanas/os.

RETHINKING RESONANCE: NEW CONCEPTUAL UNDERSTANDINGS

We are not arguing that protégés should not become proficient in the official language of schools or instruction but should develop second language skills. Rather through transworld pedagogy as proposed in this book (see chapters 1 and 2), protégés can just as easily become bilingual and feel proud of their home language and themselves while developing proficiencies in multiple discourses in English. Moreover, as we have presented, protégés clearly used Spanish as a resource to do more advanced mathematics, including problem solving and content topics often found in upper grades. The essential point here is that "learning language" and "learning through language" are simultaneous (Halliday, 1993). What a student learns and how she/he learns it depends on the context in which learning occurs. However, linguistic choices realize particular kinds of contexts. Various classroom learning experiences are socially constructed events; that is, contexts for learning created by the interactions of teacher and students (Gutierrez, 1995).

Therefore, which language and how language is used constitutes both the context that mediates learning—in this case, mathematics—and the content of what is learned. But, the power of language extends to one's definition of self, one's relationship to a community, and one's status in a wider sociopolitical and cultural milieu (Cummins, 2000). Therefore, language choices mediate the value of protégés' knowledge, how they perceive themselves and their community, and their place in the wider society. This has critical implications for Chicana/os' participation in the important areas of science, technology, and mathematics.

On the one hand, there are limited opportunities for bilingual learners to access their primary language in the mathematics meaning-making process given how little attention is paid to this. Coupled with the sociopolitical pressure in the United States for students to normalize to regular school practices and to fully adopt the dominant language (English), we perceive very limited *chanzas* for these students to promote and develop their own linguistic resources and support their own learning and integrated bilingual identity. On the other hand, we have observed and witnessed in *Los Rayos* how the Chicana/o protégés have successfully accessed their bilingual resources while doing mathematics; thus, we see them having greater *chanzas* to successfully manage their learning in both languages. In fact, we have anecdotal data from the classroom teachers of our afterschool protégés that they stand out positively from other students in mathematics.

Consequently, it becomes evident that in order to responsibly support the development of these bilingual resources, we need a supportive environment that promotes equitable *chanzas* for these students to feel successful and to fully engage as bilingual transworld citizens, students, and doers of mathematics. We call for a critical reconsideration of how we have—or have not—been integrally supporting bilingual students and their linguistic and cultural resources.

Also, we must bring to the foreground issues of language ideologies within mathematics contexts. That is, how language (i.e., Spanish) is valued, treated, promoted, or dismissed is important as students participate in mathematical activities. There is much more that we need to understand about the influence of language ideologies in mathematics and other STEM areas. As has long been established in language socialization (e.g., Ochs, 1988) and more recently articulated in mathematics socialization (e.g., Jackson, 2009), students construct meaning of mathematics as a result of a pattern of activities in which they participate, as well as the discourse that mediates and surrounds these activities. That is, meaning-making should be harmonically balanced between the acquisition of concepts and the discourse used. If, among a group of Spanish speaking learners and within a dual language school, the mathematics discourse is largely in English, this matters!

NOTES

1. We use Latinas/os and Chicanas/os interchangeably. We recognize that the issues of mathematics development pertain to the broader community of Latinas/s than just persons of Mexican descent. However, our work was conducted in a neighborhood we identify as Chicano.

2. The afterschool project was titled *Los Rayos de CEMELA*; for this discussion we have chosen to simply call it *Los Rayos*. We wish to acknowledge the National Science Foundation for funding this research under grant—ESI-0424983. The views expressed here are those of the authors and do not necessarily reflect the views of the funding agency.

3. All undergraduate students (facilitators) are native speakers of Spanish and self-identify as having proficiency in the language.

REFERENCES

Bakhtin, M. (1981). *The Dialogic Imagination*. Austin, TX: University of Texas Press.

Chval, K. B. and Khisty, L. L. (2009). "Bilingual Latino Students, Writing, and Mathematics: A Case Study of Successful Teaching and Learning." In R. Barwell (ed.), *Multilingualism in Mathematics Classrooms: Global Perspectives* (128-144). Bristol, UK: Multilingual Matters.

Cole, M. and The Distributed Literacy Consortium. (2006). *The Fifth Dimension: An After-School Program Built on Diversity*. New York: Russell Sage Foundation.

Cummins, J. (2000). *Language, Power, and Pedagogy: Bilingual Children in the Crossfire*. Tonawanda, NY: Multilingual Matters, Ltd.

De Avila, E. A., Duncan, S. E. and Navarrete, C. (1987). *Finding Out/Descubrimiento*. Northvale, NJ: Santillana Publishing Co.

Engeström, Y. (1999). "Activity Theory and Individual and Social Transformation." In Y. Engeström, R. Miettinen, R-L. Punanmäki, (eds.), *Perspectives on Activity Theory* (19-38). New York: Cambridge University Press.

Fendel, D., Resek, D., Alper, L., and Fraser, S. (2000). *Interactive Mathematics Program*. Emeryville, CA: Key Curriculum Press.

Flores, A. (2007). "Examining Disparities in Mathematics Education: Achievement Gap or Opportunity Gap?" *High School Journal*, 91(1), 29–42.

Gandara, P. and Contreras, F. (2009). *The Latino Education Crisis: The Consequences of Failed Social Policies*. Cambridge, MA: Harvard University Press.

Glaser, B. G., and Strauss, A. L. (1967). *The Discovery of Grounded Theory: Strategies for Qualitative Research*. Hawthorne, NY: Aldine de Gruyter.

Gutiérrez, K. D. (1995). "Unpacking Academic Discourse." *Discourse Processes*, 19, 21–37.

Halliday, M. A. K. 1993. "Towards a Language-Based Theory of Learning." *Linguistics and Education*, 5(2), 93–116.

Holt, R. (2008). "Using Activity Theory to Understand Entrepreneurial Opportunity." *Mind, Culture, and Activity*, 15, 52–70.

Jackson, K. (2009). "The Social Construction of Youth and Mathematics: The Case of a Fifth-Grade Classroom." In D. B. Martin (ed.), *Mathematics Teaching, Learning, and Liberation in the Lives of Black Children* (175–199). New York: Routledge.

Khisty, L. L. (1995). "Making Inequality: Issues of Language and Meanings in Mathematics Teaching with Hispanic Students." In W. G. Secada, E. Fennema and L. B. Adajian (eds.), *New Directions for Equity in Mathematics Education* (279–297). Cambridge: Cambridge University.

——— (2001). "Effective Teachers of Second Language Learners in Mathematics." In M. van den Heuvel-Panhuizen, (ed.), Proceedings of the 25th Conference of the International Group for the Psychology of Mathematics Education, 3, 225–232. Utrecht, Netherlands: The Freudenthal Institute, Utrecht University.

——— (2004a). "Language Diversity and Language Practice: Why Should Mathematics Educators Care?" Paper presented at the Social and Political Thematic Afternoon Session of the 10th International Congress for Mathematics Education, Copenhagen, Denmark.

——— (2004b). "'Los Rayos de CEMELA' After-School Project: The UIC CEMELA Activity." Unpublished manuscript. University of Illinois at Chicago.

Khisty, L. L.and Viego, G.(1999). "Challenging Conventional Wisdom: A Case Study." In L. Ortiz-Franco, N. Hernández, and Y. De La Cruz (eds.), *Changing the Faces of Mathematics: Perspectives on Latinos and Latinas*. Washington, DC: National Council of Teachers of Mathematics.

Khisty, L. L. and Willey, C. (2013). "After-School: An Innovative Model to Better Understand the Mathematics Learning of Latinas/os." In P. Bell, B. Bevan, and A. Razfar (eds.), *Learning-Out-of-School-Time (L.O.S.T.)*. New York: Springer.

Lipman, P. (2004). *High Stakes Education: Inequality, Globalization, and Urban School Reform*. New York: Routledge/Falmer.

LópezLeiva, C. A. and Khisty, L. L. (2009, May). "'Drawing Us Apart from Within Our Village': Appropriation of Exclusionary Practices in the Mathematics Education of Latinas/os." Paper presented at the 3rd Annual Conference of Critical Race Studies in Education, "Reclaiming the Village," Tucson, AZ.

Morales, H. Jr., Vomvoridi-Ivanović, E., and Khisty, L., L. (2011). "A Case Study of Multi-Generational Participation in an After-School Setting: Capitalizing on Latinas/os Funds of Knowledge." In K. Téllez, J. Moschkovich, and M. Civil (eds.), *Latinos and Mathematics Education: Research on Learning and Teaching in Classrooms and Communities*. Greenwich, CT: Information Age Publishing.

Moschkovich, J. (2002). "A Situated and Sociocultural Perspective on Bilingual Mathematics Learners." *Mathematical Thinking and Learning*, 4, 189–212.

——— (2007). "Using Two Languages while Learning Mathematics." *Educational Studies in Mathematics*, 64(2), 121–144.

National Center for Educational Statistics (NCES) (2004). "The Nation's Report Card Mathematics Highlights 2003 (2004-451)." Washington, DC: National Center for Education Statistics U.S. Department of Education.

———— (2011). "Enrollment in Postsecondary Institutions, Fall 2009; Graduation Rates, 2003 and 2006 Cohorts; and Financial Statistics, Fiscal Year 2009." Washington, DC: US Department of Education.

Ochs, E. (1988). *Culture and Language Development: Language Acquisition and Language Socialization in a Samoan Village.* Cambridge: Cambridge University Press.

Office of Research, Evaluation and Accountability, Chicago Public Schools (2008). Retrieved from: research.cps.k12.il.us/cps/accountweb.

Perie, M., Grigg, W., and Dion, G. (2005). "The Nation's Report Card: Mathematics 2005 (National Center for Education Statistics: NCES 2006–453."U.S. Department of Education. Washington, DC: Government Printing Office. Retrieved August 19, 2013 from files.eric.ed.gov/fulltext/ED486444.pdf.

Pimm, D. (1987). *Speaking Mathematically: Communication in Mathematics Classrooms.* London: Routledge.

Pitvorec, K., Willey, C., and Khisty, L. L. (2011). "Toward a Framework of Principles for Ensuring Effective Mathematics Instruction for Bilingual Learners through Curricula." In B. Atweh, M. Graven, W. Secada, and P. Valero (eds.), *Mapping Equity and Quality in Mathematics Education.* New York: Springer.

Razfar, A., Khisty, L. L., and Chval, K. (2011). "Re-mediating Second Language Acquisition: A Socioculutural Perspective for Language Development." *Mind, Culture, and Activity,* 18(3), 195–215.

Razfar, A., Willey, C., Radosavljevic, A., and Khisty, L. L. (2008). "Multimodal Problem Solving and Probability: The Counters Game." Paper presented at the annual meeting of the American Education Research Association, New York.

Robelen, E. (2011, November). "New NAEP, Same Results: Math Up, Reading Mostly Flat." *Education Week,* 31(11).

Setati, M. (2005). "Teaching Mathematics in a Primary Multilingual Classroom." *Journal for Research in Mathematics Education,* 36(5), 447–466.

Tejeda, C., Martinez, C., and Leonardo, Z. (2000). *Charting New Terrains of Chicana/o/Latina/o Education.* Cresskill, NJ: Hampton Press, Inc.

Van de Walle, J. A., Karp, K. S., and Bay-Williams, J. M. (2010). *Elementary and Middle School Mathematics: Teaching Developmentally* (seventh ed.). Boston: Allyn and Bacon.

Vásquez, O. A. (1994). "The Magic of *La Clase Mágica.*" *Australian Journal of Language and Literacy,* 17(2), 120–128.

———— (2003). *La Clase Mágica: Imagining Optimal Possibilities in a Bilingual Community of Learners.* Mahwah, N.J., Lawrence Erlbaum.

———— (2005). "Social Action and the Politics of Collaboration." In P. Pedraza and M. Rivera (eds.) *Educating Latino Youth: An Agenda for Transcending Myths and Unveiling Possibilities,* 321–343. Mahwah, NJ: Laurence Erlbaum.

Vygotsky, L. S. (1978). *Mind in Society: The Development of Higher Psychological Processes.* Cambridge, MA: Harvard University Press.

Wells, G. (2002). "The Role of Dialogue in Activity Theory." *Mind, Culture, and Activity,* 9(1), 43–66.

TWELVE

El Mundo en la Palma de la Mano [The World in the Palm of the Hand]: Bridging Families' Multigenerational Technology Gaps though *La Clase Mágica*

Margarita Machado-Casas

WORKING TOWARD HARMONY

Using the participatory perspective on parental involvement (Vásquez, 2003 and 2006), and the multigenerational community utility-based model of Latino families interactions as a theoretical framework (Machado-Casas, 2006), this chapter explores how Latino/a families involved in *La Clase Mágica* at the University of Texas at San Antonio (LCM@UTSA), an afterschool program, use technology as a bridge for connecting with their children, getting involved with the school, and become part of the community physically and digitally. Mariana, a parent participant in LCM@UTSA reflects:

> *Esta es la primera vez que una escuela quiere enseñarme algo de tecnología. Siempre lo hacen con mis niños y yo los veo como aprenden de esas cosas. Pero a mi me han dejado atrás. Yo no podía hablar con ellos de la tecnología porque no la entendía estábamos hablando diferentes idiomas.* [This is the first time that a school wants to teach me something about technology. They did this with my children and I watched them learn about those things. But I got left behind. I could not talk to them about technology because I did not understand, we were speaking different languages.]

This chapter contributes to a ground-breaking body of research on immigrant families and their access to and use of technology by studying the experiences of both Latino immigrant and native born parents. In this chapter, we examine the experiences of Latino and immigrant families who have elementary school children, Kindergarten through fifth grade, enrolled in *La Clase Mágica* afterschool technology program. Specifically, this chapter explores the ways Latino families in the program use technology to bridge existing cultural and technological divides. The term *family member* is utilized along with the term *parent*, because it better reflects the living situations of Latino students, who often are raised communally by family members such as grandmothers, uncles, and close friends who are considered relatives (Machado-Casas, 2009b).

This research chapter (a) highlights the need to involve families in the use of technology in schools and communities; (b) describes the technology resources available to families in communities and the importance of tapping into these; and (c) provides future educators and community leaders with knowledge about the ways Latino families use and understand technology. The goal is to impact current educational practices and beliefs that fail to acknowledge Latino and Latino immigrant familial differences that affect the advancement of their children and communities overall. In order to explore these issues, current research related to Latino parent involvement in afterschool technology programs, lower computer usage rates among Latinos and the importance of computer literacy will be explored.

COGNITIVE RESONANCE: WHAT DO WE KNOW?

Latinos Parent and Family and Technology Usage

Latinos are the fastest growing ethnic group in the United States (Passel, Cohn, and Lopez, 2010). Historically, computer use among Latinos has consistently lagged behind other populations. Similar trends were found on Internet usage. According to Tseng (2001), Internet access for Hispanic households increased from 12.6 percent to 23.6 percent between 1998 and 2000. Fox (2006) noted that 56 percent of Latinos in the United States use the internet, compared to 71 percent of non-Hispanic whites and 60 percent of non-Hispanic blacks. Between 2006 and 2008, another report found that Internet access for Hispanic households increased from 54 percent to 64 percent (Livingston, Parker, and Fox, 2009).

The most recent report indicates that as a group Latinos are just as connected to the Internet and other forms of social media; however, in groups, differences vary based on age, education, income, immigration status, and language dominance (Lopez, Barrera, and Patten, 2013). Additionally, recent research suggests that family status is linked to computer ownership, with lower-income, Spanish-dominant families less likely to have a computer at home (Lopez, Barrera, and Patten, 2013). Parental perceptions of computer technology may influence negative perceptions held by some Latino students. Low-income, Spanish-dominant children have been found to have greater anxiety using computers, especially when instruction is only in English (Bohlin and Bohlin, 2002). Research findings demonstrate the importance and benefits of establishing after-school technology programs for Latino students and parents that can help improve familial attitudes and beliefs about computers (Rivera, 2008; Ek, Machado-Casas, Sanchez, and Alanís, 2010). Thus, given these factors, it is even more critical for exposing low-income, Spanish-dominant students to technology in schools.

In today's global world, it is extremely important to be digitally literate, as technology affects nearly all aspects of everyday life —academically, personally, and professionally. As of 1999, 95 percent of schools in the United States had access to both computers and the Internet (National Center for Educational Services, 2002). However, since many low-income Latinos have limited access to computers at home or at school, they are likely to lack computer and technology skills, rendering them unqualified for many jobs (Pruit-Mentle, 2002). Further, computers have become a central focus of academic curricula and are a central medium for knowledge distribution. Yet, Latino students' computer access is limited or not cognitively challenged (Warschauer, Knobel and Stone, 2004).

Family Involvement in Technology and Education

Research has consistently shown that children learn well when their parents are actively involved in their learning (Delgado-Gaitán, 1990). Further, parental support and modeling helps to enhance and secure student achievement and provides long-lasting educational gains (Darling-Hammond, 1997). Latino parents have communicated a great desire to be involved in their children's schoolwork (Valdés, 1996; Machado-Casas, Sánchez, and Ek, in press), but due to English language and computer literacy challenges this becomes difficult, particularly when the subject is technology (Vásquez, 2003). In a study conducted by Wilhelm (1998), Latino parents indicated that they do not know how to use a lot of software applications and would like to take computer courses. Such findings point to the various positive implications of involving Latino parents and families in afterschool technology programs.

Duran (2001) assessed how an afterschool technology program designed for low-income Latino immigrant families enhanced computer awareness, basic computer skills, basic word processing skills, and multimedia and telecommunications familiarity. Latino parents involved in the program showed significant gains in every area of assessment over the course of the project; gains were greatest in knowledge of the Internet, specifically in familiarity with multimedia and telecommunications technology. For the parents involved in the program, computer literacy rose from 32 percent to 73 percent. This study proved that parent and family integration into afterschool technology programs can be beneficial.

Further, Duran (2001) noted that the interactions between Latino parents and their children in this program were instrumental in acquiring computer literacy. As parents and children wrote together using computers, they engaged in focused problem solving about language content, language organization, and language form, as mediated by the computer and its software. By exchanging the roles of expert and novice, parents and children were able to explore a range of dimensions relevant to literacy and literacy practice (Duran, 2001).

Overall, the study conducted by Duran (2001) determined that afterschool technology programs for immigrant Latino parents and children are beneficial, as they connect family members, teachers, university students, faculty, and others from the community. Similarly, Valdés (1996) suggested that Latino immigrant families may benefit from exposure to school personnel who might be able to help parents understand educational practices and expectations. Involvement in afterschool technology programs would allow Latino parents such exposure.

In another study, seven elementary school students and their parents were recruited to participate in a pilot afterschool program called Learning Together (Tartakov, Leigh, and Phillips, 2003). The participants were low-income families of various ethnic backgrounds, including Latinos. The aim of the program was to improve literacy and technology skills, and to commit parents to active engagement with their children. Results of the program indicated student perceptions of increased self-efficacy concerning their computer skills. All students also reported feeling excited about their new abilities to work independently on the computers and experiment with new programs (Tartakov, Leigh and Phillips, 2003).

Machado-Casas (2009a) discussed the importance of *utility knowledge,* or the knowledge and skills necessary for immigrant survival, both in the United States and in the country of origin—i.e., skills that go beyond the basic in order to become active participants of today's globalized society. The research, conducted in North Carolina with indigenous immigrants, revealed that many families were robbed and taken advantage of because they did not know how to use technological resources like computers. Many went to local people or services that charged them astronomical amounts to send emails to teachers, send money back home, or pay their utility bills. This research found that families wanted to learn about technology, but many had children who could not be left at home alone while they attended adult programs. Furthermore, there were no programs available to them and their children at the same time. Not having the opportunity to co-learn with their children created a *digital divide* between Latino parents and their children, exacerbating the sense of separation many Latino immigrant parents already feel when communicating with their children, which leads to decreased family communication and closeness, and anxiety about child rearing practices (Machado-Casas, 2009b), similar to what Wong-Filmore (1991) found among Chinese families when the children shifted to the use of English.

Overall, research consistently demonstrates lower computer and technology use by Latinos stemming from their negative attitudes and unfamiliarity associated with lack of access to computers, effectively putting them at a tenuous situation in today's globalized world. Computers and related technologies permeate nearly all aspects of life. Such considerations lead to the importance of afterschool technology programs for Latino parents and children, primarily because they allow Latinos to become familiar with computers and the overall use of technology. This interaction between Latino parents and their children contributes to the family's intellectual resources.

REPOSITIONING METHODOLOGY: BEYOND RELEVANCE TO THE SACRED SCIENCES

As UTSA bilingual education teacher candidates *(aspirantes)* and their protégé worked together during LCM (see chapters 7–9), families were invited to be part of the LCM family on the third Tuesday of every month in technology workshops called *talleres*. In Spanish, the term *talleres* conveys something beyond the simple top-down approach utilized in most workshops; it requires what Vásquez (2003) calls a "participatory approach," where researchers are mediators and families are full participants in their learning processes, collaboratively deciding on the learning process/direction to determine what they would like to learn or how they would like learn it. During these *talleres,* families were invited to reflect on their own journeys as immigrants in the United States and how using technology would help them in their new lives.

As mentioned earlier, *family members* was the term used in addition to parents since it is more inclusive and representative of the reality of our Latino families (Machado-Casas, 2006). Between eighteen and thirty family members participated in the LCM technology *talleres.* Most were Mexican nationals and Mexican Americans, but one family was from Honduras and one was from El Salvador. Each family had one or two children enrolled in the program whose ages ranged from five to ten years old. Family members ranged in age from eighteen to eighty years old, and included young mothers and fathers as well as grandparents. In an effort to increase family participation, free childcare was provided during the LCM technology *talleres.*

Families worked on a series of technology activities that went from the most basic to the use of more difficult tasks. It takes a communal approach to learning, sharing, and teaching families about technology, one that is based on the knowledge they find most useful and necessary for their everyday life (Machado-Casas, 2010). The decision on where to start was initiated using a participatory approach (Vázquez, 2003) in which families become actors in the creation of their knowledge. Families were surveyed on the process interviewed about the importance of technology in school, at work, and with their families. Once there was consensus on the desire to learn about technology, they were asked which specific skills they would like to learn. First, they wanted to learn computer and iPod basics, because those were the technologies being used by their children in the LCM afterschool program. In addition, participant's created *utility knowledge lists* (Machado-Casas, 2009a) of skills that would be useful in their everyday lives, such as sending money home online, getting a Skype account, and an international local phone number. Through this activity, LCM families were asked to become researchers/ collaborators (Delgado-Gaitán, 1990 and 2001), observers, active participants and users of technology in multi-situational spaces in everyday life.

After participating in the LCM afterschool technology and literacy program, the families engaged in monthly in-class discussions led by a researcher as participant. These discussions focused on their experiences, struggles, and lessons learned. Fifteen to twenty parents were given a pre- and post-survey and were interviewed twice about their experiences in the afterschool program.

All of the data, including interviews, researcher field notes and in-class discussion transcriptions were coded and analyzed for themes and patterns. Participant-created digital data such as videos, stories, and work done applications were also analyzed and coded as digital data. Three major themes emerged from the data: (a) technology as a powerful tool for the everyday life of Latino families; (b) multigenerational technology connections; and (c) *nuevas conexións en casa* (new connections in the home), that is moments of multigenerational and situational connections that became possible at home because of the use of technology — technology served as a mediation factor between home interactions that synchronized multiple and complex worlds.

SYNCHRONIZING MULTIPLE WORLDS: FINDINGS AND CHALLENGES

Technology as a Powerful Tool for Everyday Life

When considering technology and schools, families are often ignored. Yet, as stated by Duran (2001), using technology with families in schools is imperative to family development. And, unlike findings of several research studies published about the reticence among Latino families to approach technology, participants in this study were ready and eager to participate in this afterschool technology program. Furthermore, they expressed being "happy" about not being the "digital invisibles" in schools and their communities. This sentiment was echoed by family members who were involved in the afterschool *talleres*. Angela, an immigrant from Mexico involved in the afterschool *talleres*, said:

> *Yo estoy muy contenta que mi hija está en este programa y que ahora ya nos tienen aquí a nosotros también. Yo sentía que era algo que no iba a poder lograr que nunca fuera a llegar a ocupar estas cosas de tecnología. Pero ahora aunque no soy experta, si me siento más cómoda y aunque con miedito ahora si sé que puedo ayudar a mi hija en sus deberes escolares con la computadoras y también que gracias a Dios ya puedo hacer tantas cosas que me hacen la vida más fácil. Como por ejemplo, revisar mi cuenta de teléfono en la Internet, escribir correos a los maestros, y ahora hasta hacer Skype con mi familia en México. Eso me ha ahorrado mucho dinero. Todo porque la LCM me ayudo a conseguir mi correo y tomaron el tiempo de enseñarme.* [I'm very happy that my daughter is in this program and now we are here also. I felt that it was something I was not going to ever be able to use, technology. But now, although I'm no expert, I do feel more comfortable but with little fear, because now I can help my daughter with her homework, the computer, and that now thanks to God I can now do so many things in the computer that makes my life easier. For example, check my cell phone bill online, write emails to teachers, and Skype with my family in Mexico. This has saved me so much money. All because LCM helped me get an email and they took the time to teach me.]

Angela's experience illustrates the transformative power of technology in people's lives (Vásquez, 2008). Technology has become a tool for her everyday life and survival in the United States, and a necessary tool for everyday life that enables Angela to stay connected, both locally and globally. She has been able to open her world to a greater range of communication and understanding—she could communicate with family as well as comprehend how the world of school works. Locally, the use of technology has allowed her to save time and money by using the Internet to take care of time consuming tasks that would require the need for transportation such as going to pay bills, and going to the school to try to make an appointment with the her child's teacher. Globally, she was been able to stay connected with her family in Mexico via Skype without having to travel to Mexico; therefore, saving money in expensive phone calls, while at the same time staying transnationally connected with her family abroad. Similarly, Francisca, a Honduran woman, said:

> *Ya creo que la tecnología se necesita para todo. Y no nos podemos quedar atrás. Se necesita para hacer citas, para el banco, para mandar dinero para todo. Yo antes de estos talleres, pues no sabía de esto. No sabía que podía mandar dinero*

a mi casa en Honduras, que podía pagar el "bill" del agua, con una iPod o computadora. Como no tengo papeles, esto me ayuda mucho. Ya no tengo que salir de la casa y todo se puede hacer así. Yo aprendí que este aparato que se puede cargar en la palma de mi mano tiene adentro todo el mundo. Solo es ocuparlo. [I think we need technology for everything. And we cannot stay behind. We need it (technology) to make appointments, for the bank, to send money and everything. Before the workshops, I did not know about this (technology). I did not know I could send money to my home in Honduras or pay my water bill with an iPod or computer. Since I'm undocumented, this helps me a lot. I no longer have to leave home and I can do everything like that [via Internet]. I learned that this apparatus (the iPod) that fits in the palm of my hand has the whole world inside of it. You just have to use it.]

Francisca echoed Angela's sentiments and emphasized how technology literally places power in the palm of your hand and at the tip of your fingers. As an undocumented immigrant, technology helps her stay protected while simultaneously connecting her to the outside world. Socially, these individuals have the opportunity to get cyber citizenship rights, they get access to the host society, otherwise not available to them because they are undocumented. They no longer have to live in the shadows. The use of the Internet becomes a *cyber-puente* (cyber bridge) that allows these families to be counted, and to no longer live under the discourse of illegality and surveillance (Machado-Casas, 2010). It further makes the socially invisible, digital visible with no boundaries or borders to cross—they hold the world in the palm of their hands, and with a single click they become active participants and contributors of a *mundo cósmico* [cosmic world] where being documented is irrelevant. This idea of holding the world and its possibilities in the palm of your hand becomes an embodiment of the importance and possibilities of mobile technology. It serves as an everyday tool for families to participate and stay connected with the world.

Multigenerational Connections

Countless politicians, professionals, and scholars have explored the concept of the *digital divide,* the gap that exists between people who have access to digital technology and those who do not. The digital divide exists at work, in schools, and most importantly, at home, creating a multigenerational rift between parents and their children, a border that children have crossed and their families have not. Although understanding the impacts of this divide is important, it is even more beneficial to explore how it can be bridged, so families can begin to see technology as a resource, not an obstacle. Juana, another participant, agreed:

Antes de meterme a LCM todo esto de la tecnología me daba mucho terror. Y en casa mis hijos todos tienen teléfonos avanzados e iPod. Todos saben ocupar la computadora y yo no. Bueno que al decirle que no sabía ni como tocarle para mandar textos. Ahora desde que comencé a venir acá, me siento mejor y entiendo mejor lo que hacen los niños cuando juegan en esos aparatos. Ahora yo me siento con ellos, les pregunto que hace, y me enseñan como ocuparlo. Ellos ahora me están enseñando a mí y nos hemos podido comunicar mejor. Por ejemplo, en ver de gritarles que vengan a comer—les mando un texto-:). O les mando un correo preguntándole que quieren comer o cosas así. Ahora la tecnología nos conecta, y nos ayuda. Amazing! [Before entering LCM everything that had to do with technology frightened me. At home, my children all have advanced phones and iPods. They all know how to use the computer and I didn't. I did not even know how to send a text message. Now since I started coming, I better understand what my children do when they play with those things. Now I sit with them, and they help me use it. They are now teaching me and we are communicating better because of it. For example, instead of screaming their names when is time to eat, I send them a text. Or I send an email asking them what they want to eat and things like that. Now technology connects us and helps us.]

Juana's example highlights the reality in many Latino households and what Wong-Filmore (1991) calls intergenerational disconnect where children who are constantly connected via advanced phones, iPods, or the Internet do so at the expense of connections with their families and surroundings. This is a multigenerational gap that is both multisituational and multifaceted (Machado-Casas, 2009), as it represents the disconnection of today's technology-focused generation from their parents and grandparents, who have little knowledge of technology. For Juana, technology had created a major wall between her and her children, a wall she tore down once she began participating in the LCM afterschool *talleres*. This opportunity allowed her to overcome her fears about technology and to use it as a tool of family empowerment. By doing so, she was better able to connect with her children and regained her place as a knowledgeable member of her household—one who used technology in the twenty-first century.

Isabela, an almost eighty-year-old grandmother, came to the *talleres* every month, and although she had a hard time at the beginning mostly because of her fear of breaking the technological apparatus, she learned a lot. She indicated:

A mi me daba mucho miedo tocar todo porque pensaba que lo iba a quebrar. Mis nietos tienen todas esas cosas y yo no sabia nada. Ya tengo un ano que vengo a LCM y si he aprendido mucho. Aunque soy mucho más lenta que los demás . . . me tienen paciencia. En casa antes me ignoraban, como que no tenía nada que decir porque no sabía nada de la tecnología. Como que decían "la abuela no sabe nada de estoy" y así me dejaban, no me hablaban mucho. Ahora en mi casa tenemos algo bueno porque yo también ocupo la computadora y cuando me vio mi hija pues se animo y ahora ella va también. Yo soy bien lenta pero mi hija me ayuda, y mis nietos también me explican si algo no llego a entender. Todos y? yo creo que estamos ayudándonos y estamos aprendiendo bastante." [I was very scared of touching everything because I thought I was going to break it. My grandchildren have all of those things and I didn't know anything about it. I have been coming to LCM for one year, and yes I have learned a lot. Although I'm much slower than everyone else . . . they are very patient with me. Now in my house we have something good because I also use the computer and when my daughter saw me she got excited and she goes to LCM too. I'm very slow but my daughter helps me, and my grandchildren also explain things to me if I don't understand something. I think we are all helping each other and we are learning a lot.]

Literature on the use of technology in schools often does not mention the role of grandparents in child rearing. Isabela's story illustrates the importance of incorporating what many call extended family into school activities. Her example points to the multigenerational and multisituational gaps that are bridged when school activities go beyond the child to include the entire family. In this way, multigenerational home connections are created that enable family members to take on the roles of learner, teacher, and co-constructor of technological knowledge.

Nuevas conexiones en casa *[New Connections in the Home]*

In the digital era, the word *connection* often refers to online access, but LCM families began using this term to explain how they began to connect with each other through technology. María stated:

Ahora en la casa hablamos acerca de lo que los niños hicieron en LCM. Y nos enseñan y nos dicen todo lo que hacen con la tecnología. Ahora la tecnología ya no es para discutir con ellos—aunque a veces todavía lo tengo que hacer porque no quieren apagar la computadora. Pero en la casa ahora tenemos una conexión—nuestra nueva conexión con al computadora y con todos que ahora Ya la ocupamos. [Now in my house we talk about what the kids did in LCM. And they teach and tell us what they do with technology. Now technology is not to argue with them—although sometimes I still have to do it because they don't want to turn off the computer. But now at home we have a connection—our new connection with the computer and with everyone who uses it.]

In this example, Maria explained the shift in attitude in the home toward the use of technology. An activity that caused tension now can be shared by all in the home—what she called their *nueva conexión* [new connection] due to the way the program has incorporated families into the program.

Emilia also elaborated on how technology has given her a new way to connect with her child:

Como me gane una iPod en LCM el año pasado ya ahora en casa tengo la oportunidad de leer con mis hijas en dos idiomas, también ahora podemos hacer cuentos Justas como familias en StoryKit los cuales podemos mandar a nues-

tros familiares in México. Lo que antes hacia digamos con papel y lápiz, ahora lo hago con el iPod. Claro que no remplaza algunas cosas, pero si hace estos momentos más divertidos parar mis hijas y para mí. Ahora la rutina es la tarea y luego a jugar y aprender en el iPod. [Since I won an iPod last year, now at home I have the opportunity to read with my daughters in two languages. Now we can also create stories together as a family in Story-Kit, which we then send to our family members in Mexico. What we used to do with a pen and pencil, now I do with the iPod. Of course it does not replace some things, but it does make those moments together more fun for my daughters and me. Now the routine is homework and then play and learn with the iPod.]

Emilia's example illustrates important changes she has made in her home after participating in the *talleres*. She described a new routine that incorporates bilingual technology use into her family life. Emilia's example shows how technology literacy can serve as a way to bridge multigenerational gaps, and to empower families through fun technologically-related activities. As stated by Vásquez (2008), these technologically-mediated *talleres* are transformative in that they provide families with pedagogical tools "to achieve new ways of enhancing the intellectual capacity of learners" (p. 183). It goes beyond the basic to a greater incorporation into the learning and schooling process—it has become a truly collaborative process. A collaborative process that creates *nuevas conexiones* (new connections) or collaborative moments of multigenerational and situational bilingual connections that become possible at home through the shared use of technology—as previously mentioned—technology serves as a digital mediator between home interactions that synchronize multiple and complex worlds.

RETHINKING RESONANCE: NEW CONCEPTUAL UNDERSTANDINGS

El Mundo en la palma de la mano y en la yema de los dedos [The World in the Palm of the Hand and the Tip of Your Fingers]

By taking a participatory perspective on parent involvement, the people who participated in the LCM afterschool *talleres* were able to find new ways to connect with their families at home, bridging multigenerational and multisituational gaps through the use of play learning and technology. These families overcame fear related to technology and relied on each other's strengths in order to overcome technological barriers. One family member put it best, saying that she now holds "the world in the palm of her hand," and it is up to her to do as much as she can with it. Some families involved in this study have also realized that there are global transnational benefits to the use of technology from home. Some have been able to free themselves from the fear of going out in public, since they are undocumented and live under a constant state of surveillance. Family members in this study have become cyber citizens creating a new *raza cósmica* since they are inhabiting and crossing borders into a new world. A world where everyone who has access to technology is automatically a citizen in a borderless cyber world filled with possibilities where immigrants who are able to use technology get cyber citizenship to complete transactions from the comfort of their homes, thereby providing access to the world and minimizing the risk of getting caught by immigration officials.

Knowledge gained through the LCM afterschool *talleres* allowed family members to change how they view technology, turning what were once multigenerational and multisituational obstacles into strong familial connections. The technology *talleres* have provided families with opportunities to reconnect and share their expertise, allowing each family member to add value. The results of this program are meaningful because they can help communities and schools understand the importance of including families in technology education and can be duplicated nationally and internationally. Incorporating families is imperative, as they too are affected by daily technological changes. This program can serve as a model of how transworld pedagogy can have a global impact by empowering people and placing the whole world in the palms of their hands.

REFERENCES

Bohlin, R. M., and Bohlin, C. F. (2002). "Computer-Related Affect Among Latino Students." *Tech Trends*, 46(2), 29–31.

Darling-Hammond, L. (1997). *The Right to Learn: A Blueprint for Creating Schools that Work.* San Francisco, CA: Jossey-Bass.

Delgado-Gaitán, C. (1990). *Literacy for Empowerment: The Role of Parents in Children's Education.* Bristol, PA: Falmer.

——— (2001). *The Power of Community: Mobilizing for Family and Schooling.* Lanham, MD: Rowman and Littlefield.

Duran, R. (2001). "Latino Immigrant Parents and Children Learning and Publishing Together in an After-School Setting." *Journal of Education for Students Placed at Risk*, 6(1–2), 95–113.

Ek, L. D., Machado-Casas, M., Sánchez, P. and Alanís, I. (2010). "Crossing Cultural Borders: *La Clase Mágica* as a University-School Partnership." *Journal of School Leadership*, 20(6) 820–849.

Fox, J. (2006). "Reframing Mexican Migration as a Multi-Ethnic Process." *Latino Studies*, 4(1–2), 39–61.

Livingston, G., Parker, K., and Fox, S. (2009). "Latinos Online, 2006-2008: Narrowing the Gap." Washington, DC: Pew Hispanic Center. Retrieved June 17, 2011 from www.pewhispanic.org/files/reports/119.pdf.

López, M. H., Barrera, A. G., and Patten, E. (2013). "Closing the Digital Divide: Latinos and Technology Adoption." Washington, D. C.: Pew Hispanic Research Center Retrieved June 17, 2013 from www.pewhispanic.org/files/2013/03/Latinos_Social_Media_and_Mobile_Tech_03-2013_final.pdf.

Machado-Casas, M. (2006). "Narrating Education of New Indigenous/Latino Transnational Communities in the South." Unpublished dissertation. University of North Carolina, Chapel Hill, NC.

——— (2009a). "'Coyotes' tecnológicos: Sobrevivencia transnacional de comunidades indígenas Latinas en los Estados Unidos." *DIDAC,* 54, 13–25.

——— (2009b). "The Politics of Organic Phylogeny: The Art of Parenting and Surviving as Transnational Multilingual Latino Indigenous Immigrants in the U.S." *High School Journal,* 92(4), 82–99.

——— (2010). "The New Global Transnational Citizen: The Role of Multilingualism in the Lives of Latino/s Indigenous Immigrants in the U.S." *CIMEXUS: Revista de Investigaciones M é xico Estados Unidos,* 2(7), 99–123.

Machado-Casas, M., Ek. L., and Sanchez, P. (Accepted, 2013). "The Digital Literacy Practices of Latina/o Immigrant Parents in an After-School Technology Partnership." *Multicultural Education Journal.*

National Center for Education Statistics. (2002). "Internet Access in U. S. Public Schools and Classrooms: 1994-2001." Washington, DC: Author. Retrieved June 17, 2011 from nces.ed.gov/pubs2002/2002018.pdf.

Passel, J., Cohn, D., and Lopez, M. (2010). "Census 2010: 50 Million Latinos: Hispanics Account for More than Half of the Nation's Growth in the Past Decade." Pew Hispanic Center. Washington, D.C.: Retrieved June 17, 2011 from www.pewhispanic.org/2011/03/24/hispanics-account-for-more-than-half-of-nations-growth-in-past-decade.

Pruitt-Mentle, D. (2002). "Participation in a Technological World: the Meaning of Educational Technology in the Lives of Young Adult Central American Immigrants." confreg.uoregon.edu/necc2002/.

Rivera, H. (2008). "Bridging the Technology Gap for Low-Income Spanish-Speaking Immigrant Families." *Association for the Advancement of Computing in Education Journal,* 16(3), 307–325.

Tartakov, C. C., Leigh, P. R., and Phillips, C. B. (2003). "More than Access: Using Technology to Support a Culturally Relevant Literacy Program for Historically Underserved Inner City Children." In C. Crawford, et al. (eds.), Proceedings of Society for Information *Technology* and Teacher Education International Conference 2003 (601–602). Chesapeake, VA: AACE.

Tseng, T. (2001). *Ethnicity in the Electronic Age: Looking at the Internet Through a Multicultural Lens.* Los Altos, CA: Access Worldwide Cultural Access Group.

Valdès, G. (1996). *Con respeto: Bridging the Distance Between Culturally Diverse Families and Schools: An Ethnographic Portrait.* New York: Teachers College Press.

Vásquez, O. A. (2003). *La Clase Mágica: Imagining Optimal Possibilities in a Bilingual Community of Leaners.* Mahwah. NJ: Lawrence Erlbaum.

——— (2006). "Cross-National Explorations of Sociocultural Research on Learning." In Judith Green and Allen Luke (eds.), *Review of Research in Education: Special Issue on Rethinking Learning: What Counts as Learning and What Learning Counts,* 30, 33–64.

——— (2008). "Reflection-rules of engagement for achieving educational futures." In L. L. Parker (ed.), *Technology-Mediated Learning Environments for Young English Learners: Connections In and Out of School* (99–110). Mahwah, NJ: Lawrence Erlbaum.

Vygotsky, L.S. (1978). *Thought and Language.* Cambridge, MA: MIT Press.

Warschauer, M., Knobel, M., and Stone, L. (2004). "Technology and Equity in Schooling: Deconstructing the Digital Divide." *Educational Policy,* 18, 562–588.

Wilhelm, A. (1998). *Closing the Digital Divide: Enhancing Hispanic Participation in the Information Age* (Policy Report). Claremont, CA: The Tomás Rivera Policy Institute.

Wong Fillmore, L. (1991). "When Learning a Second Language Means Losing the First." *Early Childhood Research Quarterly,* 6, 323–346.

IV

Evolving through Innovation

"I, the singer, labor in spirit with what I heard, that it may lift up my memory, that it may go forth to those shining heavens, that my sighs may be borne on the wind and be permitted to enter where the yellow humming bird chants its praises in the heavens, ohuaya! ohuaya!"

Anonymous (1890). Ancient Nahuatl Poetry, Containing the Nahuatl Text of XXVII Ancient Mexican Poems. *Brinton's Library of Aboriginal American Literature, Number VII*. Translated by D. G. Brinton (Original work circa 1400–1800).

THIRTEEN

La Clase Mágica Goes International: Adapting to New Sociocultural Contexts

Beatriz Macías Gómez-Estern and Olga A. Vásquez

WORKING TOWARD HARMONY

In this chapter, we argue that *La Clase Mágica* (LCM) offers a powerful approach for addressing social disparities across multiple national and international contexts.[1] The embodiment of "real learning" (Simons, 2000; Van Oers, 2005, 2006, 2007; Meijers and Wardekker, 2003), a foundational characteristic of the LCM system offers researchers, educators, and community members a number of possibilities for adapting the model to serve the learning needs of participants of any age and/or sociocultural reality. A close examination of the launching of LCM-Sevilla demonstrates the flexibility by which the LCM model adapts to the local conditions, in this case a diverse and mobilized Spanish community and a recently founded public university. Organized as equal partners in meeting the social and educational needs of their constituencies, both institutions contribute physical, human and intellectual resources to the problem-solving process (similar to LCM@UTSA, see chapter 5).

This chapter focuses specifically on the initial stages of the development of a two-way partnership between a Gypsy community in Southern Spain and the Department of Social Anthropology, Basic Psychology, and Preventive Medicine of the University of Pablo de Olavide in Seville. More specifically, it documents the challenges and possibilities that an innovative research-teaching program, such as LCM, offers Gypsy women, a marginalized community undergoing social revitalization, as well

193

as university students. Our goal is to illustrate the ways that the LCM
system aligns multiple resources to support participants' commitment to
their identity group and to new ways of knowing that prepare them to
engage the new social and technical realities of today. In the process of
aligning these resources, we show how the project forms a "hub of expertise" (Kao, 2007; Marcello and Vásquez, 2009) within the LCM community, both locally and internationally contributing new understandings of
the notion of real learning.

We begin with the theoretical discussion of real learning, the frame we
use to examine our yearlong adaptation of LCM within an international
context. Then, we briefly sketch the four components that facilitate
LCM's adaptability to new contexts and lay the groundwork for real
learning to flourish. Next, we highlight other long standing projects that
have incorporated aspects of the LCM approach, focusing on a nearby
example, *La Casa de Shere Room* that has served numerous Gypsy communities for almost fifteen years in and around Barcelona, Spain. To familiarize international readers with the broader context of our partnership
with a Gypsy community in Sevilla, we provide a general background of
the Gypsy population in Spain, and the particular Gypsy community
with whom we have established a partnership. Finally, we provide a
quick survey of the first year of the implementation of the LCM-Sevilla
project and articulate a vision of a promising hub of expertise within the
LCM international community of practice, emphasize the real learning
processes taking place among two focal participants groups: the Gypsy
women and the university students.

Real learning as Identity Learning

Learning processes are always situated. They occur in specific cultural
activity settings that "always differ in terms of time, place, and power
relations" (Meijers and Wardekker, 2003, p. 156). As such, information
gains meaning and significance in a person's life when it is assimilated
into one's own life story (Polkinghorne, 1988). Real learning about the
world (Simons 2000) involves constructing new ways of looking at the
world as well as seeing oneself in a new light. Along with the acquisition
of cognitive skills, real learning encompasses the transformation of the
whole person, in much the same way that Vygotsky (1987) and other
cultural historical theorists conceive of the notion of *perezhivanie*—"the
process through which children make meaning of their social existence"
(Mahn, 2003, p. 129). Thus, the theoretical notion of real learning (Simons,
2000; Meijers and Wardekker, 2003; Van Oers, 2005, 2006, 2007) provides
an excellent framework for assessing the developmental processes of the
LCM experiences that the undergraduate students and Gypsy women
enjoy as they acquire new cultural ways of knowing.

From our perspective, all leaning requires a motive. A motive for learning may emerge from a genuine question, a quiz, or a gap between what the individual wants to achieve and what can accomplished given available resources. We can consider a genuine question as analogous to what is called a boundary experience in identity studies, Meijers and Wardekker (2003) argue. A boundary experience is a turning point in an individual's autobiography (Sarbin, 1986; McAdams, 1993; McAdams, Josselson and Lieblich, 2006) in which one fully experiences the limits of existing resources. In Erikson's terms (1968), it is an identity crisis that triggers a commitment to a goal and the social practice that supports that purpose. Within a community of practice (Wenger, 1998; Wortham, 2001; 2003; 2006), it is a commitment to a given idea of who one is in relation to the world and to oneself.

CONCEPTUAL RESONANCE: WHAT DO WE KNOW?

As a learning initiative, LCM embodies a cross-disciplinary perspective that spans a number of fields in the social sciences including cultural psychology, anthropology, linguistics, and education. LCM projects have amassed a diverse set of findings on issues ranging from computer mediated learning, community development and integration, bilingual education, and teacher education among others (Vásquez, 2003; Lalueza, Crespo, Pallí and Luque; 1999, 2001; this book). Assessing the similarities across these projects, four key properties of LCM stand out as relevant to the Sevilla context and to the sustainability of the new project: cultural relevance, dialogic learning, cross fertilization and its malleability to new sociocultural contexts.

Grounding Learning in the Intellectual Resources of the Community

Following a cultural historical perspective, LCM grounds its learning activities on the learner's prior knowledge and experiences as critical components for learning and development (Vygotsky, 1987; Wertsch, 1985; 1991; 1998). From its beginning, LCM has made the cultural and everyday knowledge of its host community a fundamental resource for constructing the program's objectives, curricular materials, activities and the adult-child interactions (Vásquez, 2008). This approach is specifically pertinent to cultural groups whose cultural knowledge has not been recognized or incorporated in the school setting as has been the case among Latinos in the United States (Vásquez, 2003; Nieto, 1996) and Gypsies in Spain (Luque and Lalueza, 2013; Martínez and Blázquez, 2012).

Multi-Disciplinary Perspectives and Cross Fertilization

LCM incorporates elements from a number of disciplinary perspectives to enhance learning across numerous social systems and settings. This gives LCM the flexibility to explore various dimensions of education and social integration. It not only offers social science researchers an enriching arena to analyze cultural, psychological, linguistic, and social processes, but also offers educators and community reformers a transworld pedagogy (that goes beyond the cultural relevance to an interculturality reaching back to the origins of the group, see chapter 2). In welcoming researchers and practitioners from multiple international, national, and disciplinary backgrounds, LCM incorporates diverse insights and lenses that make possible cross-fertilization across diverse research perspectives and disciplinary boundaries.

The Feasibility of Transportability

LCM's conceptual foundation and social justice philosophy in combination with the university-community organizational structure and other elements adapted from its parent project, the Fifth Dimension (Cole, 1996; Cole and the Distributed Literacy Consortium, 2006), are the driving force behind LCM's ability to adapt to local sociocultural ecologies (Vásquez, 2003; Marcello and Vásquez, 2009). Its initial adaptation from a Fifth Dimension activity designed to serve learners from an upper class, English-speaking community (Nilsson and Nocon, 2005) to a bilingual and bicultural project serving both Mexican immigrant children and a Native American community significantly distances *La Clase Mágica* from its parent project. LCM's research lens expands across age groups, moving beyond elementary school to preschoolers and adolescents, and finally to *La Gran Dimensión*, a parent component offering adults access to computer technology and a means for self and community empowerment (Macías and Vásquez, 2012). What distinguishes LCM from its predecessor and makes it viable for addressing the social and educational needs of distinct communities is its focus on providing nonmainstream youth with educational resources and institutional support to enhance their academic achievement in K–12 and their representation in higher education (Stanton-Salazar, Vásquez, and Mehan, 1996). These adaptations transform LCM into a model of social change applicable in other sociocultural contexts seeking social integration on equitable terms (Martínez Avidad, 2012).

By 2010, LCM had established itself in four Mexican-origin communities and a Native American reservation in San Diego County in southern California. This inspired other initiatives along diverse geographical and social landscapes including *La Casa de Shere Rom* in Barcelona, Spain working with a number of Gypsy communities. Along with the Fifth

Dimension, it also inspired the establishment of UC Links, a consortium of university-community partnerships sponsored by the University of California system to tackle the under-representation of underserved minority youth (Underwood and Parker, 2013).

REPOSITIONING METHODOLOGY: BEYOND RELEVANCE TO THE SACRED SCIENCES

The capacity of *La Clase Mágica* to adapt to the sociocultural contours of its host communities, while at the same time maintaining its basic assumptions and structures, has given form to an international community of learners involving a number of researchers, students, universities, and community partners. The networking across related projects within the broader LCM system has become a fertile ground for the emergence of vibrant international research community. Thus, in this section, we explore LCM as a case study of a venture that extends it into the international scene (Yin, 2003). Our reflections describe the planning and implementation process of the LCM-Sevilla project in relation to other implementation projects far and near. As participatory researchers, we provide a brief description of our participants, primarily focusing on the Gypsy community.

An International Community of Practice

Together, these LCM characteristics situate the Sevilla project at a vantage point for extending and enriching its own development and, thus contributing to the lessons learned across international sites. LCM-Sevilla has begun experimenting with ways to transform the original idea and offer new vistas into learning and development that also incite social action. Below, we describe the stages of the implementation of the LCM model among Gypsy communities in Spain.

La Clase Mágica *in Spain: Serving the Needs of Gypsy Communities in Barcelona and Sevilla*

As in many other countries around the world, Gypsy (their choice of ethnic designation) communities have traditionally experienced difficulty integrating into the European majority society. Commonly, they suffer discrimination every where they settle. In Spain, in particular, many myths circulate about their nomadic lifestyle and culture (Lalueza, Crespo, Pallí and Luque, 2001). Recent research, shows that over time their employment and educational situation has been improving (Laparra, 2011), although their educational integration still lags behind other groups (Laparra, 2011). Gypsy traditional professional niches continue to be associated with the non-formal economy of collecting and peddling refuse. While their informal economy may be profitable, they nevertheless reflect low unemployment rates that exclude them from social benefits such as unemployment benefits and pensions.

Gypsy women, on the other hand, face additional obstacles of a patriarchal tradition that assigns them the role of caregivers and transmitters of values. Countering this intransigence, a number of associations of Gypsy women have pushed for the right to an education, birth control, and individual freedom. However, Gypsy women claim their ethnicity in their push to modernize gender roles that fit the social realities of today (Laparra, 2011), refusing to renounce their Gypsy heritage.

La Casa de Shere Rom[2]: *Bringing* La Clase Mágica *to Gypsy Communities*

In the 1990s, the Grupo de Investigación en Desarrollo Humano, Intervención Social e Interculturalidad [Research Group on Human Development, Social Intervention and Interculturality] from the Universidad Autonoma de Barcelona established *La Casa de Shere Rom* (CSR) based on the LCM organizational structure and philosophy (Lalueza, Crespo, Pallí and Luque, 2001; Luque and Lalueza, 2013) as part of an educational project implemented in several neighborhoods with Gypsy populations in the metropolitan area of Barcelona. Over the years, *La Casa de Shere Rom* (Shere Rom's house is a fiction character in Gypsy mythology) has successfully extended to thirteen sites in different predominantly Gypsy communities, schools, and associations across Barcelona. The incorporation of Gypsy values, language, and culture, close relations between the researchers and community leaders, and the ownership of the project by the community members, makes CSR a replicable model for the Sevilla team. Although CSR serves mainly school-age children and teenagers, several community women have recently taken the leadership to organize Gypsy women using the LCM framework illustrating community uptake of a projected introduced by university researchers. They proposed two online courses to help local adults obtain a basic high school degree and a driving license. Not only do these actions call attention to the leadership role these women took, they also shed light on the first signs of long-term sustainability of the overall project, which in the case of the Barcelona has lasted almost a decade and a half.

LCM Project in Sevilla

The Sevilla case is one more example of the protean nature of LCM and its ability to adapt a new sociocultural reality. It demonstrates the continuation of its foundational ideas and objectives to serve the interests of local disenfranchised communities. In retaining its essence, LCM-Sevilla concentrates on promoting active and real learning for all its participants as a viable pedagogical strategy for addressing the social and educational disparities of a locally marginalized community.

Building on the initial LCM philosophical foundation and its adaption in Barcelona, LCM-Sevilla is in its initial stages of constructing a collaborative partnership across several community associations in the community of *Polígono Sur* adjacent to Pablo de Olavide University (UPO), the university sponsoring the research. The project builds on a history of relations across different entities within this particular neighborhood, the UPO researchers (Ramírez, 1995, 1999; Ramírez-Garrido, Cala-Carrillo, and Sánchez-Medina, 1999; Ramírez and Sánchez, 1997; Ramírez, Sánchez, and Santamaría, 1996; Macías, Amián, Sánchez, and Marco, 2010), and Macías, a member of the original *La Clase Mágica* at University of California, San Diego (Macías and Vásquez, 2012). Below, we provide a brief sketch of the collaboration between the university and the *Polígono Sur* neighborhood's social institutions and associations. Finally, we show how LCM-Sevilla weaves into a tapestry of social collaboration.

Plan Integral Para el Polígono Sur, Sevilla, Spain

Polígono Sur, a marginalized area in Sevilla, located in the southern section of the city, on the east bank of the Guadalquivir river is demarcated by clear borders (rail track, freeway, industrial area), making the transition to the rest of the city physically difficult. Polígono Sur is the home to approximately 50,000 habitants who live in an area of 145 hectares (358.3 acres) with approximately 7,000 apartments. Almost 25 percent of the inhabitants are of Gypsy background. The neighborhood is clearly low-income with substantial diversity of social class and status within the different subareas. The community where LCM-Sevilla is situated, the Barriada Martínez Montañés neighborhood, is without a doubt the most disadvantaged area in terms of social exclusion, unemployment, drugs abuse, truancy, and illiteracy (Martínez and Blázquez, 2012).

In 2003, the Sevilla city government, acknowledging the impoverished condition of Polígono Sur, launched a new initiative to coordinate the efforts of public and neighborhood associations interested in improving the social conditions of the area. The establishment of the office of the *Comisionado para el Polígono Sur* (Commissioner of the Polígono Sur[3]) grew out of this effort. The commissioner was charged with mobilizing the efforts of governmental organizations (local, regional, and national), and a number of associations to improve the social conditions of the area. The *Plan Integral para el Polígono Sur* (Integral Plan for Polígono Sur) was drawn to guide the community development through a collective process emphasizing the active participation of the communities themselves.

The plan focused on strategic areas to better enhance the social conditions of the community including issues related to urban and local coexistence, labor integration and the promotion of entrepreneurship, community health, and socio-educational and family integration. As part of the latter, the Martínez Montañés Project, an adult literacy initiative was implemented targeting the Barriada Martínez Montañés community, coordinated by The Center for Adults in *Polígono Sur* and a Gypsy women association, called *Akerdi i Tromipén*. The goal of the project was to generate community engagement and ultimately, community empowerment. It began with an opening celebration welcoming residents to visit the center and become aware of social services provided including health, social and educational programs. The opening strategy was particularly important because residents do not typically take advantage of the Adults Education Center where they can acquire basic and literacy advanced skills, in spite of the high rate of illiteracy in the community. To their credit, the women of the community proposed an agenda of ongoing activities such as sewing, dancing, computing, and literacy courses and closed the 2012 year inviting the community to enjoy a festive end of the year celebration. The new LCM project took root as part of the literacy activities of the Martínez Montañés Center.

The University Pablo de Olavide and Polígono Sur Partnership: La Residencia Flora Tristan

In 2004, the Office of Student Housing of the Universidad Pablo de Olavide opened *La Residencia Flora Tristán* as a social experiment to bring together the university and the community of *Polígono Sur*. Its broader goals were to combine university student housing and service learning (Martínez and Blázquez, 2012) placing students in the projects and activities offered at *Polígono Sur*. Flora Tristan Residence offered students the opportunity to take part in the process of change based on the idea of learning as an integral part of the whole person experience (Simons, 2000) and the concept of multiliteracies (Cazden, Cope, Fairclough, Gee et al., 1996). Thus, students had to commit to a learning plan that focused on the development of cognitive skills, and fluency in social and attitudinal competences (Martínez and Blázquez, 2012). It was established as a two-way collaboration in which the university provided a service learning experience that had transformative impact on its students (Maturana and Nisis, 2002). In return, students were awarded lower housing fellowships (at times free of charge) in exchange for their involvement and commitment to a plan that was closely supervised by professionals and university tutors (Martínez and Blázquez, 2012).

SYNCHRONIZING MULTIPLE WORLDS: FINDINGS AND CHALLENGES

The LCM-Sevilla Project: A One-Year Story

As discussed above, LCM-Sevilla was born in the middle of a strong current of social transformation that was taking place in the *Polígono Sur* area of Sevilla. Collaboration, thus, was facilitated by a history of participation in the social life of *Poligono Sur* by two university professors involved in proposing the incorporation of LCM. They acted as co-agents of social change along with the community members who experienced a disorienting, yet an exciting sea of change full of synergy.

LCM-Sevilla sparked the opportunity to develop a new university course called, "Learning Processes in Non-Formal Contexts" focused on different aspects of learning processes in communities of practices. Since it did not have a field practicum in the first semester, the professors recruited a small number of students in service-learning to establish the new LCM project, which has substantially increased overtime.

In our initial meetings with the community, we found that both parties shared common interests, but approached these from different perspectives. A plan was developed to target women in the most segregated area of town, while we, as university professors and researchers, wanted to implement a project that fortified community empowerment and adult learning within the framework of the LCM. The two efforts complemented each other well and our collaboration was charged with energy and mutual motivation. It was a perfect fit.

We began by joining the Martínez Montañés ongoing activities such as adult literacy, drivers' training, sewing, and flamenco workshops, proposed and attended by the community women. Throughout the 2011–2012 academic year, we engaged in strategizing the possibility of linking to other national networks, such as the Barcelona team as well as recruiting and placing university students in the serving-learning practicum component.

RETHINKING RESONANCE: NEW CONCEPTUAL UNDERSTANDINGS

Our overall research goal is to specialize as a hub of expertise exploring those areas that are not central to other LCM projects, such as a focus on adult community members, in particular, Gypsy women and a "service learning" component for undergraduate students. Our future project development and research goals are outlined below:

Goal 1: Development of an LCM program designed to enhance adult participants' multiliteracies with the ultimate objective of community empowerment.

The LCM tradition has focused on designing optimal learning environments to stimulate children's cognitive abilities through play and other creative activities (Vasquez, 2003). However, retooling LCM to serve adults changes the approach to skill development and community empowerment. Fantasy and play cannot be as easily integrated in the curricular activities in the same way as with children. As explained before, the experience in Sevilla is not the first adaptation of LCM to an adult population (Macías and Vasquez, 2012). Other adult LCM initiatives (e.g., in California and Barcelona) have focused specifically on enhancing basic skills among adults. The LCM-Sevilla seeks to explore the possibilities that the LCM model offers as a system for enhancing the academic and computer-related skills and knowledge that can possibly enhance the living conditions of women living in a marginalized community.

Following Freire (1970) and Vygotsky (1978), we believe that the adult's prior knowledge is foundational to all literacy learning activities (Ramírez, 1995; Wertsch, 1998; Macías and Vásquez, 2012). The adult's voices and identities are intertwined into the guiding principles in designing educational activities as part of an inclusive and liberating education, whether the learning content focuses on computer or formal literacy, driving tests, etc. Narratives have also been successfully used in adult education for the inclusion of participant's heritage and personal experience in learning activities (Birren and Birren, 1996; Birren and Deutchman, 1991; Freire, 1970; Ramírez, 1995). Drawing from narrative studies, we can affirm that personal narratives constitute a privileged tool for the expression and enactment of identities in different life settings (Bamberg, 2003, 2004; Bruner, 1986; Brockmeier and Carbaugh, 2001; De Fina, Shiffrin and Bamberg, 2006; Linde, 1993). Following previous experiences at UCSD (Macías and Vasquez, 2012), our plans for the LCM-Sevilla project are to explore the potential of women's personal narratives as intellectual tools—i.e., as referents and linkages between old and new knowledge. Following the philosophical principles of *La Clase Mágica*, we consider these personal narratives as important means to incorporate the women's previous background and motivations in the curricula to both foster "real learning" and validate their background experiences (Vasquez, 2003; Sánchez and Macías, 2009). That is, our plans are to use their narratives as teaching and learning tools in the problem-solving process in the development of the curriculum and instruction.

Goal 2: Documenting of service learning and real learning among university students at LCM-Sevilla

LCM-Sevilla aims to support the whole LCM international research community providing empirical insights into the university students' intellectual and social development as a result of their service learning experiences. The affect on university students' learning using innovative pedagogies that connect theoretical concepts with real life situations and problem solving has been one of the main contributions of LCM projects across time (Vásquez, 2003; Martínez Avidad, 2012). The aim of the university courses linked to practicum sites has been closely related with promoting experiential learning. The benefits of participation in LCM have been demonstrated in the achievements and academic careers of child participants, subsequently contributing to the social change of their minority groups (Martínez Avidad, 2012; Gallego and Vásquez, 2011). But the benefits gained by the U.S. mainstream students at UCSD and non-Gypsy students from middle class backgrounds in Spain, have not been widely documented. Yet, LCM regardless of its location, counts on the university students' personal discoveries and theoretical insights that substantiate incidence of real learning (Simons, 2000; Van Oers, 2005, 2006, 2007; Meijers and Wardekker, 2003), as well as the experience of identity changing. These reflections serve as acts of intercultural communication that position the participants in a complex world where they develop global world skills (Cazden, Cope, Fairclough, Norman, Gee, et al., 1996; Trilling and Fadel, 2009; Gallego and Vásquez, 2011). As a result, the university students learn how to interact in intercultural contexts and how to build positive relations with culturally different children and adults through their own experiences rather than from academic texts. They also learn how to apply innovative teaching methods and more importantly, they learn to work in settings where their cultural assumptions are not seen as more powerful than those of their minority counterparts. A student participating in LCM-Sevilla illustrates this point:

> Another thing that has called my attention is that they [women in the Project] are surprised that we [students] are still studying at our age, we have not married, have not had kids, and Carmen [one of the women], for example is only a bit older than us [students]. That makes me think of how different are people's life's depending on the context where they have developed.

This serves as an example of a real learning experience. Real learning grows out of a situation in which individuals recognize that their resources are not sufficiently provoking a situation in which new meanings are created. Our goals for the LCM-Sevilla are to focus our research on exploring how these services and real learning processes occur.

Altogether, LCM-Sevilla stands as a nascent example of *pedagogía transmundial* (see chapter 2). We have appropriated key insights developed across LCM's long history and extended them towards a new area of expertise that concentrates on adult learning (both students and ethnic minority members) and more directly on community empowerment. The Seville case also illustrates the protean nature of LCM to blend in to each new sociocultural milieu. Its foundational ideas and objectives continue to serve the best interests of diverse communities. In retaining its essence, LCM promotes real learning for all its participants; becoming a viable pedagogical tool inciting social change. Once again, the LCM model demonstrates its ability to powerfully adapt to the new local ecologies without losing its core values. By narrating the first steps of LCM-Sevilla, Spain, we document one of the latest LCM adaptations in a new international arena. LCM-Sevilla has achieved and built an international community of practice, with different hubs of specialization sites, each nurturing local needs and resources. LCM demonstrates a successful research and social action model to promote social and intellectual skills using *pedagogía transmundial*. We hope to co-design a new system of collaboration that commits to local and global initiatives (Chaiklin and Hedegaard, 2009), to research dissemination and ultimately to social action.

NOTES

1. The authors would like to acknowledge the wisdom of Olivia Puentes Reynolds and the Center for Academic and Social Advancement (CASA) who have promoted a vision of *La Clase Mágica* as serving both local and international communities.

2. La Casa de Shere Rom, translated as Shere Rom's home, was the name chosen by the researchers and community members for the Barcelona adaptation of LCM. Shere Rom is a character of Gypsy heritage oral tradition.

3. The complete documentation and administrative organization of Plan Integral para el Polígono Sur (Integral Plan for Polígono Sur) can be found at: www.poligonosursevilla.es.

REFERENCES

Bamberg, M. (2003). "Narrative Discourse and Identities." In J. C. Meinster, T. Kindt and W. Schernus (eds.), *Narratology Beyond Literaty Criticism* (213–237). New York: De Gruyter.
——— (2004). "Talk, Small Stories, and Adolescent Identities." *Human Development*, 47, 366–369.
Birren, J. E. and Birren, B. A. (1996). "Autobiography: Exploring the Self and Encouraging Development." In Birren, et al. (eds.), *Aging and Biography: Explorations in Adult Development*. New York: Springer Publishing.
Birren, J. E. and Deutchman, D. E. (1991): *Guiding Autobiography Groups for Older Adults*. Baltimore, MD: John Hopkins University Press.
Brockmeier, J., and Carbaugh, D. (2001). *Narrative and Identity*. Amsterdam, Netherlands: John Benjamins.

Bruner, J. S.(1986). *Actual Minds, Possible Worlds*. Cambridge, MA and London, UK: Harvard University Press.

Cazden, C., Cope, B., Fairclough, N., Gee, J., et al. (1996). "A Pedagogy of Multiliteracies: Designing Social Futures." *Harvard Educational Review*, 66 (1), 60.

Chaiklin, S. and Hedegaard, M. (2009). "Radical-Local Teaching and Learning: A Cultural-Historical Perspective on Education and Children's Development." In M. Fleer, M. Hedegaard, and J. Tudge (eds.), *World Yearbook of Education: Childhood Studies and the Impact of Globalization: Global and Local Policies and Practices.*(179–198). London, UK: Routledge.

Cole, M. (1996). *Cultural Psychology. A Once and Future Discipline*. Cambridge, MA: Harvard University Press.

———(2006). *The Fifth Dimension: An After-School Program Built on Diversity*. New York: Russell Sage Foundation.

De Fina, A., Shiffrin, D., and Bamberg M. (eds.). (2006). *Discourse and Identity*. Cambridge, MA: Cambridge University Press.

Erikson, E. (1968). *Identity, Youth, and Crisis*. New York. W. W. Norton.

Freire, P. (1970). *Pedagogy of the Oppressed*. New York: Continuum.

Gallego, M. and Vásquez, O. A (2011). "Praxis in Dis-Coordination." In P. Portes, P. and S. Salas (eds.), *Vygotsky in the Twenty-First Century: Cultural Historical Theory and Research in Non-Dominant Communities* (214–228). New York, NY: Peter Lang Publishing.

Kao, J. 2007. *Innovation Nation: How America is Losing its Innovative Edge, Why It Matters, and What Can We Do to Get It Back*. New York: Free Press.

Lalueza, J. L., Crespo, I. Pallí, C., and Luque, M. J. (1999). "Intervención educativa, comunidad y cultura gitana. Una experiencia con nuevas tecnologías: la Casa de Shere Rom." En Essombra, M.A. (ed.): *Construir la escuela intercultural. Reflexiones y propuestas para trabajar la diversidad étnica y cultural*. Barcelona: Graó.

——— (2001). "Socialización y cambio cultural en una comunidad étnica minoritaria. El nicho evolutivo gitano." *Cultura y Educación*, 13(1), 115–130.

Linde, C. (1993). *Life-Stories: The Creation of Coherence*. New York: Oxford University Press.

Luque, M. J. and Lalueza, J. L. (2013). "Aprendizaje colaborativo en de práctica en entornos de exclusión social. Un análisis de las interacciones." *Revista de Educación*, 362.

Laparra, M. (Coord.). (2011). *Diagnóstico social de la comunidad gitana en España. Un análisis contrastado de la Encuesta del CIS a hogares de población Gitana 2007*. Madrid: Ministerio de Sanidad, Política Social e Igualdad, Secretaria General Técnica, Centro de Publicaciones.

Mahn, H. (2003). "Periods in Child Development." In A. Kozulin, B. Guindis, V. S. Ageyev and S.M. Miller (eds.), *Vygotsky's Educational Theory in Cultural Context*. (119–137). Cambridge, MA: Cambridge University Press.

McAdams, D. P. (1996): "Personality, Modernity, and the Storied Self: A Contemporary Framework for Studying Persons." *Psychological Inquiry*, 7(4), 295–321.

McAdams, D. P.; Josselson, R., and Lieblich, A. (2006). *Identity and Story. Creating Self in Narrative*. Baltimore, MD: United Book Press.

Macías, B. Amián, J. G.; Sánchez, J. A. and Marco, M. J. (2010): "Literacy and the formation of cultural identity." *Theory and Psychology*, 20(2), 231–250.

Macías, B., and Vásquez, O. A. (2012). "Identity Construction in Narratives of Migration." In T. Hansen and K. Jensen (eds.), *Self in Culture in Mind. Connectional and Applied Perspectives*. Aalborg, Denmark: Aalborg University Press.

Marcello, A. and Vásquez, O. A. (2009). "Una mirada contextualizada del uso de prácticas de innovación en comunidades cultural y lingüísticamente diversas: la necesidad de adaptación mutua." *Revista de Investigaciones UNAD*, 8(2), 13–30.

Martínez Avidad, M. (2012). "Comunicación para el desarrollo y la inclusión social de minorías: La Clase Mágica, un modelo de intervención para el cambio social." Unpublished doctoral dissertation, Universidad Complutense de Madrid, Spain.

Martínez, V. and Blázquez, A. (2012). "La Residencia Universitaria Flora Tristán: un ejemplo de formación humana y de compromiso con la sociedad." *Revista de Educación*, 358.

Maturana, H. and Nisis, S. (2002). *Formación humana y capacitación*. Santiago, Chile: Dolmen.

Meijers, F. and Wardekker, W. (2003). "Career Learning in a Changing World: The Role of Emotions." *International Journal for the Advancement of Counseling*, 24, 149–167.

Nieto, S. (1996). *Affirming Diversity: The Sociopolitical Context of Multicultural Education* (second ed.). White Plains, NY: Longman

Nilsson, M. and Nocon, H. (2005). *School of Tomorrow. Developing Expansive Learning Environments*. Bern, Switzerland: Peter Lang.

Polkinghorne, D. E.(1988). *Narrative Knowing and the Human Science*. New York: State University of New York Press.

Ramírez, J. D. (1995): *Usos de la palabra y sus tecnologías. Una aproximación dialógica al estudio de la alfabetización*. Buenos Aires, Argentine: Miño y Dávila Editores.

——— (1999): "Escritura e identidad. Función de la literatura histórica en los orígenes del nacionalismo." *Araucaria*, 1, 15–34.

Ramírez, J. D. and Sánchez, J. A. (1997): "Ética, retórica y educación. El nexo dialógico." En A. Alvarez (ed), *Hacia un curriculum cultural: La vigencia de Vygotski en la educación*. Madrid: Fundación infancia y aprendizaje.

Ramírez, J. D., Sánchez, J. A., and Santamaría, A. (1996): "Making Literacy: A Dialogical Perspective on Discourse in Adult Education." In J. Y Valsiner and Voss H-G. W. (eds.), *The Structure of Learning Processes*. Norwood, NJ: Ablex Publishing Lorp.

Ramirez-Garrido, J. D, Cala-Carrillo, M. J., and Sanchez-Medina, J. A. (1999): "Speech Genres and Rhetoric: The Development of Ways of Argumentation in a Program of Adult Literacy." In M. Hedegaard and J. Lompchster (eds.), *Learning Activity and Development*. Aarhus, Denmark: Aarhus University Press.

Sánchez, J. A. and Macías, B.(2009): "Identiteit, leren en emoties." In B. Van Oers, Y. Leeman, and M. Volman, (eds.), *Burgerschapsvorming en identiteitsontwikkelin. Koninklijke*. Assen: Netherlands: Van Gorcom.

Sarbin, T. (1986). *Narrative Psychology: The Storied Nature of Human Conduct*. New York: Praeger.

Simons, P. R. J. (2000). "Towards a Constructivistic Theory of Self-Directed Learning." In G. Straka (ed.), *Self-Learning*. Münster, Germany: Waxmann.

Stanton-Salazar, R., Vásquez, O.A., and Mehan, H. (1996). "Engineering Success Through Institutional Support." In A. Hurtado, R. Figueroa, and E. Garcia (eds.), *Strategic Interventions in Education: Expanding the Latina/Latino Pipeline*. (100–137). Santa Cruz, CA: University of Santa Cruz.

Trilling, B. and Fadel, C. (2009). *Twenty-First Century Skills: Learning for Life in our Times*. San Francisco, CA: Jossey-Bass.

Underwood, C., Parker, L. and Stone, L. (2013). "Getting It Together: Relational Habits in the Emergence of Digital Literacies." *Learning, Media, and Technology*, 1–17. DOI: 10.1080/17439884.2013.770403.

Van Oers, B. (2005): "The Potentials of Imagination." *Inquiry*, 24(4), 5–18.

——— (2006). "An Activity Theory Approach to the Formation of Mathematical Cognition: Developing Topics Through Predication in a Mathematical Community." In J. Maaβ. and W. Schlögmann (eds.), *New Mathematics Education Research and Practice* (113-139). Rotterdam: Sense Publisher.

——— (2007). Helping Young Children to Become Literate: The Relevance of Narrative Competence for Developmental Education. *European Early Childhood Education Research Journal*, 15(3), 299–312.

Vásquez, O. A. (2003): *La Clase Mágica: Imagining Optimal Possibilities in a Bilingual Community of Learners*. Mahwah, NJ: Laurence Erlbaum.

———— (2008). "Reflection—Rules of Rngagement for Achieving Educational Futures." In L. L. Parker (ed.), *Technology-Mediated Learning Environments for Young English Learners: Connections In and Out of School* (99–110). Mahwah, NJ: Lawrence Erlbaum.

Vygotsky, L.S. (1987). *Thinking and Speech.* N. Minick (ed.). New York, NY: Plenum.

———— (1994). "The Problem of Environment." In R. Van Der Veer and J. Valsiner (eds.), *The Vygotsky Reader* (338–354). Oxford, UK: Blackwell.

Wenger, E. (1998). *Communities of Practice: Learning, Meaning, and Identity.* Cambridge, MA: Cambridge University Press.

Wertsch, J. V. (1985). *Vygotsky and the Social Formation of Mind.* Cambridge, MA: Harvard University Press.

———— (1991). *Voices of the Mind.* Cambridge, MA.: Harvard University Press.

———— (1998). *Mind as Action.* New York, NY: Oxford University Press.

Wortham, S. (2001). *Narratives in Action.* New York: Teachers College Press.

———— (2003). "Accomplishing Identity in Participant-Denoting Discourse." *Journal of Linguistic Anthropology, 13,* 1–22.

———— (2006). *Learning Identity: The Joint Emergence of Social Identification and Academic Learning.* New York: Cambridge University Press.

Yin, R. K. (2003). *Case Study Methodology: Design and Methodology.* Thousand Oaks, CA: Sage Publications.

FOURTEEN

Iluminadas a través de Cosmovisión: A New Age of Enlightenment for *Pedagogía Transmundial*

Ellen Riojas Clark, Belinda Bustos Flores, and Olga A. Vásquez

In our five-year quest to harness and expound upon the essence and pedagogical power of *La Clase Mágica,* we came to further understand who we are as individuals, teachers, and scholars. In John-Steiner's words, we form a truly creative collaboration with "Generative ideas emerg(ing) from joint thinking, from significant conversations, and from sustained, shared struggles to achieve new insights by partners in thought." (p. 3)

We argue that ordered logic perpetuated by our educational systems endangers languages, cultures, and our humanity. Western thinking, ideals, and logic dominate our society's thinking to the exclusion of other voices since the conquest of the New World. Regrettably, this has led to a focus on reification of these ideals at the expense of other knowledges and worldviews present in the classroom and society of today. We concur with Salazar (2013), who asserts that "superficial and uncritical focus on methods often privileges whitestream approaches aimed at assimilation, ultimately robbing students of their culture, language, history, and values, thus denying students' humanity" (p. 4). We see this leading to a focus on efficiency instead of individuality, structure over flexibility. The notion "that knowledge should be approached through the intellect leads to the belief that scholarship must be objective rather than subjective, that personal emotions, histories, and motives must be removed if the conclusions are to be valid" (Carjuzaa1 and Ruff, 2010, p. 74) severs the personal connection to one's way of knowing in relation to one's community and its ecological surroundings. Knowledge is relational, changing, and belonging to everyone; it cannot be sold as a product that is acquired though mass production.

Freire (1970) reminds us that to transform the world, we must reflect and act upon it. Our work exemplifies this philosophy—to transform education by challenging existing school structures and focusing on innovative and humanizing approaches to learning:

> Currently, most studies on humanizing pedagogy describe the role of the teacher in creating a humanizing experience for students. Some would argue that scholars continue to privilege the experience of the "oppressor" [educator] and negate or exclude the agency of the "oppressed" [learner] by strictly focusing on the educator's role in a humanizing pedagogy. (Salazar, 2013, p. 23–24)

While efforts such as bilingual education are laudatory and demonstrate the positive benefits of the use of the native language and culture (Rolstad, Mahoney, and Glass, 2005), often the delivery is embedded in traditional teacher-centered structures (Flores, 2001; Flores and Cortez, 2010). The same is true in the content areas, especially for underrepresented students, with a focus on technical and reductionistic methods prevailing over the construction of knowledge through dialogue, inquiry, and problem-solving (Salazar, 2013; Valenzuela, 1999). Even the incorporation of digital tools is often limited to basic technical skills and knowledge consumption, rather than creativity and "the use of technologies in ways that empower people to participate more fully and equitably in society" (Gorski, 2009, p. 352).

Throughout, we contemplate, communicate, learn, and are enlightened by the sacred sciences, providing us a kaleidoscopic lens to view how nature represents transformation in order to understand and relate to the world. We appropriate the communal wisdom of our *antepasados* and conceptualize a transworld pedagogy that opened our eyes to many perspectives. Thus, we came to the conclusion that if we really want to transform how children are taught, we must go beyond our comfort zone and our own ways of thinking. In our numerous conversations surrounding this book project, we came to recognize and accentuate the ideals and wisdom of *nuestros antepasados*. We are connecting with our Mayan ancestors' collective intelligence generated across time and through their *cosmovisión*—an epistemology that encompass notions of spirituality, transcendence, harmonic balance, and evolution—of living in harmony with nature and the cosmos. Through our dialogic process, we recognize that the basis of all creation is sacred and that living in harmony with the natural world as transworld citizens was not an option, but a necessity. We reaffirm our roots based on our traditions, our history, and our worldviews to be in synchrony with our fellow human beings and our natural surroundings. In losing the connection to the collective intelligence of our people, i.e., the knowledge, language, and ways of being, the "sum of the country's creative potential" (Fishman, 1996/2007, p. 71) essentially vanishes.

While all numbers are sacred, we emphasize the concept of four because it serves as the basis for many indigenous principles: of directionality—north, south, east, and west; of geometric constructs such as squares; of color—black, white, red, and yellow; of balance, physical, emotional, mental, and spiritual; of nature—wind, fire, earth, and water, of natural cycles—fall, spring, summer, and winter; the lunar cycle; the very essence of all we do in life. As we awaken our indigenous consciousness and incorporate the epistemology of *cosmovisión*, embracing the force of power as symbolized by our indigenous *antepasados* as *la solidez, la fortaleza, la felicidad, y la estabilidad* (Sabiduría Maya, 2013). These pillars of solidity, strength, happiness, and stability energize our work. We move between the cosmic world, real-life settings, activity, and pedagogy, and are guided on this journey as bilingual and bicultural beings. Through the process of collaboration in the conceptual design of this book, we evoke the power of four to represent the theoretical constructs: dialogic process, notion of culture, a bicultural/bilingual critical pedagogy, and the sacred sciences. Further, the themes of our volume are organized to frame our proposed transworld pedagogy with a focus on the learning process as an open system: embracing a transworld view, transcending borders as transworld citizens, enacting transworld pedagogy, and evolving through innovation.

Using the Mayan *cosmovisión*, we feel compelled to follow our inherent nature to seek, transcend, harmonize, and evolve anew by speaking through an ancient voice:

> *Compartimos e iluminamos el significado de las ciencias sagradas para el desarrollo de una pedagogía transmundial. Así fue como llegamos a ver nuestras raíces como un tesoro iluminando en el árbol de vida con sus ramas llenas de conceptos científicos. Así fue como llegamos a ser Magas iluminadas.* [We share and illuminate the significance of the sacred sciences in developing transworld pedagogy. That is how our roots became a treasure that illuminates the tree of life with its branches full of scientific concepts. That is how we came to be illuminated Magas.]

EMBRACING A TRANSWORLD VIEW

As we embrace this transworld view, we readily accept Cerecer's (2000) notion that: *El individuo está en el mundo, en acto y potencia, porque el mundo está en el individuo de la misma manera* ([The individual is in the world, in acts and potential, because the world is in the individual in the same way], p. 214). In our quest for *"achiev(ing) new insights,"* Anzaldúa (1987/ 1999), John-Steiner (2000), Cajete (2000), and others became beacons of light and set us toward discovery and trailblazing directions. These *iluminados* signal what was possible, what was missing and how to go about finding our way across worlds, weaving a web of new consciousness as Anzaldúa (1987/1999), so wisely foretold decades before we were able to fully understand, let alone internalize her vision:

> At some point, on our way to a new consciousness, we will have to leave the opposite bank, the split between the two mortal combatants somehow healed so that we are on both shores at once and, at once, see through serpent and eagle eyes. . . . and cross the border into a wholly new and separate territory. Or we might go another route. The possibilities are numerous once we decide to act and not react. (p. 378)

As we heard the voices of the past, we reaffirm commitment to our community, while awakening to a new age of enlightenment. Our historical consciousness then as Boix-Mansilla and Gardner (2013) purport "informs our knowledge of self and orients us toward the future" (p. 57). Thereby, capturing our sense of creativity, commitment, drive, and *compadrazgo* (sister/brotherhood). We embrace the *confianza* [trust] to challenge monolithic standards, western ideology, ourselves, and others to change. Inspired by the goodness of our community, we recommit to the power of our culture.

In the end, we learned to speak in one voice through *El Maga*, our muse, the fanciful electronic entity who reigns over *La Clase Mágica* with the essence of a spiritual, mystical guide and who moves in and out of the magical and scientific, making everything possible. *El Maga* tells us:

> *Quien soy, yo soy quien soy, y soy.* Who am I, I am who I am, and I am and my roots carry our historical cultural practices. I am the tree of life spreading knowledge through my branches that bloom social justice and social change.

In truly addressing the needs of our differing contexts and our ever-changing world, we looked into our *comunidad/familia* to see the full extent of who we are as cultural beings and recaptured what we deem important from all that has been lost through modernity and the conquest of our very essence.

We must not forget that our people, *nuestra raza*, understood the importance of harmonic balance, the power of observation and inquiry to generate knowledge, and were able to harness resources to use technology since ancient times. The Mexican philosopher and educator, José Vasconcelos (1976) aptly described these ancient cultures' scientific advancements and hypothesized that the traces of these civilizations and culture could not be adequately calculated. Using modern tools, recent massive architectural discoveries in the Guatemalan jungle confirmed that these advanced civilizations existed all the way back to the 1000-350 B.C. (Hansen, 2001). Although, these discoveries fortified Vasconcelos' perceptive vision, the last 100 years of archeological findings indicate that we have only touched the surface in discovering the extent of indigenous scientific thought and accomplishments.

Vasconcelos envisioned a utopic civilization built on the accomplishments of our *antepasados* "fashioned out of the treasures of all the previous ones" (Jaén, 1997, p. 40). He promoted a philosophy of brotherhood and a universal vision. As *mestizos*, Vasconcelos considered us to be *La Raza Cosmica* (Juárez, 1973), while some have been critical of this notion, we also recognize the time and space in which his ideas were developed. As a child, in Texas border schools, he observed that Mexican students were immersed in English and separated from their counterparts (Juárez, 1973). This alienation affected students' self-worth in a negative way. Appropriating Vasconcelos' conscious raising pronouncement, *Por mi raza hablará el espíritu [the spirit speaks for my race]*, Anzaldúa (1987) declares: "his [Vasconcelos'] theory is one of inclusivity. . . . From this racial, ideological, cultural and biological cross-pollination, an 'alien' consciousness is presently in the making" (p. 99). It is these voices and the accomplishments of the past that provoke us to expand our consciousness.

We acknowledge the power of the sacred sciences and the endless possibilities towards a new way of thinking, aligning our community's notion of *bien educados* [well-mannered] with our *antepasados'* notions of harmony and balance. Through our exploration, we became acutely aware that these sacred practices resonated with post-modern sociocultural and critical theories. For example, similar to Vygotsky's (1978) notion of expert guides, Mayan communities have sages, *ajnaab' winaq*, as the keepers of the sacred sciences:

> . . . *las personas encargadas en la construcción del conocimiento o las personas sabias son aquellas que han cumplido ciertos compromisos en la comunidad y desempeñan funciones diversas. Son los ajnaab' winaq o las maestras, filósofas, guías, parteras, las encargadas del calendario, las que guardan los documentos, las que velan por la vida en la comunidad, etc* [. . . the women responsible for the construction of knowledge are the wise people, who have fulfilled certain commitments in the community and perform different functions. They are the *ajnaab' winaq*, teachers, philosophers, guides, midwives, in charge of the calendar, which saved documents, who are responsible for life in the community, etc.] (Jiménez, 2012, p. 2)

Likewise, we found the notion of harmony and balance in Freire's (1970) work that speaks of the importance of the dialogic process as a means to achieve synthesis and an egalitarian society.

In our fast-paced world, we caution against relying on the sanctioned, while overlooking the sacred practices of our *antepasados* and dishonoring the communal knowledge that has been acquired through close relationships with the natural world. To realize a transworld vision, we are willing to transcend borders in our ways of thinking, especially in challenging Western ideology that has been imposed as our common knowledge. We value other ways of thinking and logic. For example, Fischer (1999) explained that Mayan logic is clearly distinct in that it represents the groups' way of thinking and living. In this light, we came to accept the wisdom of Benito Juárez (1867) that *El respecto al derecho ajeno es la paz [respecting others rights is peace]*. We, in a community, must teach to respect differences through a humanistic approach (Freire, 1970), while creating harmonious settings for learning. With honor, we take our role as *Magas, las ajnaab' winaq* of our communities as important, for we will serve as sages of our many worlds.

Transcending Borders as Transworld Citizens

> Bridges are thresholds to other realities, archetypal, primal symbols of shifting consciousness. They are passageways, conduits, and connectors that connote transitioning, crossing borders, and changing perspectives. (Anzaldúa, 2002, p. 243)

Nepantla, a Nahuatl word meaning *tierra entre medio* (land in between), popular today as the notion of "interstices" was the space we occupied throughout this work as we attempted to bridge the liminal (threshold) spaces that span between the worlds we were trying to reconnect. We captured, "Transformations (that) occurred in this in-between space, an unstable, unpredictable, precarious, always-in-transition space lacking clear boundaries (p. 1)" as Anzaldúa (2002) declared. Our exposure to other ideas, people, and worlds transformed our thinking, although occasionally we felt vulnerable, we recognized that change is to be expected.

To create new knowledge or to use new concepts in a new way is to use the imagination of our communities who have long used the creative act as a basis of learning. In explaining the meaning of life, Western thought places value on the written word and in an ordered logic, as the absolute truth. In contrast, Mayan logic and truth are based on the natural order of life; its ontology is biological: *Por esto los codigos de su epistemolgia son y estan en la naturaleza y su grammatical es el orden de la physis biológica* (Cerecer, 2000, p. 226). Thus, to transcend from what we know, we must engage in critical dialogue with others as we recapture the sacred sciences evident in the wisdom that is generated through our daily lives.

Moreover, rather than simply conceptualizing learning as a linear process moving from one point of development to the next, our ideas resonate closely with Engeström's (2001) notion of expansive learning occurring in continuous cycles. According to Engeström and Sannino (2010), this theory "puts the primacy on communities as learners, on transformation and creation of culture, on horizontal movement and hybridization, and on the formation of theoretical concepts" (p. 3). In the case of LCM's transworld pedagogy, as a social design experiment for preparing teachers, these ideas are further supported by Gutiérrez and Vossoughi (2010):

> Grounded in expansive notions of learning and mediated praxis funda-
> mental to a transformative education for students from nondominant
> communities, the social design experiment provides persistent oppor-
> tunities for reflection and examination of informal theories developed
> over the course of participants' experiences as students and teachers in
> apprenticeship. Such reflection is necessary for teachers to develop a
> coherent and orienting framework for teaching and learning that has
> both heuristic and explanatory power. We . . . illustrate how cultural
> historical concepts of learning and development supported "lift offs"
> (Vossoughi, n.d.) in which university students could see anew the
> teaching and learning processes at work. (original text, p. 101)

We use the Mayan's cultural historical understandings, which beheld an interdependence of the human body with the cyclical patterns of nature (Cerecer, 2000), as we borrowed from our *antepasados'* spiral symbolism depicted by the snails' shell as Lara (2013) described:

> *El ascenso sutil lo representa a través de una concha de caracol, donde es*
> *evidente también la figura de una espiral que alude a la idea de trascender, de*
> *evolucionar rumbo a otras alturas en el universo.* [The subtle rise is repre-
> sented through a snail shell, where the figure of a spiral alludes to the
> idea of transcending, where evolving to other heights in the universe is
> also evident.] (p. 13)

Using the snail as a symbolic tool of transformation, we conceptualize learning as a spiral process that begins with the individual in harmony with others —expert guides—family, teachers, friends, etc. As learners encounter others along their cyclical path, their sphere of knowledge widens and deepens. "Expansive learning is an inherently multi-voiced process of debate, negotiation and orchestration" (Engeström and Sanni-no, 2010, p. 5). This for us captured the essence of learning as *crecimien-to—* the expansion of self-awareness, values, ideals, and knowledge.

Our mind represents thinking and logic; according to Cerecer (2000), two Mayan ideological structures complement Plato's logic of the abstract notions of psyche, egalitarianism, and justice. In the Mayan *cosmovisión, el nahualismo* is a cultural dimension that expresses the actualization of self beyond real existence and represents the path towards social justice (Cerecer, p. 216). *El nahualism* is not mystical, *"es una expresión mas del espíritu cognitiva del Ser, es un mas de su posibilidades e existencia real* [It is an expression of the cognitive spirit of being, it is a more than its possibilities and real existence."] (Cerecer, p. 232) The human self, our psyche, as a construction of cultural and historical experiences is represented in *nahualismo; tonalismo* acknowledges the animal spirit/self, thereby constituting who we are in relation to the natural world. Thus, it is also important to consider *el nahualismo y el tonalismo* as part of indigenous knowledge and logic to further expand our thinking.

In attaining these new connections and understandings in relation to the cosmos, we become transworld citizens. "The result comes from a resonance with beauty. Sacred Art is a celebration of both nature and mind, phenomena and consciousness" (Creative Harmonics, 2013, para. 5). Connecting to the sacred sciences has allowed us to expand the knowledge base of *La Clase Mágica*. We, who are bilingual-bicultural, are inspired to create and to return the gift of creation back to the primal source because we understand the beauty of giving back to nature in a most visible form. As such, we have woven a transworld pedagogy that encompasses different epistemologies, community realities, and contexts so that we can learn in harmony with our academic and cultural communities.

ENACTING TRANSWORLD PEDAGOGY

Through our transworld pedagogy situated in the magical nature of *La Clase Mágica* (LCM), we see the acquisition of knowledge, confidence, and skills and the affirmation of self through a child's voice (see chapters 9–11). Teacher candidates, *aspirantes,* as learners become aware of how children learn, become cognizant of children's strengths, and appreciate how children's minds enact problem-solving through a creative and engaging inquiry process. *Aspirantes* learn to interact, to guide, and to facilitate thinking. *Aspirantes* acquire the capacity to incorporate home/community knowledge and language and to use digital tools in the creation of new knowledge (see chapters 7 and 8). Most importantly, *aspirantes* formed a strong teacher identity as they develop into cultural and professional efficacious beings with the capacity to leading their students towards successful and productive futures.

Thus, teachers and teacher educators must reconsider viewing learning-teaching as separate processes, but rather view learning-teaching as a spiraling process in which boundaries blur between learner and teacher. Moreover, they must understand the value of creating a harmonic learning environment that focuses specifically on the learner. Lastly, they must incorporate the use of digital tools as mediums for creation and empowerment. In preparing teachers for the realities of our complex world, we must provide opportunities for our teacher candidates, such as LCM, in which they are situated in context to envision themselves with the capacity for transformative change. Gutiérrez and Vossoughi (2010) capture this notion best, when they advocate:

> creating contexts where activity is guided by a mediated praxis aimed
> at the possible opens opportunities for equity-oriented and respectful
> learning to manifest concretely in the everyday social relations among

human beings. Mediated praxis promotes expansive forms of learning in which individual and collective zones of proximal developments coalesce, as individual participants "act a head taller than themselves" in ways that lift the activity towards its future, emerging form. (original text, pg. 111)

EVOLVING THROUGH INNOVATION

To change our current thinking and perspectives, we must engage in innovative practices. As Kao (2007) suggests, innovation is not only about sciences or technology:

It is about new ways of doing and seeing things as much as it about the breakthrough idea. Seen in this way, innovation is always in a state of evolution, with the nature of its practice evolving along with our ideas about the desired future (pp. 19–20).

In this volume, we note the transportability of *La Clase Mágica* (LCM) in various contexts and learners across the life-span and space. While LCM has been mostly implemented in the after-school setting, other adaptations of LCM are underway that further demonstrate the benefits of LCM, disrupting the rigid forms of learning. For example, at the University of California, San Diego, Wishard Guerra (2013), has pushed the development of *Mi Clase Mágica* (MCM) for the last four years, focusing on Latino bilingual children, and their parents in a community Head Start setting. At the Kumeyya Ipai Reservation's Head Start program, she also adapted MCM to serve Native American children, ages three to five and their parents through Little TACKLE (Technology and Cultural Kumeyaay Literacy Education). These projects use design experiment to create an optimal learning environment for young children with a focus on culturally and developmentally appropriate language and literacy activities situated in collaborative and playful learning. Specifically, young children engage with adults in activities, such as joint storytelling that promotes their development of emergent literacy and vocabulary. Wishard Guerra's (2013) preliminary analysis of the impact of *Mi Clase Mágica* demonstrates that playing with literacy with multiple agents (undergraduates, Head Start teachers, and at home with parents) results in meaning-making and expressive vocabulary development.

In Texas, as part of the Academy of Teacher Excellence (ATE) efforts, Riojas-Cortez (2013) recently piloted the implementation of LCM's basic tenets to an early childhood development center's weekly curriculum with young children and their parents. Rather than situating it in an after-school program, *La Clase Mágica Preescolar* is embedded as weekly activity during the day. Early childhood teacher candidates guide young Latino and African American children through developmentally appropriate activities using iPads. Riojas-Cortez's (2013) preliminary analysis identifies the mutual learning and socio-affective benefits for young children and candidates alike. In addition, teacher candidates' exposure to diverse learners within the daily setting has expanded their pedagogical knowledge, skills, and beliefs.

ATE also initiated *La Clase Mágica* Robotics clubs as part of the after-school program at four different schools serving Latino elementary and middle school students (Yuen, Ek, and Schuetze, 2013). They have established a community of learners, as teams consisting of engineering students, teacher candidates, and protégés (students). Teams collaboratively build and program a robot; later, the protégés participate in a robotics competition. Preliminary analysis suggests that protégés are feeling confident about themselves as learners, demonstrating vocabulary expansion, transporting what they have learned to the classroom, and considering careers as engineers (Schuetze, Claeys, Flores, and Sczech, 2013).

Another, path-breaking iteration of LCM is the creation of Pre-Columbian mathematic clubs that incorporate the sacred sciences. An initial pilot using the *Nepohualtzintzin*, a Pre-Columbian calculator (see chapter 1) has shown the academic and personal benefits for young female adolescents. With the assistance of computer science engineering students, Pre-Columbian mathematics online games were developed and piloted. We expect that these efforts may have an impact on Latinos given that they are grossly under-represented in science and technology careers.

Since modern technology makes possibilities limitless, we witness ongoing innovation and optimal learning opportunities being created in LCM. We also note the interdisciplinary approach as a means to realize creative ideas, while maintaining harmony and balance among the creators. We also observe the innovative uses of the knowledge, resources, and tools available in our multiple worlds, thus constantly generating transworld pedagogy

Toward Pedagogía Transmundial

We envision a future in which a *pedagogía transmundial* incorporates the tenets of the sacred sciences, uses knowledge as relative and dynamic, focuses on the learning process, and is reflective of the social contexts of the multiple communities it serves. Throughout, we have used the notion of indigenous knowledge and worldview as the prism for exploring a new vision of education and society to be in synchrony with the history, traditions, and heritage of the children we serve. Another aspect of the *pedagogia transmundial* is the intersection of language, culture, and technology to address the complexity of the reality we live in today. This pedagogy is greatly needed in for this new world, one that disrupts the singularity and resistance to change of existing monolithic educational structures. Traditional institutional culture ignores the needs and resources of ethnic minority populations relegating great numbers to the margins of society.

Transworld pedagogy stands in contrast to this inertia. Incorporating ancient knowledge made visible through modern technology is critical to living in harmony with our environment, and therefore to our survival as a species. Moving between our culture and other cultures, we highlight the sacred sciences to make parallels with the modern world. Knowledges, yet to be discovered, will allow us to move towards future scientific thinking and innovation. Other ways of thinking will enhance our own. This thinking is what makes *pedagogía transmundial* transportable and relevant; it builds upon the knowledge of the community while incorporating a wide-ranging worldview. The future belongs to those who set themselves on a pursuit of new ways of thinking, cultivate cultural sensitivities, values self and others, and promotes social and ecological justice. This will awaken us to a new age of enlightenment.

¡ADELANTE!

In the quest for our knowledge, the regaining of the sacred, and the recognition of who we are!

REFERENCES

Anzaldúa, G. E. (1987/1999). *Borderlands/La Frontera: The New Mestiza.* San Francisco: Aunt Lute Books.

———— (2002). "Preface: (Un)natural Bridges: (Un)safe Spaces." In G. B. Anzaldúa and A. Keating (eds.), *This Bridge We Call Home: Radical Visions for Transformation* (1–3). New York: Routledge.

Boix-Mansilla, V., and Gardner, H. (2007). "From Teaching Globalization to Nurturing Global Consciousness." In M. M. Suárez-Orozco (ed.), *Learning in the Global Era* (47–66). Los Angeles: University of California Press.

Cajete, G. (2000). *Native Science: Natural Laws of Interdependence.* Santa Fe, NM: Clear Light Publishers.

Carjuzaa, J., and Ruff, W. G. (2010). "When Western Epistemology and an Indigenous Worldview Meet: Culturally Responsive Assessment in Practice." *Journal of Scholarship of Teaching and Learning, 10*(1), 68–79.

Cerecer, G. A. (2000). "Hacia un epistemología maya." *Anales de Antropología,* 34. Instituto de Investigaciones Antropológicas Universidad Nacional Autónoma de México.

Creative Harmonics. (2013). Retrieved August 13, 2012 from creative-harmonics.org/pages/sacred-science-art-and-consciousness/sacred-art-article/indigenous.php.

Engeström, Y. (2001). "Expansive Learning at Work: Toward an Activity Theoretical Reconceptualization." *Journal of Education and Work, 14*(1), 133–156.

Engeström, Y., and Sannino, A., (2010). "Studies of Expansive Learning: Foundations, Findings, and Future Challenges." *Educational Research Review, 5*(1), 1–24. DOI: 10.1016.j.edurev.2009.12.002.

Fischer, E. F. (1999). "Cultural Logic and Maya Identity: Rethinking Constructivism and Essentialism." *Current Anthropology, 40*(4), 473–499.

Fishman, J. (1996/2007) "What Do You Lose When You Lose Your Language?" In G. Cantoni (ed.), *Stablizing Indigenous Languages,* (71–81). Northern Arizona University. Retrieved August 25, 2013 from http://jan.ucc.nau.edu/~jar/SIL/Fishman1.pdf.

Flores, B. B. (2001). "Bilingual Education Teachers' Beliefs and Their Relation to Self-Reported Practices." *Bilingual Research Journal, 25*(3), 275–299.

Flores, B. B. and Riojas-Cortez, M. (2010). "Measuring Early Childhood Teacher Candidates' Conceptualizations of a Culturally Responsive Classroom Ecology." *Journal of Classroom Interaction, 44*(2), 4–13.

Freire, P. (1970) *Pedagogy of the Oppressed.* (M. Ramos, trans.). New York: Continuum.

Gorski, P. C. (2009). "Insisting on Digital Equity: Reframing the Dominant Discourse on Multicultural Education and Technology." *Urban Education, 44*(3), 348–364.

Gutiérrez, K. D. and Vossoughi, S. (2010). "Lifting off the Ground to Return Anew: Mediated Praxis, Transformative Learning, and Social Design Experiment." *Journal of Teacher Education, 61*(1–2), 100–117. DOI: 10.1177/0022487109347877.

Hansen, R. D. (2001). "The First Cities: The Beginning of Urbanization and State Formation in the Maya Lowlands." In N. Grube (ed.), *Maya: Divine Kings of the Rain Forest* (50–65). Verlag, Germany: Konemann Press. Retrieved August 1, 2013 from goafar.org/AFAR/Reading_files/The%20First%20Cities-The%20Beginnings%20of%20Urbanization%20and%20State%20Formation%20in%20the%20Maya%20Lowlands.pdf.

Jaén, D. T. (1997). *The Cosmic Race/La Raza Cósmica: A Bilingual Edition.* Baltimore, MD: The John Hopkins University Press.

Juárez, N. F. (1973). "José Vasconcelos and La Raza Cósmica." *AZTLAN, 3*(1), 51–82.

Jiménez, A. (2012). "Epistemología y revitalización de los idiomas Mayas: La reconstrucción de significados." Proceedings from Symposium on Teaching and Learning of Indigenous Languages, University of Notre Dame, South Bend, IN, October 30–November 2, 2011. Retrieved June 17, 2013 from www.kellogg.nd.edu/STLILLA.

John-Steiner, V. (2000). *Creative Collaboration.* Oxford: Oxford University Press.

Juárez, B. (1867). Speech given July 15, 1867 in Mexico City, Mexico.

Kao, J. 2007. *Innovation Nation: How America is Losing its Innovative Edge, Why It Matters, and What Can We Do to Get It Back.* New York: Free Press.

Lara, E. G. (2013). *Nepohualtzitzin: En el modelo matemático figurativo Náhuatl: Evidencia de su existencia a través de un retrato figurativo hablado en Náhuatl.* México City: D. F.

Riojas-Cortez, M. (2013). "*La Clase Mágica* Preescolar." Presentation at University of Texas at San Antonio, Texas Child Development Center, August 20, 2013.

Rolstad, K., Kate, S., and Glass, G. V. (2005). "Weighing the Evidence: A Meta-Analysis of Bilingual Education in Arizona." *Bilingual Research Journal, 29*(1), 43–67. DOI: 10.1080/15235882.2005.10162823.

Sabiduría Maya (2013). Retrieved August 18, 2013 from www.sabiduriamaya.org/home/calculador/tuqij_inc.php?day=25&month=08&year=2013&submit=1.

Salazar, M. C. (2013). "A Humanizing Pedagogy: Reinventing the Principals and Practice of Education as a Journey toward Liberation." *Review of Research, 37*(1), 121–148. DOI: 10.3102/0091732X12462686.

Schuetze, A., Claeys, L., Flores, B. B., and Sczech, S. (2014, forthcoming). "LCM as a Community-Based Expansive Learning Approach to STEM Education."

Valenzuela, A. (1999). *Subtractive Schooling: U.S.-Mexican Youth and the Politics of Caring.* Albany, NY: State University of New York Press.

Vasconcelos, J. (1976). *La Raza Cósmica,* vol. 802 from the Collección Astral. Espasa-Calpe Mexicana, S.A.

Vygotsky, L. S. (1978). *Mind in Society: The Development of Higher Psychological Processes.* Cambridge, MA: Harvard University Press.

Wishard Guerra, A. (2013). "Linking Research to Practice: Using Child Data to Develop Best Practices in Teaching and Service." Presented at UC Links Annual Conference, April 26–27, UC Berkeley, California.

Yuen, T., Ek, L. D., and Schutze, A. (2013). "Increasing Participation from Underrepresented Minorities in STEM through Robotics Clubs." Paper presented at the International Conference on Teaching, Assessment and Learning for Engineering, August 26–29, 2013, Bali, Indonesia.

Index

About the Contributors

Iliana Alanís, PhD, is associate professor in the Department of Interdisciplinary Learning and Teaching for the University of Texas at San Antonio. Her work focuses on the effect of schooling for language minority children in bilingual programs. She is especially interested in forms of teaching that promote native language development and its correlation to second language acquisition for Mexican American children.

María Guadalupe Arreguín-Anderson, EdD, assistant professor of early childhood and elementary education at the University of Texas at San Antonio, completed her doctoral degree in bilingual bducation at the Texas A&M University-Kingsville. Her research focuses on elementary science education in dual language settings and her publications explore issues of equity in culturally and linguistically diverse environments.

Mayra Martínez Avidad, PhD, is associate professor of educational technology at University Camilo José Cela of Madrid, Spain. She joined UCJC after two years as a visiting researcher in the Department of Communication at University of California, San Diego. Her research interest includes the influence of alternative communication networks in the construction of social reality, ICT for social development and citizen empowerment, and ICT in intercultural education.

Lorena Claeys, PhD, is executive director for the Academy for Teacher Excellence at the University of Texas at San Antonio. Her research interests include teacher preparation, induction support, and school-community-university collaboration/partnerships.

Ellen Riojas Clark, PhD, is professor emerita of bicultural-bilingual studies at the University of Texas at San Antonio. Her research examines self-concept, teacher identity, ethnic identity, gifted language minority students, and efficacy.

Theresa Lara De Hoyos, MA, is a graduate of the University of Texas at San Antonio and has worked as a multimedia designer and Moodle administrator for the Academy of Teacher Excellence. Her passion for instructional design and working with emergent technologies provides an avenue for designing and developing creative and innovative digital instruction.

Lucila D. Ek, PhD, is associate professor in the Department of Bicultural-Bilingual Studies at the University of Texas at San Antonio. Her research focuses on language, literacy, and identity of students-of-color, particularly Latinos/as as well as bilingual teacher education. She has published in *Anthropology and Education Quarterly, Equity amd Excellence in Education, Bilingual Research Journal,* and *High School Journal.*

Belinda Bustos Flores, PhD, is professor and chair of the Department Bicultural-Bilingual Studies at the University of Texas at San Antonio. Her research focuses on teacher development including self-concept, ethnic identity, efficacy, beliefs, teacher recruitment/retention, high stakes testing, and family cultural knowledge. Flores is founder of the Academy for Teacher Excellence.

Adriana S. García is a doctoral student in culture, literacy, and language in the Department of Bicultural-Bilingual Studies at the University of Texas at San Antonio. She is also a Language Support Teacher for Northside ISD and works primarily with Bilingual and ESL students and teachers in grades Pre-kinder through fifth grade.

Armando Garza is a doctoral student in culture, literacy, and language in the Department of Bicultural-Bilingual Studies at the University of Texas at San Antonio.

Beatriz Macías Gómez-Estern, PhD, is associate professor at the Universidad de Pablo de Olavide, Sevilla, Spain. Her research interests are in the areas of the enactment of emotions in "narratives of migration" and the educative role of autobiographical narratives in educational settings, especially in culturally diverse classrooms and with adult minority students. She has coauthored publications on cultural identity formation.

Kris D. Gutiérrez, PhD, is professor of literacy and learning sciences and holds the inaugural provost's chair at the University of Colorado, Boulder. She is also professor emerita of Social Research Methodology in the Graduate School of Education and Information Studies at the University of California, Los Angeles where she also served as director of the Education Studies Minor and Director of the Center for the Study of Urban Literacies. Dr. Gutiérrez is the past president and a fellow of the American Educational Research Association (AERA). She is also a fellow at the National Conference on Research on Language and Literacy, and the National Education Policy Center.

Kimberley D. Kennedy, PhD, was associate professor at the University of Texas at San Antonio in the Interdisciplinary Learning and Teaching Department. Her research highlights the importance of a resource-oriented paradigmatic shift in education in order to serve all students more equitably in the ever-shrinking "mainstream"—particularly English Language Learners.

Lena Licón Khisty, PhD, is professor emerita, University of Illinois at Chicago. Her work has centered on research and teacher development within a multidisciplinary approach involving bilingual/ESL education and mathematics education. Her interests center on a sociocultural perspective to improving Latinos' schooling, focusing on classroom interactions and language use in mathematics.

Carlos A. LópezLeiva, PhD, is assistant professor in the Department of Language, Literacy, and Sociocultural Studies at the University of New Mexico. His research interests are in the social construction of culturally and linguistically diverse learners; the social dimension of teaching, learning, and doing mathematics in different educational environments and integrated with other fields; identity development of Latinas/os and/or Hispanics as bilingual doers of mathematics; mathematization processes; critical pedagogy; and practitioner and participatory action research.

Patricia D. López received her PhD in education policy and planning from the University of Texas at Austin with a portfolio in Mexican American Studies. Her research focuses on Latina/o politics and policy, critical policy analysis, political engagement, and Chicana feminist theory.

Margarita Machado-Casas, PhD, is assistant professor at the University of Texas at San Antonio. Her research interests include Afro-descendants, indigenous and Latino education, transnational communities, and technology literacy. She is currently a co-editor for the *Handbook of Latinos in Education* which was awarded the Critics' Choice Award by the American Education Studies Association.

Carmen M. Martínez-Roldán, PhD, is associate professor of bilingual-bicultural education at Teachers College, Columbia University. Approaching literacy and learning as socially and culturally mediated, her research focuses on bilingual children's literate thinking—how children construct meanings from texts, including digital texts, in English and Spanish and the contexts that mediate their interpretive processes.

Henrietta Muñoz, PhD, is the United Way Eastside Promise Neighborhood project director, a $23.7M dollar grant from the U.S. Department of Education. She received her PhD from the University of Texas at San Antonio in 2009 and was a 2010/2011 Annie E. Casey Foundation Children and Family fellow.

Patricia Sánchez, PhD, is associate professor in the Department of Bicultural-Bilingual Studies at the University of Texas at San Antonio. Her research utilizes a sociocultural lens to examine issues related to globalization, transnationalism, immigrant students and families, teacher preparation, and critical research methodologies.

Macneil Shonle, PhD, is currently a software engineer at Google and an affiliate professor at the University of Washington Bothell. His research covers programming tools, aspect-oriented programming, and language design.

Lisa Santillán is a doctoral student in the Department of Bicultural-Bilingual Studies at the University of Texas at San Antonio. She is an elementary bilingual teacher who has worked with culturally and linguistically diverse students for over ten years in South Texas.

Zayoni Torres is a doctoral student at the University of Illinois at Chicago. She is a former Center for the Mathematics Education of Latinos/as (CEMELA) fellow, a Abraham Lincoln Fellow and current research assistant for English Learning through Math, Science, and Action Research (ELMSA).. Her research interests include the mathematics education of bilingual students, students' multiple identities, and adult literacy through a feminist perspective.

Angela Valenzuela, PhD, is professor in education policy and planning in the Department of Educational Administration, University of Texas, Austin. She also serves as director of the National Latino/a Education Research and Policy Project. She is the author of *Subtractive Schooling: U.S. Mexican Youth and the Politics of Caring* and *Leaving Children Behind: How "Texas-Style" Accountability Fails Latino Youth.*

Olga A. Vásquez, PhD, Department of Communication, University of California at San Diego, is an anthropologist of education and founder of *La Clase Mágica*, a research-based after-school cultural laboratory. Her recent work highlights the urgent need and approaches that education must take to meet the challenges of the twenty-first century, particularly as it relates to U.S. Latinos.

Craig Willey, PhD, is assistant professor of mathematics education at Indiana University School of Education at Indianapolis. His research interests include the preparation and development of mathematics teachers of Latinas/os and other bilingual student populations, as well as the improvement of mathematics curriculum to increase access for and enhance engagement of bilingual students.

Timothy T. Yuen, PhD, is assistant professor of instructional technology in the Department of Interdisciplinary Learning and Teaching at the University of Texas at San Antonio. His research examines learning tools and informal learning environments to support conceptual understanding and motivate students in engineering and computer science.

CPSIA information can be obtained at www.ICGtesting.com
Printed in the USA
BVOW08*1647110214

344522BV00004B/4/P

9 780739 186831